Aristotle and the Ethics of Difference, Friendship, and Equality

Also available from Bloomsbury

Health and Hedonism in Plato and Epicurus, by Kelly Arenson
Philosophies of Work in the Platonic Tradition, by Jeffrey Hanson
Rewriting Contemporary Political Philosophy with Plato and Aristotle, by Paul Schollmeier
Skill in Ancient Ethics, edited by Tom Angier and Lisa A. Raphals

Aristotle and the Ethics of Difference, Friendship, and Equality
The Plurality of Rule

Zoli Filotas

BLOOMSBURY ACADEMIC
LONDON • NEW YORK • OXFORD • NEW DELHI • SYDNEY

BLOOMSBURY ACADEMIC
Bloomsbury Publishing Plc
50 Bedford Square, London, WC1B 3DP, UK
1385 Broadway, New York, NY 10018, USA
29 Earlsfort Terrace, Dublin 2, Ireland

BLOOMSBURY, BLOOMSBURY ACADEMIC and the Diana logo are trademarks of
Bloomsbury Publishing Plc

First published in Great Britain 2021
This paperback edition published 2023

Copyright © Zoli Filotas, 2021

Zoli Filotas has asserted his right under the Copyright, Designs and
Patents Act, 1988, to be identified as Author of this work.

For legal purposes the Acknowledgements on p. viii constitute an extension
of this copyright page.

Cover image: Drag handle, Eskimo.
Photo by Werner Forman/Universal Images Group/Getty Images.

All rights reserved. No part of this publication may be reproduced or transmitted
in any form or by any means, electronic or mechanical, including photocopying,
recording, or any information storage or retrieval system, without prior
permission in writing from the publishers.

Bloomsbury Publishing Plc does not have any control over, or responsibility for, any
third-party websites referred to or in this book. All internet addresses given in this
book were correct at the time of going to press. The author and publisher regret any
inconvenience caused if addresses have changed or sites have ceased to exist,
but can accept no responsibility for any such changes.

A catalogue record for this book is available from the British Library.

Library of Congress Cataloging-in-Publication Data
Names: Filotas, Zoli, author.
Title: Aristotle and the ethics of difference, friendship, and equality: the plurality
of rule / Zoli Filotas.
Description: London, UK; New York, NY, USA: Bloomsbury Academic, 2021. |
Includes bibliographical references and index. |
Identifiers: LCCN 2021006751 (print) | LCCN 2021006752 (ebook) | ISBN 9781350160866
(hardback) | ISBN 9781350160873 (ebook) | ISBN 9781350160880 (epub)
Subjects: LCSH: Aristotle. | Ethics. | Political science–Philosophy.
Classification: LCC B485 .F55 2021 (print) | LCC B485 (ebook) | DDC 171/.3–dc23
LC record available at https://lccn.loc.gov/2021006751
LC ebook record available at https://lccn.loc.gov/2021006752

ISBN: HB: 978-1-3501-6086-6
PB: 978-1-3502-5993-5
ePDF: 978-1-3501-6087-3
eBook: 978-1-3501-6088-0

Typeset by Deanta Global Publishing Services, Chennai, India

To find out more about our authors and books visit www.bloomsbury.com
and sign up for our newsletters.

Dedicated to my parents

Contents

Acknowledgments	viii
Note on the Texts and Translations	ix
Introduction	1
1 The Problem of Slavery and Persuasion in the Fifth and Fourth Centuries BCE	21
2 Interpersonal Causation and the Generic Definition of Rule	53
3 Kinds of Community, Kinds of Rule	71
4 Political Rule, Equality, and Equalization	97
5 Political Rule and the Good	117
Conclusion	139
Notes	147
Bibliography	187
General Index	197
Index Locorum	201

Acknowledgments

This book began as a doctoral dissertation at McGill University. I was extraordinarily lucky to have as my supervisors Marguerite Deslauriers and Stephen Menn, each of whose influence is on every page of this book and each of whom has transformed how I read, work, teach, and think.

As I've brought it to a conclusion, I've had daily reason to thank my students at the University of South Dakota. I'm grateful for the curiosity and humor with which they approach strange ideas and the patience and kindness they grant strange professors.

Thanks too to Dale Clark, Joe Tinguely, and Yishu Zhuo, my splendid philosophy colleagues at the University of South Dakota, for conversation, racquetball, and much else. Joe in particular has gone above and beyond to help with this book, looking over long stretches and discussing its ideas at length. He's a wonderful interlocutor and fellow traveler. Among the many others who have written commentaries and responses, talked through ideas, and otherwise improved the book are Andrea Falcon, Luis Fontes, Justin E.H. Smith, Josiah Ober, Hasana Sharp, and Roy Lee, as well as my astute and generous anonymous reviewers.

I thank the team at Bloomsbury for shepherding this book to publication and Kosta Gligorijevic for preparing the index.

I feel more love and gratitude than I can express to my family for their support through this project and countless other things. Thank you, Mom, Dad, Heather, and Olive.

Note on the Texts and Translations

I have used the Oxford editions of texts by Plato and Aristotle and Loeb editions of the Greek texts by Xenophon and the presocratics, with the exception of the Belles Lettres edition of Xenophon's *Memorabilia* (Louis-André Dorion and Michele Bandini. Paris: Les Belles Lettres, 2000) and Brad Inwood's edition of Empedocles (*The Poem of Empedocles* [Toronto: University of Toronto Press, 2001]).

The English translations I have most frequently consulted are Lorde's translation of the *Politics*, 2nd Edition (Chicago and London: Chicago University Press, 2013), Rowe's translation of the *Nicomachean Ethics* (Oxford: Oxford University Press, 2002), and those in Barnes's *Complete Works of Aristotle* (Princeton: Princeton University Press, 1984) and Cooper's *Complete Works of Plato* (Indianapolis/Cambridge: Hackett, 1997). Unless otherwise noted, I have either adapted their translations or provided my own.

Introduction

I. Prelude: Socrates and Lysis

At the beginning of Plato's *Lysis*, Socrates asks a teenager whether his parents love him. The boy replies that of course they do. Why then, Socrates asks, do they forbid him to drive the family chariot and to use the family donkey, though they entrust these tasks to slaves? Why do they humiliate him by forbidding him to "rule even his own self," making him obey not only the two of them but various tutors and guardians? It seems, Socrates says, that the boy is "enslaved" (δουλεύοντα) to many "masters and rulers" (δεσπότας καὶ ἄρχοντας).[1] Socrates lingers over the incongruity between the enslaved tutors and the marks of privilege that define the young man. Lysis is rich, good looking, widely admired, and destined for political power. How could loving parents give such an elite specimen such a miserable station?

The *Lysis* is a dialogue about *philia*, love or friendship, and so the conversation is framed in terms of whether Lysis' parents love him. But the immediate paradox turns on a different word, *archein*, normally translated as "rule." One reason that Socrates highlights this theme is that he takes it for granted that Lysis is already equipped with many common-sense assumptions about who can appropriately rule whom. On the one hand, Lysis thinks that parents have every right to rule over their children (even though, like any teenager, he sometimes chafes at their authority). But on the other, he also assumes that various parties—women, slaves, donkeys—have little or no claim to rule over anyone.

Characteristically, then, Socrates is forcing Lysis to confront tensions among the beliefs he has absorbed from the people around him. In particular, Socrates asks how to square the low status of many residents of classical Athens—enslaved people and free women in particular—with the respect and obedience children give them simply because they're adults.

Lysis doesn't initially find the puzzle too difficult. He simply suggests that the difference between adult and child trumps the differences between free people and slaves, men and women, and so on.[2] Free Greek men, he thinks, inherit the right to rule almost everyone else but only once they become adults.

Socrates, however, will have none of this—he rejects *all* of the differences that Lysis (and most everyone else in the classical Athenian milieu) might expect to justify the rule of some people over others. According to Socrates, there is only one criterion for rule: understanding (φρόνησις).

> In those areas where we really understand something, everybody—Greeks and barbarians, men and women—will trust us, and there we will act just as we choose, and nobody will want to get in our way. There we will be free ourselves, and rule over others. But in areas where we haven't got any understanding, no one will trust us to act as we judge best, but everybody will do their best to stop us, and not only strangers, but also our mother and father and anyone else even more intimate. And there we are going to be subject to the orders of others.[3]

In domains about which Lysis already knows something, Socrates continues, his father accepts his rule—for example, he submits to Lysis' expertise in grammar and spelling. And since rule is related in this way to knowledge, the only limit to the power Lysis might someday acquire is how much he can learn. Socrates invites Lysis to join him in a perverse fantasy. If the king of Persia thought that Socrates and Lysis knew the secrets of medicine, Socrates says, "he wouldn't stop us even if we pried his eyes open and smeared ashes in them, because he would think we knew what we were doing."[4]

Socrates here entices Lysis into an outrageous revision of fifth-century Athenian common sense. On the one hand, Socrates is implying that anyone qualified to rule over women, slaves, and children is ipso facto qualified to rule over cities and empires. On the other, he is suggesting that anyone *not* qualified to be an all-powerful king has no claim to rule even his own children. And although Socrates is happy to use practical skills like medicine as examples of *phronêsis*, he thinks the deepest and best kind of understanding is won by dedicating one's life to philosophy, dialectical examination of the Good. His suggestion, then, is that nonphilosopher Athenians have no right to rule anyone—even their children, wives, and slaves—while philosophers should be the kings of the world.

II. Aristotle's Theory of Rule

The exchange between Socrates and Lysis captures in miniature a distinctive philosophical project. That project is to develop a theory of human relationships based on 'rule' in the Athenian household and then to use it to answer much broader questions about justice, politics, and how people should live. In this book, I argue that Aristotle carries out just such a project throughout his ethics and politics.

Aristotle's view of cooperation and social relationships depends on a theory that I call "rule pluralism." According to this view, rule comes in many qualitatively different kinds or forms (εἰδή). All can be found in normal, small-scale household relationships, and most are required by justice under various circumstances, both inside the household and beyond. Aristotle's rule pluralism, I argue, has far-reaching implications throughout the *Ethics* and the *Politics*, for example on his much-loved discussion of friendship. Perhaps most notably, it sheds new light on Aristotle's treatment of political rule, the relationship suitable for free and equal fellow citizens, and on Aristotle's relationship to the liberals and other egalitarian political thinkers who succeeded him.

Rule Pluralism

It is characteristic of Aristotle that as he introduces rule pluralism, he presents himself as backing away from Platonic overreach into more familiar, reassuring territory. By the tenth line of the *Politics* he is already rolling his eyes at something very much like Socrates' provocations in the *Lysis*. "Those people," he says, "who suppose that the same person is an expert in political rule, kingly rule, managing the household, and being a master of slaves [πολιτικὸν καὶ βασιλικὸν καὶ οἰκονομικὸν καὶ δεσποτικὸν εἶναι τὸν αὐτὸν] do not argue well." He continues:

> For they consider that each of these differs in the number or fewness of those ruled and not in kind [εἴδει]—for example, the ruler of a few is a master, of more a household manager, and of still more a political or kingly ruler—the assumption being that there is no difference between a large household and a small city; and as for the political and kingly rulers, they consider a kingly ruler one who has charge himself, and a political ruler one who on the basis

of the precepts of this sort of science, rules and is ruled in turn. But these things are not true.[5]

Against those who think that there is only one kind of rule, Aristotle promises to provide his audience with "a better view concerning these kinds of rulers, both as to how they differ from one another and as to whether there is some expertise [τι τεχνικὸν] that can be acquired in connection with each of them."[6] On his view, he says, it will turn out that "despotism and political rule are not the same thing, nor are all the species of rule the same as one another" (οὐ ταὐτόν ἐστι δεσποτεία καὶ πολιτική, οὐδὲ πᾶσαι ἀλλήλαις αἱ ἀρχαί) and in particular that "the slavemaster is not so-called according to a science he possesses [κατ' ἐπιστήμην], but because of what he is *like* [τῷ τοιόσδ' εἶναι], and similarly with the slave and the free person."[7]

Aristotle, then, introduces rule pluralism in a way designed to reassure his students, against the likes of Socrates, that no one needs lessons from a strange philosopher about how to run a farm or debate his compatriots in the assembly. *Of course* a normal Athenian's day-to-day rule over his children is nothing special. *Of course* kingship is exotic and magnificent, suited only to the most exceptional people if to anyone at all.[8]

But, as we will see in Chapter 1, Plato is not Aristotle's only interlocutor. Most significantly, Aristotle also quietly rejects a much more popular way of understanding rule in his time and in ours, a more or less dualistic one. This is the simple and intuitive view that the only meaningful distinction between kinds of rule is between a good kind and a bad kind. Ancient Greek thinkers typically label the bad kind of rule *despoteia*, despotism, and contrast it with some single alternative. Some, for example, contrast barbarian empire with the political order (*politeia*) of Greek cities.[9] Others draw the line within the Greek-speaking world, between Athenian-style democracy on the one hand and Spartan-style oligarchy on the other—though they disagree about which regime amounts to *despoteia* and which does not. Either way, they talk as if rule is despotic just when it injures or mistreats its subjects in one way or another—for example when it causes harm, when it's imposed without consent, or when it isn't restrained by justice. On this widespread approach to rule, one form is slavish and degrading, while the alternative is uniquely appropriate for the free.[10]

I take it that nowadays many people, in both popular and academic contexts, accept a kind of rule dualism akin to this one. They suppose that there is one good or legitimate sort of rule that manages to avoid wronging its subjects—for example by securing their consent, by using procedural mechanisms to protect everyone's rights, or by eliminating oppression and exploitation. On such views, whenever an arrangement strays from legitimate authority, it thereby turns into domination, which is to say that it necessarily becomes unjust. This kind of dualism does not leave much room for the basic question of Aristotle's rule pluralism, namely how various forms of rule might differ one from another even if they are all just. And it has made it harder for readers to recognize that question's importance throughout Aristotle's thought.

Yet Aristotle insists that question is vitally important to his readers' everyday lives. It is true, he tells them, that a free man is naturally suited to rule over both his wife and his slaves. But since a man must respect his wife's freedom, he may not treat her as a mere tool as he does his slaves. Young boys, moreover, are also free inferiors of Greek men; to that extent they are just like women. But it would not do for a man to rule his son the same way he rules his wife. Children are suited to a further, distinct sort of rule because they are inferior only for the moment. And, furthermore, *each* of these three forms of hierarchical domestic rule (οἰκονομική) must be kept distinct from the political rule (πολιτική) exercised by free citizens when they take turns ruling and being ruled, one by the other.¹¹ And the story continues, the distinctions among kinds of rule proliferating throughout the corpus.

Aristotle returns very frequently to the concept of rule and the differences among its species. His comments go far beyond what he needs to reject Socratic rule monism, and they raise many difficulties and introduce complications into many corners of his social and political philosophy. But nowhere in the surviving corpus does he give them a unified, focused treatment.¹²

Politics I.5 1254a26–33

Yet there are many signs that he thinks they are extraordinarily important.¹³ For example, shortly after Aristotle announces rule pluralism in *Politics* I, he makes a remarkable claim:

> Wherever something is constituted as a single, common thing out of a greater number of components, whether continuous or discrete, a ruler and a subordinate come to light. This distinction exists in all living creatures, but not in them only; it is grounded in the whole of nature. Even in things which have no life there is a ruler, as in a musical mode.¹⁴

The important point for the *Politics*, of course, is the implication for human relations. Aristotle is saying that wherever two or more people make up a group with any claim to unity and commonality, they form a hierarchical structure.[15] In such cases, there can never be a question of *whether* there is a ruler, only of identifying the ruler and the kind of rule involved.

Aristotle emphasizes the vast scope of this principle. It is not just that he describes it as something like a law of nature. He also offers it up as self-evident, one on a list of simple principles drawn "both from reason and experience" that, he says, make it "easy" (οὐ χαλεπὸν) to answer trickier philosophical questions about slavery.[16] There is no reason to think it is restricted just to the household relationships or to *Politics* I.[17] Rather, the principle of rule appears to apply to all human partnerships, relationships, or communities (κοινωνίαι). To be sure, Aristotle thinks that any generalization about the natural world might admit of the occasional exception and that there might be border cases, say quasi-communities that barely involve rule. But our passage implies that whenever anyone cooperates with anyone else at all, they will form a group with a hierarchical structure.[18]

This claim would not have been as surprising to Aristotle's audience as it may be to us. One reason is that although the English word "rule" is the standard translation of *archê* and *archein*, it is not a perfect fit. In popular culture today people usually use the word "rule" to evoke hazy, vaguely medieval images of power or domination. In formal and academic settings, we regularly use it in expressions like "democratic self-rule" and "rule of law." In their different ways, both of these ways of using the word suggest that ruling and being ruled are remote from normal people's everyday lives. *Archein* and its cognates in ancient Greek had meanings along both of those lines in ancient Greek philosophy too. But for Aristotle and his audience, the word primarily suggests perfectly unromantic and pedestrian daily interactions. They would not have found it strange to say that teachers "rule" over their students, farmers over their animals, doctors over their patients, and so on. On the one hand, rule is small scale and personal; on the other, it is ubiquitous across social life.

And Aristotle's texts confirm that he thought of it that way. Aristotle appears to use the principle that every community has a ruler to criticize Plato's portrait of a fledgling city made up of a weaver, a farmer, a shoemaker, and a builder: "even among four persons, or however many partners there are, there must necessarily be someone who assigns and judges what is just."[19] More generally, as he works through various kinds of cooperation and community, Aristotle finds it natural to ask who rules and how. When in *Politics* III it is time to define the constitutions—democracy, oligarchy, and so forth—he takes it as obvious that the way to do so is in terms of who rules. Considering the various forms of family friendship in *Nicomachean Ethics* VIII, he contrasts normal marriages where the husband rules over the household to deviant cases where an 'heiress' takes over. And there are many other such cases.

Equality and Political Rule

So we may take it as an axiom of Aristotle's ethics and politics that whenever people find themselves somehow cooperating or acting together (whenever they make up a "ἕν τι κοινόν"), they must form a unit structured by rule. This claim, however, might appear to conflict with Aristotle's well-known views about two important sorts of community and association, each a paradigm ἕν τι κοινόν in its own way: the friendship of virtue and the political community.

Aristotle's comments about those two kinds of community express his deep and sustained attention to communities of free people who regard each other as equals. In the perfect friendship of virtue, described in *EN* VIII-IX and *EE* VII, a pair of friends share a single life, each admiring the other's moral excellence, the one regarding the other as a "second self." The friends' uniquely stable relationship is one of the pinnacles of human achievement and happiness, and it depends on their profound equality and mutuality. In the political communities that are the focus of the central books of the *Politics*, free citizens share alike in deliberation and decision, with each pursuing the common good of the community as a whole. It is the sort of community he most encourages his readers to foster in cities and in their own political pursuits.

Either of these sorts of relationships might seem to make it clear that Aristotle cannot seriously think all human relations involve rule. And indeed, on many readings of Aristotle's philosophy, he lingers on the rule of women, children, and slaves in *Politics* I precisely to show what people *leave behind* when they move beyond the domestic sphere into real politics and healthy, flourishing human relationships. On such readings, the relations of ruling and being ruled belong to a sordid sub-political condition. When we realize our potential for political life (so the story goes) we leave them behind in favor of relations of freedom, equality, and mutuality. On this way of reading Aristotle, he prefigures much later political thought, where equality rules the day in the public sphere and each citizen ideally enjoys a sphere of uninhibited self-rule, or else all jointly rule the whole.[20]

No one could deny that freedom, equality, and mutuality are central to Aristotle's political and ethical thought. But I argue in this book that the sorts of interpretation I have just described are anachronistic and misleading. For Aristotle never says that rule is suspended in the friendship of equals or in political communities. He never says that democratic citizens must renounce any claim to rule one another, so that each might remain unruled.[21] What he does say repeatedly is quite different: that when free people form relationships with their equals, they ought to take turns ruling and being ruled, and when they do, they must rule over each other in a particular way, namely "politically."

The clear implication is that political rule is one kind of rule among many, and that even virtue friends must, when they act together, somehow negotiate the dynamics of ruling and being ruled. It is true that Aristotle does not think that one member of a community of equals should *permanently* rule another. But his preferred alternative is that they pass rule back and forth *seriatim*, and that they make sure that whoever is ruling at the moment does so in the right way. In other words, equality and mutuality should be understood *within* rule pluralism, and the relationships of equals must somehow take their place among the many hierarchically organized composites Aristotle analyzes with his theory of rule. Communities of equals are a special case, but they are not exceptions to the principle that all communities are structured by rule. If this is so, Aristotle's conceptions of "rule" and "equality" are interrelated in complex ways, and each ought to be understood in terms of the other. On the one hand, rule cannot be the ruthless, zero sum affair it might seem. But on the other, equality must be compatible with a surprising sort of asymmetry and control.

Rule as a *Genus*

Another way to put this point is to say that at some level of description, Aristotle uses the word "rule" univocally. And so a full account of Aristotle's political and social philosophy must explain not just how the various species differ one from another but also what links them as members of a single genus.

The problem is especially acute when it comes to the political relations of equal fellow citizens on the one hand and the domination of slaves on the other. It is certainly important to Aristotle that those relationships differ. But, more troublingly for modern readers, his theory assumes that they have something in common.

As I argue in Chapter 2, an important part of the general conception of rule that ties them together is that all forms of rule involve a particular kind of *causal* connection between people. Whenever one person rules another, one of them—the ruler—acts as a certain kind of cause on the other. Now anyone familiar with Aristotle's *Physics* knows that for Aristotle the best explanation of any natural phenomenon must provide its final cause, that is, the goal or end that explains it. Although Aristotle's treatment of rule is not part of his natural science, I argue that final causes are nevertheless central to his understanding of rule. Ruling over people is a matter not just of pushing them around but rather of providing them with ends.

How, then, does Aristotle imagine one person shaping the ends of another? In the classical Greek world, many people would have answered in terms of bodily punishments and rewards. But Aristotle rejects that approach. Drawing on intellectual currents from fifth- and fourth-century Athens, he argues that pleasure and pain are inadequate for ruling any human being, even a natural slave. Anyone who seeks to rule effectively over human beings, he thinks, must not just control their bodies but somehow take hold of their souls. And that means affecting them using *logoi*, speeches or arguments. *Logoi* go beyond mere pleasure and pain. They appeal to the characteristically human desires for honor and knowledge, and they communicate what deserves praise and blame and what is just and unjust.

On Aristotle's view, ruling over people with *logoi* is not just a matter of persuading them to do things. Aristotle's examples of rule often turn on something different—the ways actions that would otherwise be pointless or random can be transformed in relation to other, higher projects. Expert bridle-makers (to elaborate on an example from the *Ethics*) are adept at finding ways to make the best bridles for certain horses, for riding under certain conditions, and so on. But the craft of bridle-making is useless on its own. If we tried to imagine the bridle-maker in a social vacuum, we might picture him making a random assortment of bridles, some ornamental, some suited to novice riders, others for ponies and zebras, etc. Or we might picture him sitting forlorn and idle, making no bridles at all. But the thought experiment ultimately fails because making bridles only makes sense, on Aristotle's view, when it has a purpose, such as contributing to a military expedition.[22] Thus the art of a military general rules over that of the bridle-maker and so too does the general himself rule over the bridle-maker. The point isn't that the general gives instructions to the bridle-maker (although he does), but rather that his military projects confer meaning onto the bridle-maker's activities and deliberations. In Aristotle's jargon, the ruler provides the decision (προαίρεσις) that establishes the goal-for-the-sake-of-which (οὗ ἕνεκα) that brings meaning to the actions of another.

And so when Aristotle talks about rule, in any of its many forms, we should think less of prisoners under the whip than of scientists working for a weapons company or of artists making corporate advertisements. In such cases, the workers may (or may not) be compelled to do things they would prefer not to do, and their labor may (or may not) enrich or otherwise benefit the bosses more than it does them. But what makes them paradigm cases of rule in Aristotle's sense is that their thoughts, ingenuity, and expertise take their meaning within a horizon provided by the bosses' goals. The workers thus contribute positively, as full human agents, to their rulers' actions. It is this teleological, psychological link that brings together the many forms of rule into a single genus.

Species of Rule

We may then return to the question of how the species differ one from another. Do they reduce to the psychological differences between people, like those that Aristotle thinks separate a Greek man, in various ways, from his wife, his children, and his slaves? Is it a matter of ruling for one's own benefit in some cases and for the common good in others? Or is the main difference ruling permanently in some cases and taking turns in others? Aristotle suggests each of these explanations in various places, but I argue in Chapter 3 that no combination of them gives a satisfying account of the differences between kinds of rule. A better source is chapters VIII.9 through IX.3 of the essay on friendship in Books VIII and IX of the *Nicomachean Ethics*, which contains the fullest version of an analogy that Aristotle returns to in all three of his ethical works, a comparison of household relationships to political regimes or constitutions (πολιτεῖαι): fatherhood goes with kingship, slave-mastery with tyranny, brotherhood with constitutional regimes, and so on.

Aristotle sometimes talks as if there were just two positions in the power structure of any community: an active one and a passive one, ruler and ruled. But the account of the *Nicomachean Ethics* makes it clear that he thinks there can be a third, intermediate station, one that is important for distinguishing among kinds of rule. People occupy the intermediate position by participating (μετέχειν) in rule, even though they are not "most authoritative" or "sovereign" or "in charge" (κυριώτατος). One example of this intermediate position is analyzed in the middle books of the *Politics*: the position of individual members of the masses in cities with powerful courts and the assemblies. These people are not "officers" or "magistrates" (ἀρχαί or ἄρχοντες—words that can also mean "rulers"),[23] and none of them rules in an unqualified sense. None has full authority over even one aspect of civic policy, as do the treasurer and the general. Still, they can have a real effect on the actions of the city by voting, recalling officials, giving speeches, and so on. In so doing, they make positive contributions to the city's actions, and they put limits on the person who is in charge. Aristotle suggests we label their ambiguous position "indefinite office" (ἀόριστος ἀρχή).[24] Free women provide another example of this intermediate place in a power structure. Aristotle thinks they should deliberate and contribute to management of the household although they should never be in charge. That is, Aristotle thinks a woman should act within a moral horizon set by the decisions of her husband, but that she nevertheless holds a kind of authority that imposes special limits on how he decides—limits absent in the rule of men over both children and slaves.

Aristotle thinks that each of the three positions in a power structure—being in charge, contributing in a way that limits and informs the decisions of the person in charge, and passively submitting—should be occupied by some people some of the time, depending on the contingencies of the people involved and the situations in which they find themselves. Together with a set of what we might call the "temporal" categories (temporary, alternating, and permanent rule) these positions in a power structure allow him to make fine-grained distinctions among many kinds of rule. "Royal" rule is benevolent but completely unrestricted. The ruler is so vastly superior to the person ruled that no trust or delegation is necessary (the paradigm of this arrangement is the rule of a father over a young child). "Aristocratic" rule is the more complex arrangement where nature puts one party in charge but nevertheless assigns the other some limited form of authority. And "political" rule occurs where natural differences fail to determine who should rule and who should be ruled. In these cases rule is assigned by turn or some other, external set of practices or institutions. Alongside these "correct" forms of rule, Aristotle's framework likewise allows him to diagnose a wide variety of "incorrect" or exploitative ones. For example, although some people have every right to be in charge, they may, like a domineering husband or an overly permissive father, trust their subordinates too much or too little.

I draw on *Nicomachean Ethics* VIII to work through definitions of no fewer than seven distinct kinds of rule. But the division into species is less a strict taxonomy than a way to acknowledge the variety of human cooperation and interaction. Following a favorite metaphor of Greek philosophers, we might imagine the many species of rule as letters (στοιχεῖα) in an alphabet. They can be used to form an indefinitely large set of human relationships, in its good and bad permutations.[25] By understanding them, philosophers might hope better to analyze the social world. Legislators, householders, and other rulers might for their part use them to spell out better lives for themselves and their subordinates.

What Kind of Rule Is Best?

Aristotle's rule pluralism, with the genus-species structure I have just sketched, offers a distinctive tool for describing, analyzing, and classifying human interactions. But for Aristotle the purpose of studying ethics and politics is not just to understand facts but more importantly to act well and pursue the good. Yet Aristotle's texts do not make it easy to say what sort of rule he ultimately thinks is best or how he thinks his readers should deploy and respond to the various forms of rule when they engage in politics.

In the *Nicomachean Ethics*, for example, he says simply that royal rule—the type held by a benevolent, all-powerful king—is best.[26] And he says that if a godlike person of surpassing virtue belonged to your community, it would be appropriate to make that person king. But it is hard to square those claims with the overall tenor of the *Politics*. Political rule plays an outsize role throughout the treatise, and Aristotle usually casts it in a very flattering light. Not only do the citizens of the "regime of our prayers" in Books VII and VIII rule each other politically, but one of Aristotle's main goals in Books III to VI is to encourage the young men in his audience to exercise political rule by participating in the political institutions of their cities.

In Chapters 4 and 5, I consider why political rule has this special status even though it is the third-best kind of rule overall and the worst of the "correct" kinds. Political rule, we will see, is partly defined by its unique relationship to one of the pillars of Aristotle's conception of justice, often called the "principle of desert." This principle requires that we treat people according to differences in what they deserve. More deserving people should get a larger share of the goods belonging to the community; less deserving people should get less. Aristotle thinks that in nonpolitical communities the principle of desert establishes who should hold what kind of power over whom. In the simpler cases, like the rule of children and slaves, superiors should rule and inferiors obey; in more complex cases, as in a marriage, one person is in charge of the other but an ethics of trust and delegation determines who should be trusted with what sorts of authority.

Political communities are special because their members, as he variously puts it, are "equal" or "similar in kind." The principle of desert therefore does not determine who rules and who is ruled, and some other set of conventions, practices, and institutions must take its place. We have already mentioned one set of political institutions, namely the "indefinite offices" of assemblyman and juror, which allow people to participate in rule even when they are being ruled. But political communities must supplement those by allowing community-members to pass rule from one member to another, ruling and being ruled "by turns" (κατὰ μέρος). Aristotle usually seems to imagine turn-taking on the model of standard political offices in Athens. Most officials there were chosen at random and held office for at most a single, one-year term. During their tenure they could expect to be obeyed, even by people better positioned to make decisions than they were. The rest of the time they deferred to whoever had been placed in power. Thus most or many people could expect to be in charge of some things some of the time.

We will see that Aristotle folds many complexities into his account of such seemingly simple practices. For example, he claims that ruling and being ruled by turn is necessary even in communities where some people deserve rule more than others. That is, he recommends that the members of political communities sometimes treat each other as equals *counterfactually*, even though they know that some deserve to rule more than others. Moreover, he holds that inequalities must be imitated (μιμεῖται, a word perhaps better translated as "faked") with titles and honors elevating rulers above the people they rule. Such practices reflect the complexities of Aristotle's notion of equality (ἰσότης), which I discuss in Chapter 4. In particular, I argue that for Aristotle, many of the kinds of equality he discusses in Book V of the *Nicomachean Ethics* are not pre-political facts about people but rather the effects of practices of "equalizing" (ἰσάζειν) performed by judges and other political actors.

When he calls a group of people a "community of equals," I argue in Chapter 5, Aristotle means their members are *similar enough to disagree among themselves about who is better than whom*. Since human beings are generally poor judges of their own value, such communities are everywhere. And everywhere people meet this condition, dangerous faction is liable to break out when someone tries to take permanent control. This danger corresponds to the main virtue of political rule—that it wards off disastrous political conflict and thereby provides people with the conditions that allow them to achieve happiness: it gives some people the leisure necessary to do philosophy while allowing others a chance to exhibit the ethical virtues by making decisions on behalf of themselves, their families, and their communities. But while he thinks political rule is therefore the best available regime for free men in most communities, its value is highly qualified. Aristotle never gives up on the idea that rigid, hierarchical rule is best, at least from the perspective of someone who has stepped back from practical life to take on an absolute perspective on the world. Political rule is merely an imperfect imitation of the royal rule suited to gods, the divine beings free of the inconveniences of human life.

We might, then, summarize Aristotle's theory of rule as follows: (i) Aristotle thinks that rule is found wherever humans cooperate, and that it is a particular kind of causal, psychological relationship in which the ruler establishes the teleological horizon in which subordinates operate. (ii) He divides it into kinds, based not only on the type of person in charge but also on an ethics of trust, qualified inclusion, and alternation of roles. (iii) And he thinks that this scheme is particularly important because it allows us to see the relationship between the absolute, divine value of rigid, hierarchical rule and the more qualified, specifically human value of politics. It allows him to recommend political rule regretfully, as the best form of rule for a sort of creature who cannot, alas, sustain the tidier, hierarchical relations of gods.

III. Overview of the Argument

In this book, I give a fuller account of this theory of rule, defending the interpretive claims I've just made, showing how they emerge from the text, and filling in details.

In Chapter 1, I consider how Aristotle positions himself within fifth- and fourth-century discussions of slavery and persuasive speech. I discuss the main alternative Aristotle would have envisioned for rule pluralism: a form of rule dualism according to which persuasive speech is suited to the free and violent coercion is suited to the slavish. And I consider the rival view that Aristotle would adapt into his own theory: that to rule someone is to act as a cause on the other person's soul. The chapter focuses especially on Aristotle's rivals and predecessors. Readers interested exclusively in his views as they appear in his own work may wish to skip to Chapter 2.

Chapter 2 turns to Aristotle's generic definition of rule, according to which one person rules another by providing a final end for activities in the other's soul. I stress that since this conception is teleological, it leaves room for considerable positive ethical, cognitive, and rational contributions from the person who is ruled. The chapter discusses how this conception of rule appears in key passages in the *Rhetoric*, the *Ethics*, and the *Politics*, and how it reflects his understanding of *logos* and *phantasia*.

Chapter 3 argues that the function of the constitutional analogy at the heart of Aristotle's treatment of hierarchical friendship (which compares fatherhood to the rule of kings, marriage to aristocracy, etc.) is to provide an all-purpose classification of cooperation and that it is our best source for a taxonomy of the species of rule. The chapter includes an extended discussion of the aristocratic rule Aristotle believes men should exercise over their wives and a long argument that Aristotle thinks all relations of friendship involve rule.

Chapter 4 opens by considering passages where Aristotle recommends that his readers engage in political rule. I then sketch the relations among political rule, equality, and justice. I explore the quasi-mathematical arguments that Aristotle uses to develop the role of equality in human interactions, and I argue that political rule involves "equalizing" differences just as much as recognizing antecedent equality.

In Chapter 5, I argue that Aristotle thinks political rule is appropriate for communities whose members vary considerably in worth, and that it also calls for considerable pretense and imitation. I argue that Aristotle thinks that these practices are appropriate for human beings because of peculiarities in our nature—but that they are, as it were, a second-best option. This chapter also considers the connections between the interpersonal relationships and formal political office.

In the conclusion, I consider Aristotle's place in the later history of political thought, especially his distance from the various forms of liberal political theory that would succeed him.

IV. Navigating the Aristotelian Corpus

In the outline I just sketched, I credit Aristotle with a theory that is consistent, complete, and clear. But it is well known that the works I am interpreting are fragmented, compressed, and sometimes baldly inconsistent. The *Politics* is, in Malcolm Schofield's apt summation, "a collection of semi-independent mini-treatises, whose interrelations, sequence, and compositional history remain matters of rather tired dispute."[27] The *Ethics* presents a somewhat more unified overall argument, but it comes in two not-quite-parallel versions, in the *Nicomachean* and *Eudemian Ethics*. Indeed the whole corpus that has been handed down to us was originally written piecemeal as lecture notes to be expanded and adapted for the classroom. Aristotle revised and added new material throughout his life, sometimes inserting new text in the margins of his work or on loose scraps of paper. The editors who put together the pieces after his death did an overall admirable job but could not avoid inconsistencies, lacunae, and contradictions.[28]

Yet if Aristotle's corpus is often a mess locally, the intellectual project it records is astonishingly ambitious and carefully worked out. Aristotle repeatedly positions his ideas within a unified curriculum, and he gives copious arguments about its method and how the parts are (and are not) connected. He assigns his inquiries to well-defined disciplines and subdisciplines, sometimes with distinct methodologies and goals, threading the corpus with cross-references that indicate not just connections among works but the order in which students should proceed. The challenge, then, is to give due weight to the overall structure of Aristotle's project without neglecting the messiness of his texts.

Practical Philosophy, Not Science of Nature

It is worth highlighting two overarching policies that I adopt in the face of these difficulties. First, while there are many distinguished commentaries and monographs just on the *Nicomachean Ethics* or the *Politics*, I do not restrict myself to the interpretation of just one treatise. Rather, I move freely between the works, treating them as contributions to the single discipline that Aristotle variously calls "practical philosophy," the "science of human affairs," or sometimes just "politics."

In the *Nicomachean Ethics*, Aristotle is particularly clear about the unity of practical philosophy. He begins Book I by positioning all human ends within politics and closes Book X with a transition to a study of legislation and constitutions—evidently the very study conducted in the *Politics*.[29] Both treatises appear to be governed—fairly consistently if not without exception—by the same methodological principles, and they are linked by many cross-references and common themes. To quote Schofield again, "For us, ethics and politics signify two distinct, if overlapping spheres. For Aristotle, there is just one sphere—politics—conceived in ethical terms."[30] Of course contradictions and gaps *within* Aristotle's practical philosophy remain. I address those as I reach them.[31]

But if I disregard the boundaries between the *Ethics* and the *Politics*, I am very cautious about the disciplinary boundary between Aristotle's practical philosophy on the one hand and natural philosophy on the other. In particular, I do not appeal here to Aristotle's zoological works such as the *Historia Animalium* and the *Generation of Animals*, which develop a detailed theory about the differences between male and female animals. Many scholars have thought that this zoological account must explain why Aristotle thinks women are naturally subordinate to men, and some have thought they may suggest a biological account of natural slavery too.[32]

But there is good Aristotelian warrant for resisting this path. Aristotle claims that political inquiry has different aims than natural science (action on the one hand, understanding on the other), and he thinks different standards apply to each. He has a maddening habit of gesturing at possible connections between the disciplines and then declining to pursue them. And because of his commitments across the philosophical disciplines to the priority of form and *telos* in explanations, there are deeper worries about how to integrate bodily (i.e., material) causes into his overwhelmingly teleological discussions of the good life.[33] So I do not think that Aristotle's natural science or his "first philosophy" can be taken as foundational to his practical philosophy. Those external texts (and the less easily classified work on *Rhetoric*) are better used cautiously and occasionally—as I do with the lexicon in the *Metaphysics* Δ in Chapter 2—as sources of clues for how to supplement a program that has its home in a different, more or less unified discipline studying how human beings pursue the good together.

Argumentative Method

I defend many of the claims in this book through a problem-posing, problem-solving method. That is, I raise focused interpretive questions and solve them by working outward to the passages that provide a full answer. Chapter 1, for example, begins by asking why, in a passing comment, Aristotle recommends (against Plato) that natural slaves be "admonished"—gently persuaded with words—considering that he also actively supports their domination by masters. To answer, I work my way through many of Aristotle's claims about slavery and related texts by his predecessors and contemporaries. That discussion adds up to one argument for a central claim about the genus of rule, namely that for Aristotle all rule over human beings ultimately operates through *logos*, not force.

This aporetic approach keeps me close to Aristotle's words, and it allows me to explore Aristotle's theory of rule with a series of focused, self-contained arguments. It also means that the book is not exhaustive in the manner of some other works of scholarship. I do not, for example, catalogue every occurrence of key words that Aristotle uses, nor do I always try to collect everything he says on a given topic. Likewise, I do not mention all of my agreements and disagreements with other scholars. My goal is, more modestly but I hope more tractably, to trace one central path through Aristotle's complex treatment of human life, showing the connections among parts too often considered in isolation and bringing into view a remarkable set of ideas that colors much of what Aristotle says about the social world.[34]

V. The Contemporary Significance of Aristotle's Theory of Rule

I have already mentioned some difficulties with the word "rule." For most contemporary English speakers, the problems aren't just semantic but also political. We would find it strange to say that teachers, parents, and doctors "rule" over their students, children, and patients. We reach for other words in these contexts—those people, we prefer to say, have "authority," hold positions of "power," and should show "leadership."[35] Our usage in such cases says something about our views on justice. If we find it odd to think of parents "ruling" over their children, bosses over their employees, and so on, the problem isn't that the expressions sound like nonsense, but rather that they suggest hierarchy, inequality, and dominance. So although we may well say that a country ought to "rule" itself through the organs of the democratic state, it's something else altogether—and something altogether unacceptable—to say that any individual ought to rule over any other.

Not only do I follow Aristotle in speaking in this troubling way over the course of this book, but I also devote considerable space to the idea that slavery benefits masters and enslaved people alike, that women are especially suited for domestic work, that farmers and menial workers should largely be excluded from politics, and that it would be best if a divine king took over, eliminating anyone else's claim to political participation. Such thoughts are obviously not politically innocent, and they are not merely historical curiosities. Quite the opposite, they continue to provide comfort and encouragement for fascists, white supremacists, and the like, as classical texts on such topics have done for a long time.[36] My goal is certainly not to support such people and their projects. Indeed, my reading of Aristotle's theory of rule rests in large part on aspects of Aristotle's theory they might find embarrassing, such as his views on the cognitive power of embodied emotion and the epistemic importance of particular perspectives. And yet I do not attempt to reclaim Aristotle for any of the rival political factions that I myself prefer, as much work on Aristotle's *Politics*—liberal, communitarian, Marxist, Arendtian, and so on—more or less explicitly does.[37]

I well understand why some readers would choose not to study anyone who said the things Aristotle did. And I well understand why others might try to redeem those claims or explain them away. But I think there is also a political value in trying to see them clearly, in connection with other texts that Aristotle would have read, in light of the typical associations of the Greek words he used, and so on.[38] I think this approach is the best way to tell the truth about Aristotle, but that does not mean that I think it is neutral or disconnected from contemporary concerns. Rather, I aim to develop what I sometimes think of as an "untimely" reading of Aristotle, useful for unsettling contemporary ways of thinking about politics.

To that end, this book, connects two figures I sometimes think of as the "Good Aristotle," responsible for the theory of virtue friendship in *EN* VIII and IX, and the "Bad Aristotle" who composed the theory of natural slavery in *Politics* I. Modern readers are inclined to keep them separate. But I try to see each as clearly as I can, the one in connection with the other. How, I ask, could both have inhabited a single, integrated perspective?

1

The Problem of Slavery and Persuasion in the Fifth and Fourth Centuries BCE

Aristotle, then, thinks a Greek gentleman should rule over his wife in one way, over his enslaved workers in another, over free citizens another, and so on. Each sort of rule, he says, differs in kind from each of the others. And he holds that some type of rule must structure human relationships whenever two people cooperate. We've started calling this position "rule pluralism."

Aristotle does not tell an elaborate story about how rule pluralism fits into the earlier history of philosophy, as he does, for example, for his theory of the soul. But in *Politics* I, he does position himself against various unnamed rivals, pitching rule pluralism as a novel alternative to their views. It's typical of Aristotle to present his ideas this way, and it's also typical that when we turn to the texts he is thinking of, they don't say quite what we might expect.

And so in this chapter I follow some of Aristotle's references outward to their sources in the fifth and early fourth century BCE. I argue that while Aristotle emphasizes his disagreement with "rule monists" who think that all rule is a unified science, this comparison is less revealing than a disagreement with the Plato of the *Laws* about the proper treatment of slaves. That disagreement weaves together strands of ancient thought that are often studied in isolation: the status difference between free and "slavish" people, the ascent of persuasive speech to the center of political practice, and the nascent science of psychology.

I. Rule Monism

As we saw in the Introduction, the most obvious opponents of rule pluralism are nameless people, invoked twice in *Politics* I, who "suppose that the same person is expert in political rule, kingly rule, managing the household, and being a master of slaves" (ὅσοι μὲν οὖν οἴονται πολιτικὸν καὶ βασιλικὸν καὶ οἰκονομικὸν καὶ δεσποτικὸν εἶναι τὸν αὐτόν).[1] These people, Aristotle implies, think of rule as a science (ἐπιστήμη).[2] I will be arguing that they do not shape Aristotle's thought nearly as much as he pretends. Still it is worth considering who they were and what they believed.

There are several ancient texts that defend versions of the position Aristotle has in mind. In the Introduction, we considered one version of the *all-rule-is-the-same* hypothesis from Plato's *Lysis*, in which Socrates urges the young Lysis to pursue wisdom on the grounds that with one stroke it will free him from all sorts of subordination and grant him authority over everyone from his tutors and his parents to the Great King of Persia.[3] This sort of view seems to have circulated widely within Socrates' circle. It is similar, for example, to a passage by Socrates' disciple Aeschines, who retells the famous story of Themistocles' improbable victory at Salamis. Themistocles, Socrates says, had vastly inferior resources to the Persians, but because he was the better man—more virtuous and more knowledgeable—the Athenians handed themselves over to him, he defeated the Great King, and he even won the king's admiration.[4] Xenophon, another Socratic to whom we will return at the end of this chapter, develops an extended variation on this theme. His Socrates tells an aspiring general that the appropriate knowledge will qualify him to rule even if he is never elected, but that "a dunce without knowledge is neither general nor doctor, even if the whole world appointed him."[5]

The Socratic version of rule monism contrasts with another, nastier version. In *Politics* VII, when Aristotle says that "most people seem to think that despotic rule is statesmanship,"[6] he is apparently thinking of something akin to Thrasymachus' claim in the *Republic* that success in politics—whether in a democracy, oligarchy, or wherever—is simply a matter of advancing one's own interest at the expense of others. Whereas on the Socratic view all (legitimate) rule amounts to kingship, on the Thrasymachean view all (actual) rule amounts to despotism.

But if Aristotle has any single text in mind as he introduces rule pluralism in *Politics* I, it is likely Plato's *Statesman*. Aristotle recalls it closely enough that many scholars have pictured it spread out on his desk as he composed *Politics* I.[7] Early in the *Statesman*, the Eleatic Stranger summarily cuts across many of the distinctions between kinds of rule his audience would take for granted. A king's advisers, he argues, must have the same kinds of knowledge and expertise that define the king himself, so there is no necessary difference between a king and subjects; running an agricultural estate (οἰκός) amounts in practice to directing slaves, so there is no difference between a slavemaster (δεσποτής) and a "householder" (οἰκόνομος); finally, large plantations and small cities are much the same thing. "It's clear that there is one sort of expert knowledge concerned with these things," the Stranger says. "Whether someone gives this the name of expertise in kingship, or statesmanship, or household management, let's not pick any quarrel with him."[8]

Aristotle stresses the distance between this view and his own, but he does not criticize or refute it. Rather he ignores its content entirely. He clearly thinks there is a simple, devastating objection to all versions of rule monism, namely that it flattens out crucial differences, both descriptive and normative. The rule monist can neither distinguish Pericles' benign rule from the disastrous reign of the Thirty Tyrants, nor recommend that a father treat his infant child any differently from fellow citizens he might have to command if he is assigned political office. And even though he attributes some version of rule monism to "most people," we should not think that it was bold or unorthodox to reject it. Quite the opposite. The *all-rule-is-the-same* position was a fringe view designed to provoke. The Socratics certainly realized how shocking it was to suggest that an inexperienced child could command armies if he learned some philosophy or that a citizen needs the mythical virtue of kings just to give instructions to slaves and children.

Indeed, Plato himself does not ultimately seem to have accepted the view, even in the *Statesman*. Midway through the dialogue, the Eleatic Stranger retreats from his earlier claim about rule, suggesting that his first attempts to characterize the statesman belonged to a naïve, utopian philosophy describing the rule of gods over humans, not the more complex political relations humans must forge when they rule each other.[9] There does of course turn out to be a single, architectonic political science. It involves, inter alia, delegating to officials, training people in subordinate arts, and the eugenic production of a populace with the right dispositions. That is a far cry from the sort of rule monism Aristotle is disassociating himself from in *Politics* I. Even the Platonic text Aristotle uses as its main source isn't too serious about rule monism.

II. The Admonishment Claim

In short, if we judge the importance of a rival view by how widespread its proponents are, and by how hard Aristotle must work to push back against it, rule monism cannot be the most important alternative to Aristotle's position. And at the end of his notorious treatment of slavery, Aristotle hints at a more important set of rivals when he contrasts himself with a group of opponents very different from the *all-rule-is-the-same* people.

> Those people [he says] who deny *logos* to slaves and assert that commands only should be used with them do not argue finely: admonishment is to be used with slaves more than with children.[10]

I will refer to this claim often, and it will be useful if inelegant to call it the "admonishment claim." Although Aristotle doesn't say so, one of the targets of the admonishment claim seems to be a passage in Plato's *Laws*. There, the Athenian stranger says this:

> We ought to punish slaves justly, and not to make them conceited by merely admonishing them as we would free men.[11]

This disagreement with Plato makes it clear that Aristotle doesn't just want to keep rule monists from running different forms of authority together. For when it comes to admonishing slaves, it is not some rival but Aristotle himself who presses his contemporaries to treat slaves more like free citizens than they typically do. And he does so in response to a passage from Plato—whose *Statesman*, again, is the presumptive locus classicus of rule monism—stating that political and despotic rule differ not just in the number of people ruled but in the ways they should be enforced.

Aristotle's position here is quite surprising. He only rarely uses the word *nouthetêsis* and its cognates, but they are widespread in other classical texts, and Plato uses them often. *Nouthetêsis* is a gentle response to mistakes and bad behavior using reason and education rather than force. In standard translations it finds English equivalents ranging from mild—"rebuke," "reproach," or "chastise"—to *very* mild—"convince" and "advise." In Plato, admonishment is particularly associated with education in virtue. For example, the *Sophist* defines it as "our forefathers' time-honored method of now scolding, then gently encouraging" (τὰ μὲν χαλεπαίνοντες, τὰ δὲ μαλθακωτέρως παραμυθούμενοι);

they "used to employ it especially on their sons, and many still use it on them nowadays when they do something wrong."¹² Along the same lines, Socrates also says in the *Apology* that if he has ever acted unjustly then he did so unintentionally, and the city should admonish and instruct (διδάσκειν) him instead of just dishing out punishment.¹³

So when Aristotle says against Plato that slaves should be admonished, he means that slaveholders should persuade their slaves with rational arguments and ethical education; this, he says, is the best way to respond to the slaves' rationality. This may seem like an obviously progressive, even proto-liberal position. William Fortenbaugh has argued that it is. In what is surely the most influential of the relatively few discussions of the admonishment claim, he writes that *nouthetêsis* gives slaves "their due." It "honors" and "respects" the slave's cognitive abilities such as they are, and it allows the slave to "partake in reason as best he can." Thus, he says, Aristotle has developed "a new and more thoughtful view" than his predecessors on the subordination of slaves.¹⁴ For Fortenbaugh, the admonishment claim amounts to what later philosophers would call a negative claim right, according to which slaves' status as rational beings places a moral restriction on what their masters may do to them.

There is an obvious objection to this kind of reading. It is not clear how, after developing his notorious theory of natural slavery, Aristotle can coherently ask masters to "respect," "honor," or otherwise attach noninstrumental value to their slaves' interests. After all, Aristotle famously thinks that a natural slave is the "living property" of another, like a part of his master, a living tool, or a bodily organ.¹⁵ That is, slave masters need never credit the slaves' interests with any intrinsic value and should instead rule "despotically." Masters, that is, should fix their attention on their own projects, using slaves purely as means to other ends.¹⁶ How can Aristotle recommend this kind of unrestricted domination, yet still say that masters must respond to their slaves' capacity for reason by admonishing rather than commanding?

Few scholars suggest an answer, because few discuss the admonishment claim in any depth. Those who do mostly seem both to accept Fortenbaugh's liberal reading and to agree with the suggestion that I have just mooted, namely that if Fortenbaugh is right about the admonishment claim, then Aristotle is inconsistent.¹⁷ They do not, however, dwell on this contradiction. This is in part because the admonishment claim is just one of many puzzles and textual problems in Aristotle's extremely schematic treatment of slavery. Until recently, the consensus was that Aristotle's whole discussion of natural slavery was an irredeemable mess, created by the opposing forces of Aristotle's ideological commitments on the one hand and his burgeoning insights into moral truth on the other.[18] Several important recent articles have argued, however, that Aristotle's defense of slavery is more continuous with his overall philosophy than his modern sympathizers might hope.[19] Along the same lines, I would like to argue that (however things stand with the many other puzzles and contradictions) the admonishment claim is entirely compatible with the domination of so-called natural slaves. It will be a long argument, but by the end of Chapter 2, we will see that in making the admonishment claim Aristotle is indeed marking an important departure from the views of his contemporaries, including Plato—but not in the direction of increased freedom for slaves or increased regard for their interests.

III. Slavery and Violence, Freedom and Persuasion

Aristotle directs the admonishment claim at people including Plato who "tell us to use command only" on slaves. Notice that these people don't merely say that it's sometimes acceptable to command one's slaves. They say that slaveholders must use *only* commands and therefore that it is always at least prima facie wrong to give them reasoned arguments. Commanding slaves isn't just permitted but required.

This position is quite striking, considering that the "commands" Aristotle has in mind are evidently backed with violent force. But Plato's position would not have been as surprising for Aristotle's audience as it is for us. Although household slaves in Athens were treated more gently than in other cities—the bar was low—and although some currents in Athenian thought encouraged still gentler treatment, it remained perfectly standard to use violence to keep them in their place. Bernard Williams offers a concise survey of some central pieces of evidence:

> It was a joke that παῖς [a casual term for slaves, literally "boy"] came from παίειν, "to beat." Public slaves, at least, were marked with a brand, which as Xenophon observed, made them harder to steal than money. The overwhelming difference between free and slave, Demosthenes remarked, was that the slave was answerable with his or her body. Evidence from slaves was acceptable in the courts solely on the condition that it had been

extracted under torture. In a speech of Lysias, a man's reluctance to allow his slave concubine to be tortured is cited as evidence against him.[20]

Of course, slaveholders benefited materially from these beliefs and practices—they kept enslaved people in a state of terrified obedience. But it is worth noting that even from this perspective Athenian ideology was even crueler than it needed to be. In particular, classical Greek attitudes to slaves went beyond the kinds of exploitation (perhaps exemplified by sweat-shop labor today) regarded by their beneficiaries with indifference or even regret. The majority of free Athenians seem to have been actively *in favor* of the violent abuse of slaves, quite aside from its instrumental value. They laughed when it appeared in comedy, and there is some evidence that they made themselves out to be rougher with their slaves than they were in practice.[21]

To be sure, some people did argue that masters must be careful not to be excessively brutal with their slaves. Some gave instrumental arguments, notably that excessive violence makes slaves more likely to revolt, that if people routinely beat up unknown slaves they will end up hurting free people, or that when slaves die they may end up bringing *miasma* down on the community of free people. Others argued that excessive violence displays *hubris*.[22] But with few exceptions if any, these are positions about *how*—rather than *whether*—masters should use violence against their slaves, and they give a good sense of the bounds of the debate.[23]

In short, it would not be too strong to say that fourth- and fifth-century Greeks generally didn't just tolerate violence against slaves as a necessary evil but actually endorsed it as a matter of principle. I'd like to take a moment to ask why they would think using violence on slaves is not just permissible but obligatory.

An important source of evidence lies in the fifth-century political uses of the language of slavery and freedom.[24] In fifth-century Athenian discourse, the words related to slavery did not just evoke the perhaps 100, 000 people enslaved in Athens and their counterparts in other *poleis*. It was also used much more broadly as a term of abuse for free people with unacceptable political views or alliances. For example, Athenians invoked slavery to condemn the over-ambitious (such people sought to "enslave" good and noble people) as well as the under-ambitious (these people would be called "slavish"). In earlier texts, Greek writers had applied this sort of language to non-Greeks. One of the themes in Herodotus, for example, is the downfall of the Persians, once free but later so diminished that they could no longer comprehend the freedom of the Greeks.[25] Opponents of oligarchy and democracy soon enough began arguing that the Greek governments they opposed likewise reduced citizens to slavery. Demosthenes, for example, says that people who support Philip and the Macedonians have given up on the traditional love of freedom and are instead "eager for slavery."[26] The tyrant, he says, rules with force, as if his people were slaves; the good ruler, on the other hand, uses persuasion to secure his people's consent. Likewise, in the *Constitution of Athens*, Aristotle (or whoever the author is) writes that the most grievous feature of Athens' original constitution was that the people were enslaved; this, he says, led to the crisis that could only be resolved by Solon: "the many being enslaved to the few, the people rose up against the nobles."[27] Slavery, in this tradition, is seen as a threat not because of the misery of actually enslaved people but rather because of the shame tied to their status. As Thomas Wiedemann puts it, the Greeks are "not thinking *about* slavery so much as using the concept 'slavery' to think *with*."[28]

It does not follow that this discourse had no implications for the lives of actual enslaved people. On the contrary, the ideology made it natural to think that slaves belonged to a completely distinct class of persons and to treat them accordingly. In particular, it suggested something like the following argument.

Premise 1: Slaves and free people are opposites, suited to opposite kinds of treatment.[29]

Premise 2: The treatment appropriate for free people is persuasion with arguments.[30]

Premise 3: Force is the opposite of persuasion.[31]

Conclusion: Slaves must be treated with force rather than persuasion.

Now even if the premises were true, this argument would have serious problems. The most damaging from a strictly logical standpoint is that the idea of "opposite treatment" is vague—if we took it literally, we might have to conclude that the Greeks were committed to eating slaves, since they are committed to *not* eating the free. Still, each "premise" is found in several places in the literature, and it's not hard to see how those who accepted all of them might think they had strong reason to support ruling slaves with nothing but violent force.

What can this argument tell us about the admonishment claim? Evidently Aristotle rejects the conclusion. It follows by something like *modus tollens* that he departed from his contemporaries in rejecting at least one of the three premises. Which one or which ones? Fortenbaugh-style interpretations suggest one answer. On these readings, since Aristotle thinks free and enslaved people both have a share of reason, they are relevantly similar. This makes it unjust to deny slaves the treatment appropriate for the free. If this is correct, Aristotle rejects the first of our premises, the one suggesting an essential difference between free people and slaves, a difference justifying different treatment.

But that cannot be right. Aristotle specifically opposes himself to a set of people who seem to reject our first premise. He reports that they think that "for one man to be another man's master is contrary to nature, because it is only convention that makes the one a slave and the other a freeman, and there is no difference between them by nature, and that therefore it is unjust, for it is based on force."[32] We do not have much of an idea of who these people were and what they thought; I am inclined to think Aristotle exaggerated their importance, the better to make his own position seem moderate.[33] But we know for sure that he disagrees with them. While he concedes that some people are unjustly enslaved, his central claim about slavery is that some people are *natural* slaves, who ought to be ruled differently than free people.

Indeed, Aristotle never questions our first premise. Quite the opposite, it provides one of the main reasons that Aristotle endorses rule pluralism. And, as we will see throughout the rest of this chapter, there is little to no evidence that anyone at all sought to reject the basic distinction between slaves and the free or the practical distinction between how the two sorts of people should be treated.

IV. Lysias: *Logoi* and Rule by the Truth

To get a better sense of standard classical way of linking slavery to violence, consider a passage from Lysias' *Funeral Oration*. Early Athenians, Lysias says,

> were the first and only people in that time to drive out (ἐκβαλόντες) the ruling classes (δυναστείας) of their state and to establish a democracy, believing the liberty of all to be the strongest bond of agreement; by sharing with each other the hopes born of their perils they had freedom of soul

(ἐλευθέραις ταῖς ψυχαῖς) in their civic life, and used the law for honoring the good and punishing the evil. For they deemed that it was the way of wild beasts to be held subject to one another by force (ὑπ' ἀλλήλων βίᾳ κρατεῖσθαι), but the duty of men to delimit justice by law, to convince by argument (λόγῳ πεῖσαι) and to serve these two in act by submitting to the sovereignty of law and the instruction of reason.[34]

This speech clearly endorses the claims (or "premises") we are considering. In the final sentence, Lysias treats persuasion with *logos* as the only treatment appropriate for men and he opposes it to the force appropriate to wild beasts. The men he has in mind are the free citizens of Athens; he doesn't mention slaves, but for the reasons we just saw, there's every reason to think that when it comes to force and persuasion he and his audience members would class them with beasts rather men.[35]

Now this passage exploits the contrast between force and persuasion to advance the idea that democracy is the form of political association that best recognizes freedom—and it suggests a very particular understanding of what freedom involves. Like the *Constitution of Athens*, Lysias' funeral oration tells us that the first Athenians won their freedom by getting rid of despotic rulers. But Lysias stresses an important twist: this does not mean that Athenians now have *no* masters or that each Athenian rules himself. Likewise, by no means can the Athenians do whatever they want.[36] On the contrary, the Athenians secured freedom by replacing one kind of master with another—they demonstrate their freedom precisely by "serving" (ὑπηρετεῖν) reason and law.[37]

Why is it any better to serve *those* masters than the old tyrants the early Athenians drove away?[38] Surely there are supposed to be obvious answers to this question. For a start, there is the matter of what reason and the law are *not*. They are not, like tyrants and the masters of slaves, human beings who can exert their arbitrary, individual preferences on those in their power. Thus on Lysias' view slavery amounts not to having a master, full stop, but rather to having a particularly nasty kind of master—a *person*, that is, someone liable to use coercion to advance his or her perhaps arbitrary preferences. But law and reason also have positive features that make them good masters. The law "delimits" justice, honors the good, and punishes the bad, and Lysias evidently assumes that reason too necessarily expresses the truth about what people should do, as the whims of a tyrant likely do not. That is, the Athenians, in accepting democracy, subordinate themselves to the rule of impersonal facts about what should be done. They subordinate themselves, as we might put it, to the truth.

Now Lysias thinks that the way to secure the rule of reason and the law is through a particular kind of constitution, democracy. This raises the obvious objection that no form of political organization can *directly* put moral truth in control of its citizens. Rather, even the most democratic regimes will give some people the power to restrict and direct the actions of others.[39] Athenian democracy had many distinguishing characteristics, including institutions allowing citizens to censure officials if their tenure proved unsatisfactory and to bring their neighbors to trial at will, but nothing in Lysias' discussion here suggests that he has those in mind. He focuses on two practices, that of following the law (which minimally restricts the ability of rulers to impose their arbitrary preferences on the people and ideally leads them to act according to the insights of wise legislator from the distant past) and—more importantly for our purposes—that of persuading with *logos*, by which he means persuading the majority with speeches in the courts and Assembly. And on Lysias' account, even when people exert a great deal of influence over each other with *logoi*, the people who are influenced are ruled by truth, not their neighbors.

Lysias, then, attaches himself to a tradition, going back at least to Parmenides, according to which persuasion "attends on truth."[40] This expresses the point—we might loosely call it a "phenomenological" observation—that being talked into going somewhere feels a lot different—a lot freer—than, say, being carried away. And the reference to law and reason suggests an explanation of this intuition. When someone addresses you with arguments, they potentially contain information about the world. When you consent to their arguments, it is because they seem to tell the truth. Your relationship to a speaker is not political but cognitive—you are using him to acquire facts relevant to your actions, in the same way as you might use a guide dog or a blind person's cane. The persuader, like these perceptual aids, is a mere intermediary transmitting facts that you might, ideally, have grasped directly. We may see in this view of persuasion an early version of the later idea of the "unforced force of the better argument." The slogan suggests that the better argument is nothing to be scared of; persuaded action is unforced or uncoerced because it expresses a relationship you would ideally have had with your environment anyway.

Lysias doesn't take himself to be saying anything radical or philosophically deep. Rather, since he presumably designed his oratory to resonate with a varied, uneducated Athenian audience, we can assume that it would seem widely plausible and perhaps familiar. Nevertheless, he expresses a distinctive view of freedom, one that is similar only in some respects to later versions of that concept. It is a conception of freedom that allows the democratic city to treat its citizens in a manner befitting the free, even though it empowers some people to control other people's actions. And it also gives substantial support to the idea that persuasion is uniquely suited to the free—a view which, as we have seen, in turn, helps to support the treatment of slaves that Aristotle rejects with the admonishment claim.

V. Gorgias: Persuasion as Force

Although Lysias' picture of the relationship between persuasion and truth presumably had considerable support, it failed to account for some worrying features of real-life persuasion. As Thucydides, Aristophanes, and Plato never tire of repeating, persuasive speech allowed some people—notably orators and sophists—to acquire frightening power in politics and education, even when they seemed to have sketchy characters and bad arguments.[41] So there was every reason to question the way people like Lysias understood persuasion and freedom.

Such challenges came in many forms, but I would like to focus on one in particular. We find it vividly expressed in Gorgias' *Encomium to Helen*. There, Gorgias argues that Helen is blameless for her role in the Trojan War. He considers various reasons that she might have left—she might, for example, have been physically compelled or gone because of love—and argues that whichever was in fact her reason, Helen is blameless. The speech's core is a long section where Gorgias considers persuasive argument, which he refers to variously just as λόγος and as πειθώ.[42] He argues (or perhaps jokes) that if we would forgive Helen for getting dragged to Troy by force—as of course we should—then we should also forgive her if someone persuaded her with *logos*.

Gorgias begins his argument by dismissing an idea that we have just seen in Lysias: that when someone uses *logos* to get us to do things, our master is the truth (or at least the apparent truth), not the person. Real knowledge, Gorgias says, is extremely hard to come by, mistakes and illusion are widespread, and we must therefore often depend on mere opinion rather than knowledge.[43] His idea seems to be that if we could easily decide which speakers were telling the truth, we could indeed use speeches as aids in coming into correct relationship with the truth. But as things stand, most people are exposed to all kinds of testimony whose truth they cannot evaluate with any confidence. These speeches are politically important even when their truth is completely uncertain, and these conditions call for an analysis of *logoi* independent from whatever truth they might contain.

When we look at *logos* from this perspective, he says, we find that persuasion and force are not opposites. Rather, the one is a particularly dangerous and powerful subspecies of the other. Persuasion, he says, is "a powerful master" (δυνάστης μέγας), and Helen left "just as unwillingly under the influence of speech as if she were seized by the violence of violators (βιατήρων βία)."[44]

The Greek language makes it particularly easy to identify persuasion with force. Although sometimes the word πειθώ means much the same as the English "persuasion," it also refers to other kinds of influence such as bribery, blackmail, and especially seduction—whatever it takes to get someone else to submit, acquiesce, or obey.[45] Gorgias repeatedly reinforces these associations. He says, for example, that *logos* "forced" Helen's soul to be persuaded and that a persuader is an aggressor whose words "mold" the listener's soul.[46] The fact that such metaphors of physical transformation are even intelligible suggests that the old opposition between force and persuasion cannot be as clear cut as Lysias makes it out to be.[47]

The point is not just linguistic. Rather, Gorgias suggests that this language reflects an intuitively plausible picture of persuasion, which we can again think of in terms of its phenomenology. As we have seen, Lysias and others like him depend on one aspect of the experience of being persuaded: when we are persuaded to do things, we often continue to feel like our own masters. But the *Helen* reminds us that is by no means *always* how it feels to be persuaded. When we hear a powerful practical argument for a position we are inclined to reject—and all the more so if it is made using techniques and jargon that we haven't mastered or where we're uncertain that anyone in the conversation has a firm epistemological footing—we *don't* in fact always feel as if the persuader is shining a light on the truth. Instead, we may feel confused and upset. We may feel that we have come under the persuader's power, even if we see no problem with the other's reasoning. Under these circumstances, a skilled user of *logoi* may leave us completely disoriented and confused or make us feel that there is no choice but to concede the argument. To these first-personal observations, we might add a similar third-personal variation: sometimes when we watch one person persuading another it *looks* like the exercise of power.[48]

While Gorgias accommodates such features of persuasion, he does not lose track of the features that distinguish persuasion from the more straightforward, physical kinds of compulsion. Losing an argument sometimes feels like losing a fight, but this doesn't mean it feels just like suffering physical blows. This, I take it, is Gorgias' point when he identifies the effects of *logos* with those of one particular distinctive kind of force rather than others: the compulsion exercised by drugs and magical spells. *Logos*, he says,

> injects pleasure and rejects pain, for in associating with the opinion of the soul, the power of an incantation enchants, persuades, and alters it through bewitchment. The twin arts of witchcraft and magic have been discovered, and these are illusions of mind and delusions of judgment. . . . The power of *logos* has the same effect on the disposition of the soul as the disposition of drugs on the nature of bodies. Just as different drugs draw forth different humors from the body—some putting a stop to disease, others to life—so too with words: some cause pain, others joy, some strike fear, some stir the audience to boldness, some benumb and bewitch the soul with evil persuasion.[49]

By treating persuasion as a kind of magic or medicine, Gorgias keeps a grip on the close relationship between force and persuasion, but also points out that it has a distinctive nature of its own—its effects seem more diffuse and as it were more internal than those we would normally call violence. Gorgias stresses that this kind of effect on a person's soul opens up something that is normally thought to be protected within the individual—a person's "private feelings"—to vicissitudes of the lives and affairs of others.[50] Thus not only is persuasion a kind of force rather than an uncoercive alternative to it; it is in some respects a particularly powerful kind of force. And it is a force that, like drugs and magic, gives some people the power to impose their preferences, if they choose, on other people.

Gorgias has an explanation of why *logos* acts so differently than other kinds of force. There is a distinctive *object* for that force: the soul. He summarizes this doctrine when he says that persuasion "has the same power but not the same form as compulsion."⁵¹ We are familiar enough with what violent force does to the body; Gorgias suggests that persuasion does just the same thing to the soul.⁵² Thus we have a clear account of both how force and violence are in a sense the same phenomenon, and how they nevertheless differ in their particulars.

Many scholars treat the *Helen* as a "defence" or a "celebration" of rhetoric. There is something right about that—indeed, Plato says something similar about his version of Gorgias, who praises oratory for giving people "freedom in their own persons" and "the power of ruling over others in their several states."⁵³ But it's worth noting that this is a highly qualified kind of praise: while it suggests that it's good to be able to persuade others, it emphatically does not make it seem like a good thing to *be persuaded* by someone else.

Quite the opposite, Gorgias casts serious doubt on the kind of praise lavished on persuasion by people like Lysias. If, as Gorgias suggests, persuasion is in fact a way that individuals may reach into the souls of others and manipulate them as they choose, then there is no difference in terms of freedom between submitting to an orator and a tyrant—except perhaps a difference in degree, since to have your very soul enslaved might seem *even more invasive* than restrictions on the body. Moreover in challenging the opposition between persuasion and force, he makes trouble for the association we have seen between persuasion and freedom. Persuasion is not, after all, exclusively a dignified treatment suitable for the free. It follows that the norm of persuading citizens but beating slaves is pointless.

It's not clear how seriously Gorgias took these ideas, but for our purposes it doesn't matter much whether he is showing off his skills by arguing for a position he takes to be absurd, using inconsequential content to illustrate formal aspects of rhetoric, or instead earnestly advancing his considered views of knowledge, belief, and language. In any case, the speech has traction because it points out an apparent problem with the treatment of persuasion by people like Lysias. And it is a problem that others seemed to be taking increasingly seriously for some time. Already in the early fifth century, Empedocles could promise that he had mastered principles that could not only cure his disciples' diseases but explain materially how persuasion affected their "thought organ."⁵⁴ This sort of view was soon developed by the likes of Democritus, who argued that while medicine cures bodily disease, wisdom can penetrate through to the sufferings of the soul.⁵⁵ Such thinkers, optimistic about the prospect of extending the technical achievements of medicine to the manipulation of the soul as well as the body, formed a body of advice manuals for the political elite, using the materialist mechanist language of early natural philosophy.

VI. Plato: Logos Good and Bad

Recall that we have been considering Aristotle's gestures at the opponents of rule pluralism, trying to uncover the dialectical pressures Aristotle is responding to and the intellectual resources he will develop. In particular, we have been considering why Aristotle departs from the common sense of his time with the "admonishment claim," according to which slaves should be ruled with persuasion, not violent force. We have seen that Aristotle's contemporaries are for the most part not just sanguine but downright enthusiastic about treating slaves violently. And I have argued that this view belongs to a kind of "rule dualism": on the view exemplified by Lysias, persuasion is the special province of the free, while the subordinate status of slaves must be maintained by assigning them the opposite treatment, violence. Gorgias' treatment of speech and persuasion in the *Encomium to Helen* challenges this view by painting linguistic persuasion in the same colors as violence.

Plato is abundantly sensitive to the idea that *logos* is a sneaky kind of force, affecting the soul rather than the body. He too is convinced that verbal persuasion is a powerful and dangerous cause of change in people's souls, and that there is good reason to fear persuasive people.[56] Indeed, he often reproduces Gorgias' identification of discourse with potions, poisons, and magical spells. In the *Sophist*, for example, the Eleatic Stranger says that sophists "belong to the class of wonder-workers" (τοῦ γένους εἶναι τοῦ τῶν θαυματοποιῶν)[57] and even Socratic discourse seems to have upsetting magical or physiological effects, as we learn when Meno complains that Socrates has "beguiled him," "put him under a spell," and numbed him like a poisonous fish.[58] In other words, Plato has his own version of the idea that *logoi* sometimes feel like force.[59]

But where Lysias and Gorgias alike understand *logos* as more or less homogeneous, Plato divides it into kinds. Although the details vary from dialogue to another, he consistently distinguishes not just between good and bad kinds of rule but between a good and a bad kind of *speech*. The overall picture is very familiar: The bad kind of speech—call it sophistry—traffics in appearance rather than reality, and the people who use it pay too much attention to spirit and the appetites, and not enough to reason. Sometimes the bad kinds of *logos* seduce young men, leading them away from virtue, as they do to Euthyphro; sometimes they also wreak political chaos, allowing the basest appetites of the *demos* to set policy, as we learn in the *Gorgias*. Like the *logoi* in the *Helen*, the bad speeches in Plato's dialogues influence people in ways that have no particular connection to reality and truth.

By contrast, good *logos*—call it dialectic or philosophy—escapes these dangers and allows speakers and listeners alike to be ruled by the truth rather than irrational impulse. Throughout the *corpus*, Plato variously tries to show how this is possible with his accounts of Socratic refutation and Academic dialectic. According to dialogues like the *Republic* and the *Phaedrus*, good *logoi* are essential to the educational process that culminates in fleeting glimpses of the Forms, familiarity with which is the only real knowledge. Thus Plato's account of philosophy gives new content to the idea we saw in Lysias: that *logos* is impersonal and intellectual, that it respects the ideal of rule by truth rather than by individuals.[60]

In the *Republic*, Plato famously connects this thought to an idea we found in Gorgias' *Helen*: that we understand *logos* best when we consider its effects on the soul. One of the three parts of the soul—the λογιστικόν or "rational" part—is capable of responding directly to the better kind of *logos*. The other two, spirit and appetite, are particularly susceptible to manipulation by sophistical arguments and thus to the sophists themselves, who are expert in the moods and pleasures (ὀργὴν καὶ ἡδονάς) of their audience.[61]

The tripartition of the soul allows Plato to explain both why speeches can be powerful even when they are false and irrational and why the people with the truest and most rational speech—notably including Socrates, the only person with the true political art—are often so ineffective. The sub-rational parts of the soul only come to have an appropriate relationship with the truth once they have undergone a rigorous training regime and are properly subordinated to the λογιστικόν. And the rational part itself can only do its characteristic work after an even longer, more arduous educational program outlined in *Republic* VII.[62] Thus the tripartition of the soul informs the political program of the *Republic*, which is in part to spell out the cultural and institutional conditions that will allow good speeches (as we might say, the objectively persuasive ones) actually to persuade.

A couple of observations about these ideas are in order. First, for reasons I have just sketched, the "force of the better argument" is indeed an honest-to-goodness force in Plato, but it can only win the day under some political circumstances. This explains a feature of Plato's philosophy that has been particularly worrisome for modern readers. In the *Republic*, Socrates says that the goal of the laws is to secure happiness for the city, and it gradually emerges that he is rather sanguine about doing this deceptively, through both "persuasion and compulsion."[63] It sometimes seems hard to reconcile his coercive politics with the flattering light he elsewhere shines on Socrates' open-ended style of discussion, which forces nothing on anyone, proceeding as long as necessary to discover the truth.

But Plato's emphasis on "musical" education—the control of culture and the mandatory extended education leading up to dialectical training—suggests part of the answer: that the not-quite-rational forms of manipulation we find in the *Republic* are preconditions for Socratic discussion to arise and find an audience. That is, philosophical discourse only works on cities and souls when specific conditions obtain, and (even under the idealized conditions assumed in the *Republic*) they can only be secured using various kinds of manipulation and coercion—the bad kinds of speech in some cases and outright violence in others. Neither bad speech nor outright force connects people directly to truth, but both can be used in service of good speech, making it possible for at least some people to produce and respond directly to true discourse while putting everyone else under its influence indirectly.[64]

Second observation: We saw a moment ago that Plato defends a version of a view we found in Lysias. In the ideal case—for example, in philosophical discussions in the Academy—the makers of arguments influence each other with dialectic, which by revealing contradictions somehow or other leads to knowledge of the good. This leaves them free from arbitrary preferences and subordinates them not to human beings but to the truth. But Plato only manages to defend an attenuated version of Lysias' thesis. Recall that Lysias' approach seemed appealing partly because it reflected a phenomenological difference between being violently forced to do something and being persuaded—which, as it were, *feels* as if it preserves our freedom. But on Plato's account, only a very rare, specialized kind of speech actually manages to leave people free from arbitrary preference. When nonphilosophers secure your consent, however, they are pushing you around with mere appearances, whether you feel free or not. And if your soul is in bad shape (and it probably is) that is all anyone can do for you. For Plato, Gorgias is quite right that the kinds of persuasion exercised in the assembly and the agora—indeed, the only kinds of persuasion most of us have ever experienced—are not in principle much different from violence.

Such considerations sometimes lead Plato to talk as if nonphilosophical free citizens are essentially the same as slaves.[65] Very few people will ever experience the kind of discourse he calls "the free man's knowledge."[66] Gregory Vlastos makes the point well:

> The absence of self-determination, so striking in the case of the slave, is normal in Platonic society. The fully enlightened aristocrats are a small minority of the whole population (e.g. *Statesman*, 292e). All the rest are in some degree *douloi* in Plato's sense of the word: they lack *logos*; they do not know the Good, and cannot know their own good or that of the state; their only chance of doing the good is to obey implicitly the commands of their superiors. Thus Plato speaks currently of the subjection to the reasonable discipline of rulers, human and divine, laws, parents, and elders as servitude.[67]

Plato delights in this provocative way of talking, and it is in this vein that early in the *Statesman*, the Stranger makes the comment that we saw at the beginning of this chapter, namely that there is just one kind of rule. Indeed, Plato might lead us to think that for Plato there are just two kinds of people, philosophical masters of the craft of rule and everyone else—and that we might as well call the two groups "natural rulers" and "natural slaves." Along the same lines, we might think that Plato endorses a kind of unmitigated paternalism: that when rulers know what's best for their subjects they may do anything at all to force it on them.

VII. Plato: Mixing Compulsion with Persuasion

In the *Laws*, the Athenian Stranger introduces a final twist:

> It's likely [he says] that none of the lawgivers has ever reflected on the fact that it is possible to use two means of giving laws, persuasion and violence (insofar as the uneducated condition of the mob permits). They have used only the latter; failing to mix compulsion with persuasion in their lawgiving,

they have employed unmitigated violence alone. But I, blessed ones, see the need for yet a third way of handling laws.[68]

He goes on to spell out this third way, which combines force and persuasion. It is one of the guiding principles in the dialogue. Just as speeches and songs are preceded by warm-up exercises, the laws should be accompanied by preludes (προοίμια). These explain the moral point of the law in question. Their goal is that "he who receives the law uttered by the legislator might receive the command—that is, the law—in a frame of mind more favorably disposed and therefore more apt to learn something."[69] This doctrine makes it clear that, in the *Laws* at least, Plato thinks that the free citizens who make up the "mob"—incapable though they might be of fully achieving the rational freedom of philosophers—nevertheless can receive a partial measure of rational persuasion.

The preludes themselves, which are scattered throughout the dialogue, demonstrate that this involves a wide variety of arguments, some rigorous and others very sketchy, as well as various kinds of myth and rhetorical appeals to emotion. Clearly, these do not always meet Plato's highest aspirations for rationality, but neither are they simply "lying propaganda," as Karl Popper thought.[70] Rather, they suggest that for Plato some kinds of treatment are intermediate between philosophical discourse and bare compulsion. They draw citizens into good behavior not merely through threats but also by helping them grasp some version of the reasons that support virtuous action.

It seems plausible that Plato intends much of Socrates' practice in other dialogues in much the same spirit as the preludes: through myths and suggestive argumentative sketches, he allows readers a glimpse of philosophical truth that they would see much more fully in serious philosophical training. This is the best way to understand his claim in the *Republic* that while it would be best if everyone were ruled by the rational part of his or her own soul, this is impossible for some—and for those people, rule by the rational part of another person's soul is a good alternative.[71] Those incapable of ruling themselves certainly can't receive the rational part of their leaders' souls through dialectic. Rather, they must get it through more or less manipulative means ranging from instruction at the theatre to the noble lie.

We saw earlier that it was a widespread democratic view that persuasion bestows honor on its listeners, treating them like the free, by contrast with the disgrace of being subject to force like beasts and slaves. And we saw that Gorgias challenges this view by dragging persuasion down to the level of violent force; his account suggests that being persuaded is little better than being enslaved. We can now see that Plato does just the opposite—he argues that free citizens sometimes have no reason to complain about being manipulated and controlled by human rulers, for this can put them into the correct relation to the truth. Where Gorgias links persuasion to force (thus degrading it, at least in Plato's eyes) Plato elevates compulsion, deception, manipulation, and other force-like kinds of speech by connecting them to an idealized form of persuasion.

Plato, then, argues that many nominally free people are suited to slavish treatment. And he often seems to accept the implication that this makes them slavish—most of the citizens of even the best cities will turn out to be somewhere in between slavery and freedom. And if in the *Republic*, he stresses how these intermediate people differ from philosophers, in the *Laws* the most pronounced contrast is with foreigners and especially slaves.[72] And this brings us back to his claim that slaves should always be commanded and never admonished. Plato, it is true, is critical of the sadistic treatment of slaves that sometimes occurs in Athens—he rails against those who "treat them like brute beasts, [and] with goads and whips make the slaves' souls not merely thrice but fifty times enslaved." He argues that masters should show their respect for justice by being even more reluctant to harm their slaves than they are to harm their equals. But it is clear that by "harm" he means something like "going beyond the force that is appropriate for them" or perhaps even "harming them for no good reason." He certainly doesn't think slaves should never be beaten, nor that they should be treated like the free. Quite the opposite—for example, he consistently calls for enslaved people to be beaten as punishment for any wrongdoing, consistently with Athenian law. Rather, Plato recommends punishments more severe than seem to have been current in Athens. If, for example, a slave harms a free man, that man may beat him as much as he likes (although he must compensate the slave's owner for whatever damage he does to this piece of his property).[73]

Plato rehearses this difference between slaves and the free again and again throughout the *Laws:* a full statement of most any law will distinguish between its application to slaves and the free. The principle motivating him is the one that has guided our entire discussion, namely that free people are to be persuaded rationally, while slaves are suited to manipulation and compulsion. If the qualified forms of persuasion embodied in the preludes place free citizens somewhere in the middle of a spectrum between rational persuasion and violent force, the people literally enslaved in Magnesia are distinguished by their position at the very bottom of that spectrum. Thus for Plato as for the Athenian mainstream, slaves and the free are different kinds of people (although in degree if not in kind), the ones especially well-suited to rule by force, the others to at least some measure of rule by rational persuasion.[74]

Plato, in other words, like most of his fellow Athenians, sees a version of the first of our three "premises"—that slaves are different from the free, and the two classes must therefore be treated differently—as obvious. We have seen that he accepts only weak versions of the other two: he does not see force and persuasion as clear-cut opposites, but grants that much persuasion is morally equivalent to force, and that other kinds are somewhere in between the two extremes. And he thinks that while the freest people are ruled only by persuasion, nonphilosophical free citizens should sometimes be ruled with various kinds of force and compulsion. Still, he retains versions of all three of our premises strong enough to justify the violent treatment of slaves. There is, as he puts it, a "necessary distinction" between free people and slaves, and this follows the pattern that was standard in Athens—slaves are to receive less persuasion and more violent force than the free.[75] This, then, is the context for his claim in the *Laws* that we should never admonish slaves, thereby treating them as if they were free. However startling it is to modern readers, for Plato it is a safe, offhand comment, one that he can toss off in a passage that also exhorts slaveholders to be kinder and more moderate.

Aristotle ultimately thinks this position botches *both* the division of rule into its species *and* their collection in a coherent genus. On the one hand, as we have seen, he thinks it is absurd to lump together free Greek men (even philosophically unsophisticated ones) with their slaves and other subordinates. But on the other hand, where Plato *does* distinguish between appropriate rule of the free and the slavish, Aristotle thinks he makes the division in the wrong way, based on a false view of persuasive speech. Aristotle thinks, against Plato, that persuasive speech is the best way to rule anyone, even a natural slave; yet he also sees robust natural differences among the normal residents of a city like Athens. Aristotle was not the first to advance these theses. Indeed, they both appear in the work of the rule monist par excellence, Xenophon.

VIII. Xenophon's Theory of Rule

For Xenophon, as for Aristotle, rule is a universal and fundamental feature of all human relationships.[76] For both thinkers, rule is an activity by which one person causes changes in another person's soul using *logos*. For both, using *logoi* does not mean casting off the causal and personal dimensions of rule onto an abstract, otherworldly, and therefore impersonal authority.[77] And for Xenophon, as for Aristotle, this fact provides more or less instrumental grounds for recommending a new, gentler treatment of slaves.

Rule or Be Ruled

In *Memorabilia* II.1, Socrates is talking to Aristippus, a well-known hedonist and one of Xenophon's rivals among Socrates' disciples. Aristippus is a kind of quietist. It is, he says, "the height of folly" to try to rule over anyone. Not only do effective rulers need uncomfortable levels of self-control and discipline, they must inevitably neglect their own needs to attend to others.[78] The better path, he says, is to abandon any social or political ambitions and instead to pursue one's pleasure as an individual. Xenophon's Socrates assumes this kind of withdrawal would amount to throwing oneself into the rule of others. He asks if Aristippus could really prefer the station of a barbarian—that is, a subject of rule—to that of a Greek—a ruler. Aristippus rejects the implication:

> I am no candidate for slavery (οὐδὲ εἰς τὴν δουλείαν ἐμαυτὸν τάττω) but it seems to me that there is a middle path between the two (μέση τούτων ὁδός); I strive to walk it, avoiding rule and slavery alike. It lies through freedom—the high road which leads to happiness.[79]

Socrates argues that no such path exists, at least for those of us who find ourselves "among human beings" (ἐν ἀνθρώποις). Those of us who don't rule display weakness that others will be sure to exploit, so we must either rule or, failing that, submit to being ruled.[80] Like Aristotle, then, Xenophon's Socrates thinks that interacting with others necessarily entails ruling or being ruled. For Aristotle, the point is metaphysical or mereological. Xenophon, by contrast, offers it up as an empirical generalization about human behavior.[81] In both cases, though, the question becomes *how* to engage in the economy of ruling and being ruled rather than whether to do so. That question appears in every work in Xenophon's corpus, which overflows with portraits of exemplary rulers, cautionary tales of failed rule, and instructions for ruling (and to a lesser extent, being ruled) well. Throughout his work, Xenophon paints a remarkably consistent picture of what Xenophon sometimes calls the "royal science," the βασιλικὴ τέχνη.[82]

Rule Monism Redux: The Royal Science

The royal science is a τέχνη or ἐπιστήμη (Xenophon uses the words interchangeably), and Xenophon emphasizes that although there are many spheres in which one person can rule another, there is just one such science. If you have the expertise to rule over people in one domain, you thereby have what it takes to rule over anyone anywhere. In *Memorabilia* III.4, for example, Socrates defends a certain Antisthenes who has just been appointed general with little to no military experience. Antisthenes, Socrates argues, just led a choir to victory in a musical competition—and he did it without knowing anything about singing or the administration of choirs. Rather, he brought together various musical experts and coaches and directed money where he needed to bring them to victory. Those maneuvers promise success on the battlefield as well as the stage.

> Whatever someone leads [Socrates says], if he knows what he should have and is able to get it (ἐὰν γιγνώσκῃ τε ὧν δεῖ καὶ ταῦτα πορίζεσθαι δύνηται), he will be a good controller (προστάτης), whether he controls a chorus, an *oikos*, a *polis*, or an army.[83]

The exchange highlights an obvious objection to the idea of an all-purpose science of rule. It would seem that any such science is bound to be empty, evacuated of the specialized knowledge that characterizes people actually qualified to lead any specialized activity. After all, we normally make sports trainers leaders because of their knowledge of *sport*. We assign wall-building to people who know something about building materials and construction techniques, and so on. Xenophon does not dismiss specialized knowledge like this. Indeed he writes about it in laborious detail in the sections on planting and fertilizing in the *Oeconomicus*, in manuals like *On Horsemanship* and *On Hunting with Dogs*, and elsewhere. But he thinks the best rulers can delegate it to subordinates and put them out of mind. They may, for example, spend an afternoon chatting with Socrates about leadership, as Ischomachus does in the *Oeconomicus*.

But what special content can then remain for the kingly art? Socrates' gloss, "knowing what he should have and being able to get it," evokes a familiar thought from the period but is not much immediate help.[84] The solution, rather, comes in two parts. First, aspiring rulers may turn inward toward individual virtue. This is necessary because, for Xenophon, it is ultimately virtue that allows people to benefit from whatever objects, activities, and people inhabit their lives. Thus the Socrates of the *Oeconomicus* claims that money, horses, and land are only "goods" when they benefit the person who owns them. People should therefore be considered "wealthy" just when they have more goods than they need.[85] Ischomachus, who manages a bustling estate (largely, as we will see, by carefully educating and moralizing to his wife and slaves), seems to satisfy that definition; he is therefore a successful ruler. But, so the argument goes, he is no more "wealthy" than the penniless Socrates, whose possessions outstrip his needs just because he scarcely needs anything. To *become* wealthy, you need not accumulate possessions but rather eliminate needs. Xenophon's Socrates concludes that self-control (ἐγκράτεια) turns out to constitute not only the "greatest of the virtues" but the royal science itself.[86]

So long as the gods are agreeable, Xenophon thinks, those who master themselves can then expect all other goods to follow through an automatic sequence of causes and effects. The argument, sketched repeatedly throughout Xenophon's corpus, runs like this: since virtuous people know what is really good (recognizing, for example, when and whether money is a good useful under given circumstances), and since they have the discipline to pursue it, they reliably also seek the good for everyone working under them. For example, as we see in great detail in the *Cyropaedia*, an imperial commander feeds, houses, equips, and educates his soldiers until they're at their best. He keeps them away from temptation, rewards their efforts, responds to complaints, and takes heed of their insights. So the soldiers are happy, successful, and productive (*eudaimôn*), and their happiness soon enough redounds back to the general, since he now has highly motivated, capable, and loyal force fighting for him. Xenophon frequently describes this sort of mutually beneficial relationship, in which virtuous, happy leaders inspire virtue and happiness in their subordinates, so that each "uses" the others to maximum benefit, as friendship, *philia*. And it is what he means when he says that philosophical inquiry into good leaders ends up stripping away everything else, leaving only the happiness of followers.[87]

This view—that the effective pursuit of a ruler's advantage tends to track the happiness of a subordinate (and vice versa), so that many hierarchies might become not just positive-sum games but loving, universally advantageous feedback loops—obviously involves robust empirical views about human motivation and interests. And those point toward the second major solution to the problem of the seeming emptiness of the royal science. On Xenophon's view, the royal science may leave behind climate, fertilizers, and horse-rearing to replace them not only with virtue but also with psychology.

Xenophon's human psychology is grounded in a broader theory of animal behavior. "Living creatures," Ischomachus says in the *Oeconomicus*, "learn obedience [τὸ πείθεσθαι] in two ways: by being punished when they try to disobey, and by being rewarded when they are eager to do as they are told." After noting that rewards and punishments secure obedience in colts and puppies, he concludes that the same mechanism works for human beings:

> In the case of human beings it is possible to make them more obedient merely by talking to them (ἀνθρώπους δ' ἔστι πιθανωτέρους ποιεῖν καὶ λόγῳ), pointing out that it is to their advantage to obey. But for slaves the method of training that is accepted for wild animals is very effective in teaching obedience. For if you gratify their desires by filling their bellies, you may get a great deal out of them. Those who are naturally ambitious become even keener with praise; for some natures hunger for praise as much others do for food and drink. These methods, then, are exactly the ones I use myself, because I believe I shall have more obedient people in my employ as a result.[88]

With human beings, then, the basic principles of animal training should be supplemented with λόγοι and τιμαί, which are particularly effective on some people.

Perhaps the most important psychological effect of good rule is that subjects obey willingly (ἐθέλουσι πείθεσθαι),[89] enthusiastically (προθυμεῖσθαι),[90] and without resentment (οὐκ ἄθυμός).[91] Virtuous rulers sometimes secure this effect simply because their excellence is visible to the people around them.[92] But the main way that Xenophon's rulers transmit their virtue to the ruled is—how else?—with *logoi*.

Socrates stresses this point to a newly elected cavalry commander. After dispatching some of the finer points of managing horses on various kinds of terrain, he turns to the commander's duties in psychological influence: "Have you thought about sharpening the soldiers' souls (θήγειν δὲ τὰς ψυχὰς)," he asks, "enraging them against the enemy, and thereby making them more robust (ἀλκιμωτέρους ποιεῖ)?"[93] Once the new commander admits he hasn't considered that but promises to do so, Socrates turns to the question of "how to make them obey" (ὅπως δέ σοι πείθωνται).[94] The answer involves many elements of the theory that we've just surveyed, and its heart is persuasive oratory: "Are you saying," the commander asks once he catches on, "that on top of everything else, the cavalry commander needs to cultivate the power of speech (ἐπιμελεῖσθαι δεῖν καὶ τοῦ λέγειν δύνασθαι)?" Socrates replies:

> Did you think that a commander should keep silent? Haven't you considered that all of the best things we've learned from our culture (νόμος)—that is, knowledge about how to live—we learned through *logos* (διὰ λόγου ἐμάθομεν)? And if you learn some other fine lesson, it will be through *logos* too? And the best teachers use *logos* most of all, and those with the best knowledge discuss it the best (κάλλιστα διαλέγονται)?[95]

Likewise the exemplary householder Ischomacus argues that a man should rule his wife by persuading her with *logoi*. Although he says women are less able to endure cold and heat and more inclined to care for children than men, he claims they are identical in terms of receptivity to moral instruction: the God, he says, gave "equal powers of memory and concern to both of them" (τὴν μνήμην καὶ τὴν ἐπιμέλειαν εἰς τὸ μέσον ἀμφοτέροις), and it is thus best to persuade them to obey with verbal lessons by explaining to them that their own benefit depends on the good functioning of the household.[96] Elsewhere, Xenophon explicitly contrasts the power of persuasion with violence. The latter, he says, is inseparable from "enmity and danger" while persuasion "gives rise to the same things safely, and in the context of friendship."[97]

It should be clear that Xenophon blurs the traditional opposition between force and persuasion in much the same way we have seen that Gorgias does in the *Helen*. In Xenophon's view, a technical or scientific approach to happiness requires that rulers everywhere draw on the power of speech to influence their subordinates.

Natural Slavery and Violence

Xenophon would surely endorse the admonishment claim and perhaps he helped inspire it. His theory of rule presents an obvious challenge to the violent treatment of slaves idealized by classical Athenians. And many of his characters lean into this implication, to the astonishment of their interlocutors. Ischomachus, for example, goes so far as to say that he rewards the most devoted foremen by treating them like free people and with the honors due to gentlemen, καλούς τε κἀγαθούς.[98]

What then becomes of the special association between slavery and violent subordination, and of the ideal of freedom it helps to underwrite? Some scholars have argued that the whole hierarchical structure dissolves, just as we have seen that Fortenbaugh imagines it does in Aristotle. Sarah Pomeroy, for example, writes that in the *Oeconomicus*, "there is no natural hierarchy among human beings according to gender, race, or class" and that "although Xenophon, like his contemporaries, took slavery for granted, he did not have a theory of natural slavery." Indeed, she says that with regard to slaves Xenophon is "liberal, even radical."[99]

Xenophon is admittedly a better candidate for this sort of reading than Aristotle. The best evidence is the handful of named and unnamed enslaved characters in his dialogues whom he credits with intelligence, virtue, and the other powers and abilities of the best free people. We've already mentioned the highly competent foreman in the *Oeconomicus*. Just as impressive are the Syracusan acrobats and dancers in the *Symposium*, Panthea and her loyal eunuchs in the *Cyropaedia*, and various others.[100] Xenophon doesn't just urge his readers to be kind to such slaves; he invites them to honor and admire them, marvel at their excellence, and perhaps free them if they distinguish themselves enough. And so, to be sure, Xenophon's approach to the education of slaves (and similarly of free women, menial workers, etc.) is unusual in fifth-century Athens.[101] Like the Socrates of Plato's early dialogues, Xenophon's Socrates attacks traditional aristocracy, advocating to replace it with a new, intellectual, and moralistic aristocracy. On his view, the people who take their elite status for granted—war heroes, well-born oligarchs, and so on—may or may not deserve it. The real elites may on the contrary be the penniless Socrates or Panthea, captured by the Persians as a slave. But it is worth stressing that Xenophon leaves it rather unclear how far to extend the lessons of these exemplars. Here too, there is a parallel with Aristotle, whose theory leaves it open that some of the enslaved people of Athens may be "naturally free" and therefore victims of injustice—but gives no indication of how many (if any) are unjustly enslaved or what (if anything) anyone ought to do to help them.¹⁰²

In any case Xenophon's radicalism has significant limits. Not only does Socrates blandly characterize slavery as just; in the *Poroi*, Xenophon develops in his own voice a program according to which each Athenian citizen owns three slaves. Moreover, it is clear that he expects very many of the people held in slavery to remain slavish. In a revealing passage, Xenophon rails against the degraded manual tasks (βαναυσικαί) that must be performed by enslaved people. He writes that these cramped indoor tasks make people's bodies "effeminate" and (therefore?) their souls weak.¹⁰³ So alongside the positive feedback loop through which rulers and subordinates serve each other's happiness, there also seems to be a negative one, where necessary work in unpleasant places ensures that some people become worse and worse, body and soul.

Xenophon is quite comfortable with the violent treatment of such people. He evidently approves of a certain Nichomachides, who brags that he makes his slaves' lives "a burden to them until I reduce them to submission."¹⁰⁴ This sort of domination through force is, for Xenophon, appropriate for *bad* slaves. And bad slaves are apparently very common.¹⁰⁵ All bad masters, Ischomachus argues, have bad slaves, since they don't have the knowledge or self-control needed to train them properly. Thus, he says, he has never found a bad master with good slaves. And he quickly adds that even good masters have bad slaves at least sometimes, "though at least they don't go unpunished" (οὐ μέντοι ἀζημίους γε).¹⁰⁶ The typical range of punishments includes a list from the *Oeconomicus*: "Do they not starve them to keep them from immorality, lock up the stores to stop their stealing, clap fetters on them so that they can't run away, and beat the laziness out of them with whips?" No matter how much a good master may benefit his slaves, and no matter how impressive the best of them are, it seems that there exists a seemingly large group of slaves constitutionally unable to be good, and they should certainly be brutally punished by their masters. Perhaps this is not a theory of natural slavery, but it is closely akin to one. It is at any rate nothing like an argument for the equal dignity of all human beings.

In short, Xenophon exemplifies the pattern that we will see in Aristotle: using *logoi* to secure consent and understanding from slaves without thereby granting them the status or dignity of free people. It may be useful here to consider the analogy between Xenophon's approach to slaves and women in the *Oeconomicus* and Plato's discussion of female guardians in *Republic* V. That argument, as Julia Annas writes,

> is not based on, and makes no reference to, women's desires or needs. Nothing at all is said about whether women's present roles frustrate them or whether they will lead more satisfying lives as Guardians than as housebound drudges. . . . Of course Plato is not bound to be interested in the psychology of women, but his complete lack of interest underlines the fact that his argument does not recommend changing the present state of affairs on the ground that women suffer from being denied opportunities that are offered to men.[107]

Annas concludes that this is sufficient grounds to say that whatever its merits, *Republic* V is not a feminist text. Xenophon, as we have seen, is interested in the happiness of slaves. But his approach is, in the end, likewise instrumental.

IX. Conclusion

It is in this light that we should take stock of the admonishment claim in Aristotle himself. Like Xenophon, Aristotle never says that it is impermissible to use force on slaves if admonishment fails or if they deserve to be punished. And we would not expect him to—even with free people, Aristotle thinks arguments are often of little use. "In general it is not talk that makes emotion yield," he says, "but force."[108]

Giving arguments to enslaved people is for Aristotle a good idea, not because it gives them a choice about what to do but because, as Gorgias had suggested, *logoi* are efficacious if you are concerned not just with controlling people's bodies but also their souls.[109] The admonishment claim amounts to something like instructions about how to use a tool in light of its peculiar properties. Since a violin bow has a certain elasticity and you don't want it to bounce around too much, you should put your little finger on the frog like so; since a slave is a human being who performs cooperative actions with you, you need to control not just his body but also his soul, and that requires persuasion with language.

Needless to say, Aristotle has his own version of the Platonic thesis that *logos* has special connections to the true and the good. Nevertheless, for Aristotle as for Gorgias, *logos* is ethically neutral in the narrower sense that we cannot say in general whether it is a good thing or a bad thing to be influenced with words. Likewise, for Aristotle *logos* is important to rulers—whether or not they are concerned with the well-being of their subordinates—because of the usefulness of willing or enthusiastic obedience. We will see in Chapter 2 that Aristotle's objective, as he considers the various kinds of rule, is to develop these insights according to the lights of his other theoretical commitments. In particular, he thinks that immanent, individual, and habituated perspectives are central to practical reasoning. And so he believes that they must ultimately direct the natural hierarchies that he, like so many of his predecessors and contemporaries, sees as essential to justice and human life.

2

Interpersonal Causation and the Generic Definition of Rule

When Aristotle says that rule is divided into *species* (εἴδει διαφέρει),[1] he invites the thought that they belong to some common genus. If so, we might ask—in line with the famous arguments from the beginning of the *Meno*—for a single account tying them all together.[2] If there is such an account, it will imply surprising connections among relations that otherwise seem very different, like those of free citizens on the one hand and the domination of slaves on the other. Is there a generic account? In this chapter I argue that there is. Aristotle's division of rule into species depends on a determinate, psychologically rich conception of rule as a genus. It is a definition he offers outright in the philosophical lexicon of *Metaphysics* Δ, although what he says there calls for considerable elaboration.

I argue that Aristotle's generic definition of rule expands and transforms an idea that we encountered in Chapter 1: that *logos* is a tool allowing one person to effect changes in the soul of another. For Aristotle, I argue, this thought takes a specific form: when one person rules another, the decision (προαίρεσις) of the ruler establishes the "goal-for-the-sake-of-which" (οὗ ἕνεκα) that acts as a final cause for the actions of the person who is ruled. At the end of the chapter I consider a possible objection: that this sort of interpersonal causation turns people into puppets or automata. We will see that, on the one hand, Aristotle's conception of rule leaves it open that subjects of rule make considerable positive and independent contributions to shared action. Yet there remains a sense in which whenever one person rules another, the one quite literally does some of the other's thinking.[3]

I. Practical Truth and the πίστεις

Let's return to two rival views of persuasive speech we encountered in Chapter 1. In one approach, explored by the likes of Lysias and Plato, *logoi* at their best connect listeners to an impersonal truth; in the second, explored by Gorgias and Xenophon, they are causal instruments that subordinate one person's soul to another. Aristotle takes both traditions on board in the *Rhetoric*, a treatise that is a useful starting point because (whatever its exact relationship to the rest of the corpus) it discusses without too much theoretical elaboration views that Aristotle takes to be practical and generally persuasive.

Their importance to his thought is especially clear in the doctrine of the three πίστεις—the three "means of persuasion" or "styles of proof," namely *logos*, *pathos*, and *ethos*. Recall that according to that doctrine there are exactly three things that rhetoricians may use to persuade their audiences (and indeed three things at work in any effective piece of oratory).[4] Orators demonstrate their points not only (i) with facts and their logical relations but also (ii) by influencing listeners' emotions and (iii) by convincing the audience of their own good character. Now points (ii) and (iii) are less banal than they might seem. Aristotle doesn't just mean that orators sometimes can cause their listeners to agree with them by moving them emotionally or by coming across as good people. Of course he recognizes that those things happen all the time, but he thinks that most often the persuasion is "*atechnic*"—that is, the supposed proofs don't belong to the art of rhetoric properly speaking.

Persuasion through emotion and character is only truly rhetorical when it is provided διὰ τοῦ λόγου, "through the *logos*."[5] Orators violate this requirement if they shape the feelings of their audiences with tricks irrelevant to the case at hand (such tricks, Aristotle says, are the *only* thing covered by the rhetorical handbooks of his day). To use *ethos* and *pathos* consistently with the art of rhetoric, they must use character and emotion only in ways that rationally support the judgment (κρίσις) that the speech is trying to secure.[6] In other words, the listener's emotion and the speaker's character must somehow operate as evidence—even proof—of whatever judgment the listener is supposed to make. In this way, although public speeches will not achieve "scientific exactness" (ἀκριβὴς ἐπιστήμη), rhetorical appeals to emotion and character can transmit the honest-to-goodness truth from speaker to listener no less than the content of a speaker's argument.

It's easy to point out cases that fall short of Aristotle's standard. The speaker may not, for instance, bring crying children into the courthouse, nor recruit friends to warm up the audience by telling them how wise and accomplished he is. Likewise, a charming smile and a resonant voice are (excluding special cases) incidental to the speaker's argument and therefore to the art of rhetoric as Aristotle understands it. But it's perhaps harder to say what uses of character and emotion might *meet* Aristotle's standards. Orators seek to bring about some judgment relevant to the political life of their community: that they should demand tribute from such-and-such a colony, that the defendant committed the murder, that the dead were exceptionally heroic, and so on. Once again, how can listeners' emotions and speakers' personalities count as rational support—or indeed *proof*—of conclusions like that?[7]

In the case of emotion, there is fairly straightforward answer. As any reader of the *Nicomachean Ethics* knows, Aristotle holds that the virtues are dispositions not just toward certain actions but also to certain affective responses—indeed, he defines the virtues as "being well or badly off with regard to emotions": ἕξεις δὲ καθ' ἃς πρὸς τὰ πάθη ἔχομεν εὖ ἢ κακῶς.[8] Thus courage is a matter of how you experience fear—whether you feel it under the right circumstances, in the right amount, and so on. When you get everything right, your fear may be said to agree with or share in a true *logos* about the situation.[9] My anger is not just the boiling of blood in my heart; it also signals that that I have perceived someone dishonoring me or a person I care about.

We will return to psychological responses to *logoi* soon, but for now suffice it to say that proof through *pathê* happens just when a person responds emotionally to a situation presented in speech, not grasped with the senses.[10] When I convince you that that we need to mollify the masses with a public feast, this may involve scaring you with the prospect of their rising up against us. Part of my *point* in such a speech is that it is wholly appropriate to be afraid in this situation. If you aren't afraid, this is a sign that you haven't been persuaded; if you are, then your fear supports the desperate measures I am recommending.

So much for the rationality of persuasion through emotion. Persuasion through character—the "most effective" of all the *pisteis*[11]—is trickier. A speaker's character will often have no obvious connection to the subject matter. If I set out to persuade the city that it's time to go to war with the Persians, the peculiarities of my character are not likely to be relevant to the war itself.[12] Of course, if I have good judgment about military matters, then you have some reason to take my advice. But if I *tell* you that, perhaps by pointing out that the recommendations I made last time worked well, then my character has entered the argument itself—the *pistis* I am using is now *logos*, not *ethos*. So it may be hard to see how Aristotle can think that a person's character can persuade "through" an argument, without entering as a premise into the argument. On the one hand, speakers cannot rely on their reputation or on external evidence of their expertise (for this would not persuade through the *logos* as all three *pisteis* must do); on the other, they cannot either implicitly or explicitly use their own good character as premises (since this would use the wrong *pistis*—*logos* rather than character). What remains?

Aristotle suggests the answer when he lists the three "causes" of persuasion housed within the speaker: they are *phronêsis* ("practical wisdom"), virtue, and goodwill.[13] The idea seems to be that just as the facts you present to me can change the way I see the world, and just as the emotions you evoke in me can do the same, so too can your character directly reconfigure the way I understand a practical situation. After all, when you talk about a difficult practical situation you downplay some features of the situation and highlight others, you present events under some descriptions rather than others, and so on. If I step back to think about those factors, I will have good evidence concerning your character. But, more immediately, if I am persuaded, I may in a sense have directly *taken on* your way of processing the situation. Your *phronêsis*, virtue, and goodwill cause me to see the world differently.

We may sometimes find good advice persuasive in this way. That is, sometimes it doesn't provide us with new facts or alert us to their logical implications (as it would if it were primarily persuading us with the argument); and sometimes it doesn't change how we feel about our situation (as it would if it were persuading us with emotions); rather, some of the best advice helps us because it makes it obvious that the adviser sees the situation more clearly than we do and makes that perspective available to us. Similarly—though the details of the example are not Aristotelian—many people have had the experience of "receiving" the aesthetic eyes and ears of a friend with good taste. Listening to music with you, I find myself hearing it differently and better than I normally would. Indeed, I finally hear it rightly, because I have so to speak borrowed your ears.

I think such examples help to clarify the links between the three kinds of *pistis* and the three elements that Aristotle says come together in every speech: the speaker, the topic (περὶ οὗ λέγει), and the listener.[14] Each *pistis* ties the persuasion to a different element. Persuasion through emotion is "in" the listener, *logos* is "in" the argument itself, and proof through character is "in" the speaker. Both *logos* and *pathos* give listeners materials allowing them to form a judgment that is ultimately fully grounded within their own souls. But this is not the case with persuasion through character. As Aristotle also puts the point, when one person persuades another through character, the "speaker himself" is persuasive.[15]

These locutions suggest that the speaker provides something more—and the listener something less—in persuasion through character than in the other two proofs. If I am persuaded through *logos* and *pathos*, I take the speaker's argument into my soul, consider it by my own lights, and reach a decision that is in some sense fully my own. But with persuasion through character, I respond to the speaker's wisdom, virtue, and goodwill—but they do not thereby become *my* wisdom, virtue, and goodwill.[16]

If this reading is on track, then so long as the speaker isn't lying or mistaken, persuasion through character is (i) guided by the truth (since the speaker really does perceive the relevant features of the situation more clearly than the listener, as the speaker recognizes), but it also (ii) puts one person squarely and personally under the power of the other. When I take good advice, I receive the speaker's ethical outlook as if it were my own—and that means I am not submitting, say, to an impersonal form of the good, mediated by a philosopher king, but rather to a specific person *qua* individual.

II. Relationships between Souls in Aristotle's Ethics and Politics

The same phenomenon, through which one person takes the ethical perception of another, is crucial too to the philosophy of human affairs developed in the *Ethics* and the *Politics*. Consider, for a start, Aristotle's famous pronouncement about the role of language in human life at the beginning of the *Politics*, where he argues that human beings are the "most political" of all animals:

> The human being alone among the animals possesses *logos*. The voice indeed indicates the painful or pleasant, and hence is present in other animals as well; for their nature has come this far, that they have a perception (ἔχειν αἴσθησιν) of the painful and pleasant and signal these things to each other. But *logos* serves to reveal the advantageous and the harmful, and hence also the just and unjust. For it is peculiar to human beings as compared to the other animals that they alone have a perception of good and bad and right and wrong and the like (τὸ μόνον ἀγαθοῦ καὶ κακοῦ καὶ δικαίου καὶ ἀδίκου καὶ τῶν ἄλλων αἴσθησιν ἔχειν), and it is partnership in these things that makes a household and a city (ἡ δὲ τούτων κοινωνία ποιεῖ οἰκίαν καὶ πόλιν).[17]

In this passage, we learn (i) that *logos* draws from the uniquely human capacity to perceive the good, bad, just, unjust, and other such things; that (ii) making *logoi* allows us to transmit such perceptions to others (i.e., it has the character we found in ideal cases of rhetoric, of passing moral perception from one person to another); and (iii) that sharing "these things"—evidently not just the good and the bad but the perception (αἴσθησις) of them—produces both the *polis* and the *oikos*. This passage makes it clear that "indicating" (σημαίνειν) justice and injustice with *logoi* is central to human life and particularly to our interactions with each other.

Several passages from the *Ethics* provide evidence about how he sees the psychology of this process. At the end of Book I of the *Nicomachean Ethics*, Aristotle introduces the psychological framework that informs the rest of the treatise. It centers on the crucial distinction between the *logistikon*, the part of the soul equipped to produce *logoi* concerning the practical domain of things that could be otherwise, and the *alogon*, which may resist *logos* but can also "participate" in it by attending to it (κατήκοον) and obeying it (πειθαρχικόν). This division of the soul is central to many of the main themes of the treatise, notably Aristotle's treatment of ethical (as opposed to intellectual) virtue and of *akrasia*. But Aristotle's defense of this partition also provides crucial information about possible relations between the souls of different people.

One helpful piece of evidence is a brief argument showing that the soul must have a reason-responsive part. It turns on the way we—or at least our reason-receptive part—can "have" the *logos* of our father or friends (τοῦ πατρὸς καὶ τῶν φίλων φαμὲν ἔχειν λόγον). He offers:

> That the *alogon* is in a way persuaded by *logos* is shown by our practice of admonishing people, and all the different forms in which we reprimand

and encourage them. If one should call this too [i.e., responding to the admonishment of others] "possessing *logos*," then the aspect of soul that possesses *logos* will also be double in nature: one element of it will have it in the proper sense and in itself, another as something capable of listening [or obeying: ἀκουστικόν] as if to one's father.[18]

On a first reading, we might think that Aristotle mentions the familiar interpersonal phenomena of admonishment and persuasion as a metaphor, to make it easier to imagine the more obscure psychological processes he wants to discuss. But as Sarah Broadie points out in an illuminating discussion of the passage, this isn't right. Rather, the passage shows that he sees the interpersonal cases as *evidence* supporting a certain conception of the soul: the normal practice of interpersonal admonishment somehow "shows" that there is a reason-receptive soul-part within the individual.[19] This argument only works if the rational part of the soul can do the same thing to the reason-receptive part of someone else's soul that it does to its own.

Aristotle makes this argument immediately after pointing out the ways that nonrational impulses interfere with reason, observations that could invite the thesis (advanced, for example, by Plato's Socrates in the *Phaedo* and elsewhere, though not in the *Republic* and the *Laws*) that any nonrational parts of the soul are merely and entirely obstacles to rationality. If this were true, then we could not strive for partnership or harmony between reason and the emotions. Rather, reason at its best would suppress, eliminate, or subsume the irrational passions and desires, effectively eliminating any division within the better sort of soul. This gives him a reason to offer arguments that there is a distinct, reason-receptive part of the soul not only within *enkratic* or *akratic* people (in whom the *alogon* can be easily distinguished from the *logistikon*) but also in the souls of people who are entirely virtuous.

Aristotle, however, points out that in youngsters, students, and other impressionable people, appetites and passions can be made harmonious with other people's reasons, and in those cases the good nonrational impulses clearly remain distinct from the rational impulses that direct them. They are, after all, housed in entirely different bodies. This shows that reason can interact with the not-fully-rational parts of the soul without suffocating or destroying them, and it leaves the door open for a single virtuous soul that is nevertheless composed of distinct parts (even when the difference between them isn't made manifest by conflict). The argument, then, runs roughly as follows: indisputably, people receptive to admonishment have a reason-responsive part, since it can respond to *someone else's* reason; why not admit, then, that this part coexists with reason in the souls of virtuous people as well, even if it is not as evident there as in the souls of the *akratic*? The central point for our purposes is that when the semi-rational part of my soul submits to someone else's *logoi*, it is in some sense doing the same thing as when it submits to my own.[20] In fact it is *clearer and less controversial* that one's *logistikon* can domesticate and subordinate the *aloga* of others than it is that it can domesticate and subordinate one's own.

When Aristotle describes the workings of psychic processes in the *Ethics*, he also discusses not just individual souls but the ways psychic phenomena can bridge the souls of several people. This is clear in a little-noticed series of claims in his discussion of deliberation in *EN* III.3. At 1112b27, Aristotle says that the objects of deliberation consist of things that are possible. The notion of possibility here isn't metaphysical but personal. Possibilities are things "that could come about through our own agency; for things which come about through the agency of our friends do so in a way through our own agency, since their origin is in us" (δυνατὰ δὲ ἃ δι' ἡμῶν γένοιτ' ἄν: τὰ γὰρ διὰ τῶν φίλων δι' ἡμῶν πως ἐστίν: ἡ γὰρ ἀρχὴ ἐν ἡμῖν).[21] A few lines later, he says that we seek out not just instruments or means to our ends but also "someone through whose agency it could come about" (ὁτὲ μὲν δι' οὗ ὁτὲ δὲ πῶς ἢ διὰ τίνος).[22] And finally he closes the discussion of deliberation with an example of this sort of outsourced agency: the Homeric forms of government in which "the kings announced to the people what they had chosen to do."[23]

Commentators usually let these passages slip by without comment, and this is not entirely unreasonable, since they don't contribute directly to Aristotle's main concern in the *EN*, his argument about the happiness and virtue of individual agents.[24] But Aristotle is nevertheless communicating very clearly that he takes it for granted that agency can flow through other people. In the *Ethics* he is mostly concerned with producing decisions and using *phronêsis*, not receiving them. But in his list of intellectual virtues, he describes one—σύνεσις, "comprehension" or "understanding"—which is concerned with judging the decisions that issue from someone else's practical wisdom. Aristotle introduces it by pointing out that it is concerned with just the same things as *phronêsis*, things that could be otherwise, in the realm of what should and what should not be done—the things "about which we are puzzled, and we might deliberate." Nevertheless, although it is about (πρός) the same things as *phronêsis*, the two virtues are not the same.[25] The difference is that comprehension consists in using the faculty of belief to judge the things "said by another" (ἄλλου λέγοντος).[26]

If Aristotle makes it clear in *Nicomachean Ethics* III that one person can deliberate about an action that will flow through the soul of someone else, in *Politics* I, he suggests that in some cases *deliberation itself* can be outsourced. Notoriously, when he explains why he thinks some people are naturally subject to rule, he says that slaves lack the deliberative faculty (βουλευτικόν), that women have it but that it is unauthoritative (ἄκυρον), and that in children it is incomplete.[27] Moreover, none of them have *phronêsis*, which Aristotle says at *Pol.* III.4, 1277b25-9, is "the virtue peculiar to the ruler." Deliberation and practical wisdom are essential for human virtue, and Aristotle thinks that slaves, women, and children lack them or can't exercise them properly. And yet he insists that they all have human virtue. The implication, as Marguerite Deslauriers has argued, is that free men lend their own deliberative capacities and practical wisdom to their slaves and other natural subjects. Thus their virtues are "relative to the master" (πρὸς δεσπότην);[28] they live a life according to reason when their desiderative faculties submit to (and in the best cases only produce desires in accordance with) the reason of their rulers.[29] And although Aristotle does not put the point in terms of soul parts, we might note that when a city does something (as, for example, when Athens declares war) the citizens are divided into people who rule and people who are ruled; those who are not ruling do not need to exercise *phronêsis*, but *all* citizens must by definition be involved in judgment and deliberation.[30] It would seem, then, that some are under the power of others but nevertheless contribute to collective action by judging and deliberating.[31]

It is by no means un-Aristotelian, then, to think that a person could use *logoi* to affect and indeed take hold of someone else's *alogon*. Quite the opposite, this kind of relationship between souls is a persistent theme in his practical philosophy. If anything, Aristotle finds these causal links between parts of different people's souls more transparent, and hence less in need of lengthy explication, than the causal relationships among parts of the soul of an individual. One important implication is that engaging in conversation does not necessarily direct one's relationships toward greater equality—quite the opposite, engaging in conversation can on this view deeply subordinate one person to another. (We will need to wait until Chapters 4 and 5 to discuss what *does* amount to equal relations in Aristotle's theory of rule.)

III. Ruling

It will come as no surprise that I think the phenomena I have been discussing amount to examples of rule. Although Aristotle does not define "rule" anywhere in his practical philosophy, he does offer a list of preliminary definitions of ἀρχή in *Metaphysics* Δ, alongside similar lists for such terms as "unity," "element," and so on. Most of his definitions of ἀρχή are only indirectly related to our question here, treating the word in its impersonal senses, which call for English translations like "principle" or "beginning." But he does dedicate two sentences to the specifically social or human senses of the word that we are concerned with. As Kirwan has pointed out, they are distinct in grammar, not just meaning, from the others: the impersonal senses of the word correspond to the verb ἄρχεσθαι in the middle voice, the personal to the active ἀρχεῖν.[32] Here is what Aristotle says:

> [ἀρχή means] the one in accord with whose decision what is moved is moved and what is changed is changed—for example the rulers in cities, dynasties, and kingships. And crafts are called ἀρχαί, especially architectonic ones.[33]

To rule over other people is on this definition to bring about motion (κινήσις) and change (μεταβολή) in them. These effects take place "according to [the ruler's] decision" (κατὰ προαίρεσις) and can be interpreted in terms of crafts (τέχνη). Both parts of this definition—the part concerning decision and the part concerning the crafts—are quite significant, and I'll consider them one at a time.

Decision

Προαίρεσις, "decision" or "policy," is richly theorized in the *Eudemian* and *Nicomachean Ethics*. It is part of the same psychology of action that runs through the passages we just looked at. A decision is a "considered desire" (ὄρεξις βουλευτική)[34] and one of the defining features of a bona fide action (by contrast, for example, with a spasm). It is also the summation and end point of deliberation, the knot tying together one's various desires with other relevant features of one's outlook, including (other) standing goals, the insights acquired through experience, and the specific features of one's immediate situation. Thus decision includes deliberation, but also moves beyond it to all of the desires and ends an agent may have, including hypothetical prescriptions like those provided by crafts—that I should reinforce this saddle *if* I want it to support a particularly heavy rider. It provides a final, all-things-considered judgment about what to do.³⁵

Hippocrates, let us suppose, is a just and giving doctor who has learned to spot opportunities to bring about the good. He sees health as a particularly valuable end, and he has practiced medicine for a long time. Confronted with a snake bite, he sees an opportunity.³⁶ Perhaps he determines that leeches would effectively remove the poison. This is important information but not yet a decision. After all, there may be no leeches available or the patient may have other, more important injuries that should be treated instead. Most importantly, moral considerations might enter the picture as well—some nonmedical action may be more important than treating this patient, or the patient just might not deserve to be treated. It is when Hippocrates decides that the leeches will best realize his commitment to the good, all things considered, that he has reached a decision and is ready to act.³⁷ He has completed a set of deliberations about "how and by what means" to realize his commitment to some good, considering his specific circumstances.³⁸ He now has a considered policy in place and is ready to act.

Decisions, then, are characteristic products of the virtues and vices, and they are among the most reliable indications of the agent's character as a whole. It is natural, then, that the more technical definition of the *Metaphysics* would appeal to them when it discusses the phenomenon covered more loosely under the heading "persuasion through character" in the *Rhetoric*.³⁹ But what can it mean for someone *else* to act "according to" a ruler's decision? In a simple case, we might imagine Hippocrates directing an apprentice's every movement, perhaps even guiding his hand.⁴⁰ But rule cannot always be so immediate and comprehensive. In many of Aristotle's examples of rule, subordinates have considerable discretion in executing their rulers' ends. In fact, it would be degrading for slave-masters even to *know about* the day-to-day activities of the slaves they rule.⁴¹ How can subordinates act according to a ruler's "decision" if they regularly and autonomously choose to do this rather than that?

Architectonic Crafts

Recall now the second sentence from the definition in *Metaphysics* Δ: "Crafts, too, are called ἀρχαί, especially architectonic ones." Many readers suppose that

Aristotle here moves on from his political definition of ἀρχή to a different, artisanal or technical one. The most frequently used English translations, by Ross and Tredennick, both supply numbers to distinguish among the definitions throughout *Metaphysics* Δ—and both thereby imply that our two sentences are separate, independent definitions. But Aristotle is better understood to be expanding on the same sense of the word we have been discussing.

In particular, here as elsewhere he uses the figure of the ἀρχιτεκτῶν (construction supervisor) to flesh out the teleological relationship between ruler and ruled. "The subordinate (ἀρχόμενος)," as he puts the point in *Politics* III, "is like a flute maker, while the other [sc. the ruler] is like a flute player, the user of what the other makes."[42] Aristotle's idea is that the "users" provide an end or goal for the "makers"; the former confer meaning and indeed intelligibility on the activities of the latter. There would be no point at all in making flutes if no one would ever play them, and the various skills involved in flute-making are directed toward players' needs.

Imagine a flute-maker cut free from any of the higher arts, including even flute-playing. Such a person might randomly begin constructing various flutes, some sized for children and others for giants, tuned to a variety of different pitches and scales, and generally disassociated from the needs of players, the interests of listeners, or the role of music in education and public life. Then again, all of that might be so pointless that the flute-maker would just give up, sitting idly or taking up some other activity. When Aristotle imagines a subordinate without a ruler, he pictures someone who is not so much liberated from constraints as stripped bare of context and meaning.

Of course, on Aristotle's view the flute player is not at the top of the hierarchy. Other experts provide an end to the flute player, including the composer, the arranger, the concert programmer, the impresario, and so on. But none of those people can provide goals for themselves either. The only people who can do that must escape from the realm of mere production and ascend to action in its full sense. Such people must be able to perform "unqualified" deliberations, taking into account whatever "conduces to the good life in general."[43] The paradigm case is the "political expert" (πολιτικός), who coordinates the values of musical performance with other values in the political community and ultimately with the common good and the *kalon*.[44] Such people are necessary because rule over human beings involves animating them with the kinds of goals embodied in *phronêsis* (or its vicious analogues).

Those goals—unlike either the goals embodied by the appetites of a beast or the principles of flute-playing—are distinctively moral. Another way of making this point is to say that architectonic rule amounts to *phronêsis* (practical wisdom), the virtue that allows people to *make* good decisions. Aristotle defines *phronêsis* with just the same concepts (deliberation and apprehension of the good and useful) that he uses to explain decision.[45] And in fact he says simply that political expertise *is* "the same disposition as *phronêsis*."[46] In communities pursuing not just life but the good life, the ruler will have *phronêsis* and will provide an end for the person or people ruled that benefits them, not just the ruler.

And indeed if *phronêsis* is necessary for ruling, Aristotle argues that it is strictly superfluous for being ruled. In particular, *phronêsis* is not necessary *for* subordinates[47]—even, to anticipate a point that will become important later on, for free members of a community of equals, at least insofar as they are taking their turns being ruled. By the same token, the three types of people he thinks are naturally suited to being ruled—namely slaves, women, and children—all have some sort of failure of deliberative capacity (βουλευτικόν).[48]

Virtue and Goals

I have been arguing that Aristotle understands rule as follows: the ruler causes the actions of the subordinate by providing the latter with a practical goal or *telos*. In particular, the *logos*-making part of the ruler's soul communicates decisions that animate the activity of the *logos*-receiving part of the subordinate.

This schematic account raises questions about the origins of our goals or values. The biggest problem is that Aristotle repeatedly says that our goals and values originate in our ethical virtue, not reason. Virtue—that is, the largely habituated dispositions of the *alogon*—provides the ends of human action. Deliberation and *logos* then concern themselves with figuring out how to realize those goals in a particular situation, perhaps by finding means to the end or specifying activities that would constitute the good in question.[49] Thus it is natural that on Aristotle's overall view education, habituation, and nature play expansive roles in orienting us toward virtue or vice with a rich set of values. *Phronêsis*, for its part, brings those pre-existing values to bear in a given situation. So it might seem that when rulers transmit *logoi* to their subordinates (crystallized, in the ways we have seen, into decisions), they cannot thereby be transmitting ends.

Now some scholars reject this view, arguing that notwithstanding Aristotle's claims to the contrary, rationality—and *phronêsis* in particular—must play some role in determining ends. If we follow them, we may say continue to say summarily that the ruler's *logistikon* animates the *alogon* of his subordinates just as it does his own. But if we accept that Aristotle imagines human goals originating mainly in habituated dispositions (as I think we should), we ought to treat this as shorthand for a slightly more complex account.

When one person rules another, the ruler's *logistikon* and *alogon* both inform the subordinate's actions. Aristotle writes, after all, that decision springs from both desire and *logos*, and that it is therefore "neither without intelligence and thought, nor without ethical dispositions" (οὔτ' ἄνευ νοῦ καὶ διανοίας οὔτ' ἄνευ ἠθικῆς ἐστὶν ἡ προαίρεσις).[50] The decision contributed by a ruler to shared action is a psychological composite, just like human virtue itself. Suppose Hippocrates submits to a general's rule. The story begins with the general's ethical character, which produces some wish for a real or apparent good. The general's environment and situation (including, say, Hippocrates and a snake-bitten soldier) provide various constraints on how that good might be realized. The general seeks a way to realize his ideals, perhaps means to the end, perhaps activities constitutive of the good. A solution materializes: "*This* will do it!" And the general's *logistikon* may now produce spoken *logoi* that set Hippocrates into action.

IV. Being Ruled

Following Aristotle's lead, I have been stressing the contributions of the ruler to shared action. Along the way, I've said a lot about what subordinates do *not* contribute: they do not exercise *phronêsis* or its vicious analogues, nor do they provide the decisions that make their actions and psychic activities meaningful—that is, by articulating it with the (real or perceived) good. What remains?

A great deal.[51] We will see in Chapter 3 the great variety of contributions subordinates can make to shared activity, but for now we may restrict ourselves to the comparatively simple case where the psychic activities of subordinates are completely dominated by rulers. We may begin by observing that although, on Aristotle's view, *phronêsis* is extremely important, it accounts for only a small portion of anyone's psychic life.

It is worth recalling here the cognitive capacities of animals as Aristotle describes them in his biological works. The faculty of "imagination" or "representation" (φαντασία) allows animals to recall and reconfigure their sensations in complex networks of desires, associations, fears, expectations, and plans. A rabbit sees radish leaves behind the fence. The sight evokes any number of images or representations: he recalls other radishes, pictures the root emerging from the earth, and imagines struggling to get through the fence. Provided nothing else interferes—a painful *phantasia* stirred up by the scent of coyote, for example—he heads off toward the gate.[52] These sorts of operations amount to "thinking of a sort."[53] (And since humans can shape them, we can thereby exercise a qualified kind of rule over nonhuman animals.)

More importantly for our purposes, imagination provides an important part of human cognition too. When we are very angry or drunk, Aristotle seems to think that the rational part of the soul is crowded out entirely, and our *phantasia* uses perception, memory, and so on to run the show on its own just as it does in animals (though its desires will be imprinted by reasoning we have done at other times).[54] But more typically, our imaginations operate alongside and under the influence of rational activity. Indeed, Aristotle writes that we cannot think without also making images and representations.[55] Aristotle works out the details in the *De Anima* and the *De Motu*, but an image from Plato's *Philebus* may suffice to capture the dynamics Aristotle has in mind. Sensation, perception, and experience (παθήματα) act like "scribes" in the soul, writing texts there (λογοί) that make up our beliefs and reasons (also λογοί). There is also a second worker in the soul, a painter. His pictures sometimes depict the objects of perception directly, but sometimes they are "illustrations" (εἰκόνες) of the scribe's words.[56] So a person's mental life is in large part a complex of nonrational words and pictures that issue from *logos* as well as from other sources. In interpersonal cases, we may picture the painter in a subordinate's soul producing *phantasiai*—that is, nonrational but cognitively rich networks of images and associations—that "illustrate" the *logoi* composed by the ruler's scribe and delivered by his speech.

The faculty of *phantasia*, then, allows subordinates to contribute a rich array of intelligence and cognition to the decisions of their rulers. But that is not the end of the story. There is also a great deal of rational activity that subordinates can perform for the sake of other people's decisions. Here it is useful to think about natural slaves who, since Aristotle says they lack the deliberative capacity (βουλευτικόν), might seem to be exempt from rationality altogether.⁵⁷ Some scholars have suggested that this is Aristotle's way of describing people who we would today describe as mentally disabled, or as "dysfunctional people who cannot begin to make it on their own out in the world."⁵⁸ But that cannot be right. Aristotle believed that many or most non-Greek people were natural slaves,⁵⁹ but it was beyond any doubt obvious to him that very many non-Greek people could perform any number of complex technical and cognitive tasks. Malcolm Heath points out the main evidence:

> Some of them could plan and execute logistically complex projects (such as Xerxes' invasion of Greece). Some of them had technologically advanced cultures. The Egyptians invented mathematics (*Met.* I.1, 981b13-25); they and the Babylonians were good astronomers (*DC* II.12, 292a7-9).⁶⁰

Thus although Aristotle thinks natural slaves can't develop their own *logoi* about living well (i.e., they can't perform *all-things-considered* practical reasoning), they can perform complex instrumental calculations and even reason theoretically. Applying the case to everyone else, we can say that while other subordinates *could* exercise global practical rationality, they do not do that when they submit to the rule of another. Instead they perform more limited cognitive operations within an ethical horizon drawn by someone else. (We will see in Chapter 3 that in the cases Aristotle calls "aristocratic" and "political" rule, the subordinate can to a limited extent influence that horizon from within, "participating in rule" in the way that so-called indefinite officers participate in the rule of their cities.)

On Aristotle's view, final causes always work together with efficient and material causes. And it is possible to find clues in the *DA*, the *DM*, and the *PA* about how to flesh out the material substrate against which this process works. Presumably when ruler's speech causes representations and further *logoi* to form in subordinates' souls, they thereby initiate tiny movements in their hearts, and the story continues from there.⁶¹ But we should follow Aristotle's lead by declining to pursue such questions.⁶² As long as we are doing moral and political philosophy, we need not venture very far into natural science.

Rather, it will suffice to say that the basic mechanism of rule is persuasive speech.[63]

V. Thinking for Someone Else

From a certain point of view—we might loosely call it the "Kantian" point of view—Aristotle's position will seem bizarre. On that view, your mind cannot cause my actions, and certainly not those based on reasons I have accepted for myself (for example, because you have persuaded me to see things your way or because I have consented to your wishes). Partisans of that view might worry that the account I am attributing to Aristotle would turn mundane human interactions into occult mind control, reducing people to automata whenever they submit to the leadership of others and transforming them into puppetmasters whenever they exercise any leadership of their own.

Aristotle's teleology provides an important partial response to this worry. Heirs that we are to the scientific revolution, we tend to think of all causation as efficient causation.[64] But for Aristotle, as I have been arguing, rulers provide the *final* cause of the actions of the ruled, and so it's precisely wrong to imagine the ones pushing the others around. It's true that for mechanists like Gorgias and his many modern successors, speech gives people power because it literally pushes around other people's bodies. But for Aristotle words are apt to pull rather than push, and to take hold of the formal and rational, not merely material, aspects of human life. This difference partly accounts for the substantial contributions that subordinates can make to shared action.

A second part of the difference between the Kantian and Aristotelian point of view concerns the connections between agency and responsibility. In the classic silent horror film *The Cabinet of Dr. Caligari*, a hypnotist, Caligari, acquires mental control over a young man, Cesare, making him commit various crimes in his sleep, including murdering the town clerk. Caligari sets Cesare's objectives, but the sleepwalker then independently figures out how to achieve those objectives. Bernard Williams' account of their relationship is relevant here.[65] No one, Williams argues, would deny that Caligari is morally responsible for the clerk's death and ought to be held legally responsible too, while Cesare should not. But although agency is often thought to be a necessary and sufficient condition for responsibility, here they come apart:

there is no denying that Cesare killed the clerk (or at least *stabbed* him, since Caligari clearly did not do that). In other words, notwithstanding his peculiar circumstances Cesare remains in a robust sense an *agent*, and the killings are therefore *actions* that *he* has performed.

Although the actions are not voluntary (among other things, Cesare's state prevents him from summoning up "thoughts that would relate the killing to the rest of his life"), we should not imagine that this turns him into a robot. Cesare, Williams writes, belongs on a continuum with "people who are for various reasons in extremely suggestible states in general or in relation to a particular dominating person."[66] According to the Aristotelian theory we are considering, subjects of rule are evidently on this same continuum. Barring extraordinary circumstances, we all are often under the direct and unmediated influence of others, at least with regard to some parts of our lives and at least some of the time.[67]

Clearly Aristotle would classify most of the actions of subordinates as voluntary.[68] And as we have seen, they can and often must involve rich forms of human thought, including technical and instrumental reasoning. Thus when Aristotle speaks about rule, we may think less of prisoners and servants than of teenagers when their collective exploits reflect the worldview of a charismatic ringleader or of employees who thoroughly internalize their bosses' values. To understand these cases in Aristotle's terms would not mean denying any and all agency and responsibility to the subordinates. But it would mean giving up on many of the ideals contemporary Kantians (and contemporary Aristotelians) hold dear.

Consent is a case in point. Aristotle agrees that a *lack* of consent is often a serious problem for justice. It is unjust and lawless, for example, for a doctor to use force and manipulation on his patients.[69] Yet it does not follow, as the Kantian might easily imagine, that securing consent solves the problem. Rather, the consent of the subordinate might be evidence of how completely the ruler is in charge.[70] For Aristotle, as we will see in Chapter 3, assessing the justice and injustice of people's relations involves the more difficult practice of looking at the similarities and differences among parties to rule and using those to judge the specific—and always asymmetrical—ways each contributes to shared action.

3

Kinds of Community, Kinds of Rule

I. *Nicomachean Ethics* VIII.9–IX.3: Asymmetrical Friendship

Sometime in the 1970s, after a long period of neglect, scholars rediscovered the essays on friendship that make up Books VIII and IX of the *Nicomachean Ethics* and Book VII of the *Eudemian Ethics*. As almost everyone points out, the Greek word φιλία is broader than the English "friendship." Aristotle's discussion includes, among other things, relations with merchants and business partners, the fun but fleeting connections between teenagers, the love of mothers for infant children, and the mutual regard of fellow citizens even when they don't know each other. From this capacious material, most of the topics that have captured scholars' attention—for example, the connection between friendship and self-interest, the seemingly paradoxical slogan that the friend is "an other self," the roles of pleasure, utility, and virtue in friendship—are closely tied to what Aristotle calls "perfect friendship," the rare connection between supremely excellent people, each immersed in the other's extraordinary worth.[1]

In a paper that set the agenda for this body of work, John Cooper makes a point that has since been repeated very often. The *Nicomachean* treatment of friendship, he points out, occupies a fifth of the *EN*, more space than Aristotle reserves for any other single topic. This, Cooper says, is "a fair measure of the importance of this subject to the complete understanding both of Aristotle's overall moral theory and even of many of the more circumscribed topics (moral virtue and pleasure, for example) to which so much scholarly and philosophical attention has been devoted."[2]

But this line of thought is complicated by a fact that is hardly ever mentioned. Aristotle almost entirely restricts his account of virtue friendship, other-selves, and such topics to the very beginning and end of his treatment of friendship. The rest—almost everything from VIII.7 to IX.3, seven out of seventeen Bekker pages—is dedicated to asymmetrical relationships, including especially those Aristotle calls friendship "based on superiority," in which one friend is a better person than the other. In the main, the interpretive tradition has not taken this section very seriously. Two classic translations of the *Nicomachean Ethics* (by Gauthier and Jolif on the one hand and Ross on the other) express what seems to be a consensus when they dismiss the middle chapters of the essay on friendships as "casuistry." Of course, it might not quite be unprecedented for Aristotle to fill a lot of pages with fine details and special cases. But if we *did* take the space Aristotle gives to a topic to indicate importance, then we would have every reason to conclude that asymmetrical friendships have a major role to play in Aristotle's argument, at least locally in the essay on friendship and maybe more globally in his practical philosophy as a whole.

And indeed I want to show that the discussion of asymmetrical relationships is of considerable importance to Aristotle's theory of rule and, not coincidentally, to his practical philosophy more generally. In this chapter I will argue that, far from the miscellany commentators have so often found, the middle chapters of the *Nicomachean* essay on friendship use the concept of rule to develop Aristotle's broadest and most systematic treatment of the varieties of human cooperation and friendship. This account—call it "Aristotle's sociology"— amounts to his fullest treatment of the doctrine that there are many kinds of rule, not only in cities or in the family but throughout the social world.

II. The Constitutional Analogy

At *EN* VIII.9, Aristotle suddenly begins talking about the six *politeiai* ("constitutions" or "regimes"): monarchy, aristocracy, timocracy, democracy, oligarchy, and tyranny. He opens with a sketch of the ways each "correct" *politeia* deviates into its opposite and then moves on to what seems to be the main attraction: the comparison between each constitution and some relationship in the household. Fatherhood, he says, resembles kingship when it's good and tyranny when it's bad, brotherhood degenerates from timocratic to democratic when no authority figure keeps it under control, and so on. Before moving on, Aristotle also stops to say something about the kinds of friendship found between rulers and the people they rule *within* certain constitutions, such as the friendship of a king for his people.

The constitutional analogy is certainly the center of gravity for this stretch of argument, but at first sight it is not at all clear what purpose it is supposed to serve. It is not connected in any obvious way to the puzzles and pieces of accepted wisdom that open and motivate Book VIII nor to the development of the following chapters. Yet Aristotle leaps into exposition, foregoing his standard devices for marking a transition and setting a new agenda. Once the discussion is complete, he does not explain what lessons have emerged or use them to motivate any further stage of the argument.

An initial question, then, is simply what this part of the *Nicomachean Ethics* is supposed to be *about*. We might suppose that the topic must be one of the two poles of the analogy: either (i) the various constitutions themselves or (ii) the four family relationships he compares to them, namely fatherhood, marriage, brotherhood, and mastery of slaves. Or we might suppose along the same lines that (iii) the topic is the *relationship* between those two poles, perhaps the causal relationship between households and cities.[3]

But none of these interpretations works out. For one thing, the discussion cannot be about the constitutions per se. Aristotle's practical philosophy is designed to be taught in a specific order, and students will only learn the full story about the constitutions later, once they've already covered the contents of the *Ethics*, including friendship.[4] And his tour of constitutional theory in the *EN* is brief and schematic—indeed very crude—compared to the detailed discussion developed in the middle of *Politics* III and through *Politics* IV–VI.[5] Thus we should read Aristotle's appeal to constitutional theory along the same lines as his well-known appeal to psychology at *EN* I.13.[6] In both places, he offers only a rough sketch of material that gets a proper scientific treatment elsewhere. In both places, he exploits material that his audience will find familiar and intellectually serious (indeed, material that he indicates will be familiar from "the exoteric texts," whatever those are).[7] And in both places, although he tries to avoid saying anything that contradicts the rigorous account he gives elsewhere, he shows little interest in completeness. Rather, he takes on whatever aspects of the familiar material will best pique his students' interest and illuminate his real topic.

Does he, then, invoke the constitutions just to shed light on the four relationships he singles out in the analogy—on the friendships between fathers and sons, husbands and wives, masters and slaves, and brothers?[8] He does after all linger on specific features of these friendships, like the qualities of mothers' affection for their children and the ways that various family relationships "depend on" fatherly friendship. Perhaps, then, in keeping with the casuistry interpretation, Aristotle is indulging his inclination to catalogue, finding something to say about all the friendships he can find. If this is right, the friendship of fathers and sons would be just one more specimen, taking its place alongside the friendship of criminals, lovers, old people, sailors, and on and on. Or again we might take Aristotle to be looking at those four relationships as members of a distinct group—the household, or the private sphere. After all, Aristotle does think that the city and the household differ in kind, which might in turn suggest that household *relationships* are completely different from all other relationships. If this were so, then the constitutional analogy might be intended just to illuminate them.[9]

But by his own account Aristotle is not mainly concerned with household relationships for their own sake, but rather because of the ways they illuminate a broader set of relationships. He first indicates this when he introduces household relationships to his treatment of friendship, at the beginning of *EN* VIII.7:

> A different form of friendship [he says] is that based on a superiority (καθ' ὑπεροχήν), such as the friendship of father with son, and generally of an older man with a younger; of husband with wife; and of any sort of ruler with his subject. These friendships differ from each other, since that of parents with children and that of rulers with subjects are not the same. . . . In fact, the friendship of father with son is not even the same as that of son with father, nor that of husband with wife and of wife with husband. For each of these has a different virtue and function; and that on account of which they love differs as well; therefore, both the friendly affections and the friendships are different.[10]

Far from treating household friendships as distinctive specimens that need a freestanding treatment of their own, here he introduces them (with οἷος, "such as") as particularly vivid *examples* of the broader class of hierarchical friendships. He intends to use them (and in particular the variety they exhibit) to illustrate something about relationships spread much more broadly through the social world: namely that these relationships differ from each other and in complex ways. In the pages that follow this quote, Aristotle touches on a bewildering variety of relationships between rulers and the inferiors over whom they have or should have authority: gods and humans, ancestors and descendants, the powerful and their lackeys, magistrates and criminals, and so on. Aristotle thinks that reflecting on the case of household friendships can shed light on all of these.

The household relationships, then, are neither irreducible special cases, nor do they belong to a special domestic subspecies of *philia*. Rather, they introduce a vast range of relationships spread through every avenue of the social world. And this bewildering variety, I would like to argue, provides Aristotle's reason for introducing the constitutions. The six constitutions—and their similarities with household relationships—allow him to confer order on the various hierarchical friendships by providing an accessible scheme for sorting them into kinds.

III. Kinds of Community, Kinds of Friendship

It may seem unlikely that Aristotle would use the constitutions to provide a typology of friendship. For by the time he introduces the constitutions, he has already gone to considerable lengths to defend a different distinction between kinds of friendship—the famous threefold distinction between friendships based on pleasure, utility, and virtue. Why would he now introduce a new, different classificatory scheme based on the six constitutions?

To see the answer, recall that at the very beginning of Book VIII, Aristotle explains that he now needs to explore friendship, "because it is a kind of virtue, or something involving virtue" (ἔστι γὰρ ἀρετή τις ἢ μετ' ἀρετῆς). This signals that he will make sense of friendship using the philosophical machinery set up in *EN* II–VII to deal with familiar virtues like courage and wisdom—he will treat it, as he says a few lines later, in terms of character and emotion (τὰ ἤθη καὶ τὰ πάθη).[11] And indeed as the discussion progresses we learn that like the other virtues, friendship is a state of character that shapes a person's goals, emotions, and dispositions, and that over the course of a lifetime, it partly constitutes *eudaimonia*. This approach—an examination of friendship as it appears in an individual's character and emotions—leads naturally to the question why individuals love or care about their friends and thence to the threefold classification that sets the agenda until *EN* VIII.9. We love people,

Aristotle argues, for the same reasons we desire other things: variously because we think they are useful, they cause pleasure, and they are good. Aristotle's treatment of friendship as a quasi-virtue also leads naturally to the argument that a disposition to be friends with someone must be more or less regularly *active*, although it can be dormant at particular times, just like courage or the ability to speak German.[12]

Much of the discussion of friendship fits easily into what we might call the "methodological individualism" of the *Nicomachean Ethics*. That is, it studies actions, motivations, and states of character insofar as these belong to individuals one at a time. But Aristotle does not think that the individual is the only entity worth studying in practical philosophy. After all, he treats the *polis* as a perfect whole, teleologically prior to its parts; and on at least one of his accounts, he treats even its most basic parts as collectives rather than individuals—the relationships between master and slave, husband and wife, and father and child.[13] Although the *Ethics* fixes its gaze by and large on the individual, Aristotle is by no means averse to a kind of "methodological holism" treating communities as beings worthy of study in their own right.[14]

I don't want to get distracted by the question of whether Aristotle is an *ontological* individualist—whether he thinks the properties and actions of communities could always be reduced in principle to the properties and actions of individuals.[15] However we come down on that question, there can be no doubt that he often thinks it is legitimate and illuminating to treat communities and relationships as entities in their own right, speaking holistically at least for heuristic and methodological purposes.

I would like to argue that starting in chapter 9, Aristotle begins a line of argument (making prominent use of the constitutional analogy) that treats *philia* not *qua* virtue but *qua* community. We may think of *koinônia* as a concept concerning cooperation or of shared agency. For a *koinônia* is any group of people who share goals and act together to pursue them. Although not every relationship between human beings belongs to this category—the relationship between enemies does not nor does that between a tyrant and his subjects—they provide the context for a great deal of human life. We must, for example, belong to a community in Aristotle's sense (and so rule or be ruled) whenever we act in the marketplace, the gymnasium, the courts, the battlefield, and whenever we socialize with close friends. Some communities are hierarchical, others egalitarian; some are forced, others consensual; some are connected to the institutions of government, others private and idiosyncratic.[16]

The focus on *koinôniai* per se is new in the *EN*, but the currents of Aristotle's argument make it natural. By the end of chapter 8, he has used the threefold analysis of friendship to resolve many of the puzzles that he introduced at the outset (about the roles of similarity and difference in friendship, the friendship of wicked people, etc.). Now his original line of inquiry is trailing off, leading beyond the bounds of ethics into natural philosophy.[17] So he starts on a new problem: "It seems, as we said at the beginning, that friendship and the just are concerned with the same things and exist in the same persons." The backward reference is to his initial catalogue of *endoxa* about friendship and particularly to the widespread view that there is some kind of connection between friendship and justice. Aristotle is announcing that he will explain the connection in proper philosophical detail.[18]

If our goal is to understand friendship in its connection with the just, there are reasons not to think of friendship as a quasi-virtue held by individuals one at a time. The expression Aristotle uses for "the just" is "τὸ δίκαιον," which refers to just *situations*, as opposed to "διακαιοσύνη," which indicates a virtuous *disposition*, held by individuals. And, as we will see, he goes on to focus on fair exchanges in which everyone gets what he or she deserves (i.e., what Aristotle labels "narrow" justice in *EN* V)—and this is in its most basic sense a four-place relationship between two sets of goods and two people, and only derivatively a state of character.[19]

In this context, it is apt to introduce the notion of *koinônia*—community, partnership, association, or (where there are two members) relationship. The root of the word is κοινός ("shared" or "common"), and so it generally suggests groups of people who share something or have something in common. But in Aristotle it means especially people who share an end and act together to accomplish it.[20] Aristotle introduces this theme to the stretch of text we are considering with a very compressed argument that community, friendship, and justice are coextensive.[21] The idea seems to be something like this: in every community—that is, wherever people cooperate—it's a matter of observable fact (i) that people both make certain claims of desert on each other (τι δίκαιον εἶναι), so community implies justice; and (ii) that they regard each other with an eye for each other's good, so, according to the definition from the beginning of *EN* VIII, community implies friendship. So community entails both justice and friendship. Furthermore, friendship involves some sort of fair exchange, where people give to others what they deserve, so friendship also entails justice (i.e., the standards that determine how much one should give and take). Why does justice entail friendship? Perhaps because it requires attending to what people deserve and interacting with them in ways that help to secure it. That is very close to a definition of φιλεῖν that Aristotle offers at *Rhetoric* II.4: wishing for someone what one thinks is good, for that person's sake and not one's own, and being inclined to do those things, as far as possible (τὸ βούλεσθαί τινι ἃ οἴεται ἀγαθά, ἐκείνου ἕνεκα ἀλλὰ μὴ αὑτοῦ καὶ τὸ κατὰ δύναμιν πρακτικὸν εἶναι τούτων).[22]

Aristotle goes on to say that the *typology* of one domain will shed light on the typology of the others. In the *EN*, he points to this connection quite briefly: "The kinds of friendship," he says, "will follow the kinds of community" (ἀκολουθήσουσι δὲ αἱ τοιαῦται φιλίαι ταῖς τοιαύταις κοινωνίαις).[23] In the *Eudemian Ethics*, he develops the idea at greater length.

> It is thought that what is just is something that is equal, and also that friendship is based on equality, if there is truth in the saying "amity is equality." And all constitutions are some species of justice (αἱ δὲ πολιτεῖαι πᾶσαι δικαίου τι εἶδος); for they are communities, and everything communal is founded on justice, so that there are as many species of justice and community as there are of friendship, and all these species pick out the others (καὶ πάντα ταῦτα σύνορα ἀλλήλοις) and have their differentiae closely related (ἐγγὺς ἔχει τὰς διαφοράς).[24]

The idea is that if we understand the typology of one phenomenon, then we will have access to the typology of the others. And so we may start with whatever is easiest to analyze and use it to get a foothold on the rest.

This, I submit, is the purpose of the constitutional analogy. There are six intuitively accessible kinds of *politeia*. These can be used to indicate differences between kinds of community which would otherwise be hard to make out. And these in turn shed light on distinctions between kinds of justice and friendship that aren't so easy to tackle head-on. The analysis as a whole is ultimately valuable to a study of friendship because it clarifies the widespread but rarely understood view that justice and friendship are somehow intimately related.

There is reason to think that Aristotle's students would have agreed that the constitutions provide an easy way to get this complicated ball rolling.

For by Aristotle's time, the constitutions were a familiar lens through which to look at the social world, indeed the basic tool with which Greek political thinkers arranged themselves into political factions—notably Athenian-style democrats and Spartan-style oligarchs. The constitutions built on powerful civic stereotypes: the chaos and faction of Athenian democracy, the wise stewardship of Homeric kings, the militaristic virtues of Sparta, and so on.[25] And this tradition was also sometimes redirected—most notably but not only by Plato—to express the idea of varied ways of life on a smaller scale. Thus, for example, we can explain certain people's behavior by saying that it expresses a tyrannical or democratic personality. Aristotle likewise thinks that the real and imagined differences between cities and peoples—between Athens and Sparta and Persia and so on—are so vivid to a politically curious audience that they provide a model for something less intuitively available, the patterns distinguishing different ways that we can work together on shared projects. It is as if a modern speaker said "parents and their children often end up like *Russia*, but really they should be more like *Sweden*."

IV. Communities and Power Structures

As a tool to sort *koinôniai* into kinds, however, the analogy with constitutions might seem completely unpromising. Aristotle's best-known scheme for classifying *politeiai* is a two-by-three grid based on the number of people who rule (one, many, or all) and whether the rule is self-interested or on behalf of the people ruled. Monarchy is benevolent rule by one person, democracy is self-interested rule by the many, and so on.[26]

	One Ruler	*A Few*	*Many*
Benevolent Rule	Kingship	Aristocracy	Polity/timocracy
Exploitation	Tyranny	Oligarchy	Democracy

In *Politics* III, Aristotle treats this as the starting point for understanding the differences between constitutions of cities. Soon enough, though, he modifies it in various ways, ultimately leaving it pretty well entirely behind. Thus, for example, while he starts out by defining oligarchy as the rule of the few, he soon goes on to say that it is better understood as rule of the *rich* (of whom there are typically very few).

How, if at all, is the grid supposed to illuminate the kinds of friendship? Partway through his explanation of the analogy, Aristotle appeals to one consideration drawn directly from it: the distinction between beneficent and self-interested rule. He says that fathers resemble kings because they rule with an eye to their children's advantage; masters, by contrast, are like tyrants because they rule in their own interest. But this distinction does not serve Aristotle's main purpose in this section: the distinction between benevolence and exploitation does not indicate the boundary between two *kinds* of friendship but rather between friendship and its absence. For Aristotle, regarding someone as a friend entails pursuing his or her good for its own sake.[27] Thus since slave masters and tyrants are defined as people who rule to benefit themselves (and therefore only concern themselves with the good of their subjects for instrumental reasons) they cannot be friends with their subjects (at least *qua* subjects—a master may not be friends with his slave *qua* slave, though perhaps he can be friends with him "as a human being," if, for example, they sometimes play games or chat about public affairs).[28] This is the idea underlying his claim in *EN* VIII.11 that in the most deviant cities, there is hardly any justice or friendship.[29]

So insofar as the constitutional analogy is supposed to offer an analysis of various kinds of friendship (rather than a distinction between friendships and other kinds of human interaction—a distinction I'll return to later) it cannot draw on the distinction between benevolent and exploitative rule. Once we have abandoned this distinction, all that remains of the two-by-three grid is a threefold division of constitutions according to the number of their rulers. But this is scarcely better than the correct/deviant distinction as a tool for sorting friendship into kinds. Although Aristotle recognizes that groups of friends come in various sizes, he consistently treats relationships between *two* people as capturing everything worth saying about them. In short, to use the constitutions to categorize the various kinds of friendship, Aristotle must abandon the criteria both of beneficence and of number of rulers and exploit some other aspect of constitutions.[30]

Happily, a more promising idea is ready to hand. Consider this general definition of *politeiai*, which appears shortly after the three-by-two grid in *Politics* III.6:

> A constitution is the structure (τάξις) of a *polis* with respect to its offices (τῶν τε ἄλλων ἀρχῶν), and most of all the one that has authority over all matters (τῆς κυρίας πάντων).[31]

This definition characterizes a πολιτεία roughly as a "power structure." Strictly speaking, only cities have *politeiai*. In *Politics* III "ἀρχαί" means "magistracies" or "offices"; κυριώτατος is often translated as "sovereign." But these terms have analogues in smaller relationships that are illuminating here. In its political context, each ἀρχή typically has a mandate or sphere of responsibilities—for example, to preside over a court or to impose fines for certain transgressions.[32] For its part, κυριώτατος means "ultimately in charge" or "most authoritative"; I will argue below that in its political context, that word does not have the psychological implications I assign to it here.[33]

To consider relationships in terms of their power structure requires considering who has what responsibilities and (more narrowly) who has the highest level of responsibility and therefore runs the whole operation. The terms Aristotle uses make it particularly natural to look for constitutional analogues in the household. "Κύριος," which means "supreme," "sovereign," or "authoritative," can also be used as a noun referring to the *pater familias*, simultaneously husband, father, and slaveholder, and can generally indicate anyone in control.

V. Does Friendship always Involve Rule?

I have been arguing that the treatment of *politeiai* in *Ethics* VIII looks to the kinds of rule in order to make sense not just of some limited range of communities but of human relations generally. Immediately after giving the definition of *politeia* as a τάξις of ἀρχαί, Aristotle suggests that the definition of *politeia* as power structure is suited to precisely this task. In studying the constitutions of cities by looking at the household, he says, we will see "how many forms of rule there are for human beings and for communal life" (καὶ τῆς ἀρχῆς εἴδη πόσα τῆς περὶ ἄνθρωπον καὶ τὴν κοινωνίαν τῆς ζωῆς).[34] Again, the idea is that the constitutions aren't relevant only to cities and household relationships, or to some restricted set of hierarchical communities, but rather to power structures that underlie all human cooperation, structures that allow us to distinguish human relations quite generally into qualitatively different kinds.

Many will find it easy to accept that power structures provide a sensible way to categorize city-states. And anyone familiar with Aristotle's practical philosophy will recognize (however regretfully) that he thinks that rule is at the heart of household relationships.³⁵ But it may seem like a stretch, both by Aristotle's standards and by modern ones, to categorize all kinds of *friendship* in terms of power or rule. We might suppose that many—indeed, most—friendships and other small social groups can't be categorized by kind of rule because they don't involve rule at all.

In the Introduction I discuss one passage that suggests that Aristotle doesn't think that way—the text in *Politics* I.5 where he treats it as an *a priori* axiom that wherever things come together into a composite whole, a distinction between ruler and subordinate comes to light. And we know that by Aristotle's lights it would be a real misfortune if a community had no human rulers, for (as we saw in Chapter 2) Aristotle thinks that *phronêsis* is "unique to the ruler" (ἄρχοντος ἴδιος), and indeed that it is "the same state as politics" and therefore that it is required to achieve virtue and the human good.³⁶ A community with no ruler is thus a community where no one can exercise human virtue in its fullest form.

Still, the view is strange by modern standards, and perhaps it is appropriate to return, halfway through this book, to the question of whether it's really plausible that all human community must be in some sense hierarchical. We are, after all, now equipped with a fuller definition of rule. Recall that the paradigm case of rule occurs when you exercise *phronêsis*, thereby establishing a decision about how to pursue the good in a given situation. That decision reflects your distinctive character and outlook on a given situation. You communicate your decision in words to someone else, and it takes shape in the images and associations within that person's mind. And that person thinks and acts in a way that is oriented toward the goals identified by your decision.

Consider, in this light, Plato's depiction of Socrates. When Socrates describes himself as a midwife, he is presenting his interlocutors as rulers and himself as a subordinate collaborator—though as we see him in action, we quickly see why his interlocutors (and most undergraduate students who encounter him in Plato's work) think he has taken a dictatorial stranglehold on the direction and the spirit of every conversation he has.³⁷ Or consider some examples from contemporary academic life. When you think about philosophy, maybe you're lucky enough to have friends who set aside their own tastes, preoccupations, and idiosyncrasies, offering questions and suggestions that improve the work by your lights rather than theirs. Such people reflect and act for the sake of *your* decisions. They are in Aristotle's sense your subordinates. Maybe, on the contrary, your friends sometimes pull you *out* of your habitual ways of thinking, showing how the topics you have been considering fit into a different, better way of seeing the world that reflects *their* values. Consider academic talks and the ways various parties can reframe the conversation, for better and for worse. Again, we use the titles "thesis advisor," "thesis supervisor," and "thesis director" interchangeably, but each suggests a different view of how phenomena that Aristotle would have considered "rule" should operate. We don't talk about these issues in terms of ruling and being ruled, of course—but then again, perhaps we don't talk about them clearly or often enough at all.[38]

Perhaps some range of examples along those lines captures something of the power dynamics Aristotle finds not only within the household but wherever people act together. And perhaps they lend some plausibility to the idea that he might take the central question for understanding a community not to be "Is it free or oppressive?" but rather "Who is ruling here, and how?"[39]

An Impersonal Ruler?

Could it be that between friends and within communities of equals, no party rules, but all are ruled by some nonhuman entity, perhaps reason or the law? The principle that in every composite whole a "ruling element must come to light" does not specify that the ruler must be a person. And indeed Aristotle frequently discusses rulers of human communities that *aren't* human individuals. *Poleis*, for one thing, are often ruled by groups, like the many, the virtuous, and the rich. Furthermore, he says at several junctures that the *law* can rule a city—and indeed that it is better for the law to rule than it is for a person to do so.[40] Could it be that among friends a smaller-scale analog of the laws—perhaps a plan that they have adopted together—might rule over each, so that none need either rule or be ruled?[41]

No. Even under ideal circumstances, Aristotle does not believe the law can rule without human help. Someone must always step in to fill the gaps, adapting it to specific circumstances, recognizing exceptional circumstances in which it must be suspended, and so on.[42] On one possible view, those who interpret or apply the law thereby submit to *its* rule. On this view, legal officials would then identify and take as their *telos* ends contained in the law, not in any individual's perspective. When officials faithfully interpret the law, on this view, their interpretations may *sound* like commands, but it is the law itself setting the goals.[43] Although the content of the law may be informed by history, context, and individual decisions, those are all anchored in a higher, transcendent end. We saw in Chapter 1 that is something like Plato's view. And Aristotle's references to the rule of law are sometimes ambiguous enough that they leave room to imagine that he accepts something like it.[44]

But where Aristotle discusses the rule of law more explicitly, he does not suggest that it could have the kind of decision-giving power Aristotle assigns to rule in personal relationships. He accepts the views of those who say that the laws "only speak of the universal and do not command with a view to any circumstances"[45] and describes the law code as something like a technical manual.[46] In other words, when people interpret and apply the law and its analogues they are not necessarily engaged in ruling—but they are not submitting to superhuman, impersonal rulers. We should rather take the law and its analogues as constraints on human rulers, not as entities that engage in the practice of ruling as Aristotle understands it.[47]

A Community of Self-Rulers?

One final possible counterexample to our principle that all *koinōniai* involve rule is the possibility of communities in which people share and cooperate although no one produces *logoi* that produce a decision for anyone else. The most promising candidate would be a purely commercial community. Perhaps a Persian merchant is in the *agora* with appealing clothing and clearly indicated prices, and an Athenian arrives with money to spend. They make the exchange, but each is his own master.[48]

The basic response to this counterexample is that a pair of such people might be said in English to be cooperating, but they do not have the shared goals and activities necessary to count as members of a real community, nor are they equipped to value each other's good as they plausibly must to be friends—even utility friends.[49] Insofar as market relations are not always relations of ruling and being ruled, that is only because they are not always relationships at all.

So much, then, for the hypothesis that every community—that is, every friendship—has a ruler. It seems to me that Aristotle asserts this point fairly clearly and that he has compelling if not dispositive answers to the main objections critics might raise against it. And so let us now return to the argument. Aristotle, you will recall, is pursuing the possibility of classifying all friendships—notably, friendships among equals—by identifying the sort of the rule that they exhibit.

VI. Kinds of Rule

If my argument so far is correct, the constitutional analogy of *EN* VIII is designed to sort human communities into kinds, and it does so in terms of different kinds of rule. This means that we can mine the passage for information about the different kinds of rule in order to fill out the pluralism that, as we have seen, Aristotle announces in *Politics* I with plenty of fanfare and little detail.

When scholars consider the differences among specifically interpersonal kinds of rule, they typically focus on some combination of three ideas, all stressed in *Politics* I: first, there is the distinction we have already considered (and to which we will return) between benevolent rule and exploitation. Second, there are what we might call "temporal" categories: a free man's rule over slaves and women is permanent, his rule over his sons is temporary, and his rule over his fellow citizens is intermittent, since everyone will take turns ruling and being ruled. And third, there is the difference between kinds of people: women, children, and slaves have different cognitive abilities and are therefore suited to being ruled in different ways; since Aristotle stresses that rule does not amount to holding any particular kind of knowledge but depends on natural differences between rulers and subjects, we might easily conclude that the differences between kinds of rule are *constituted* by natural differences between kinds of people.[50]

But it would be disappointing if these options exhausted Aristotle's views about the various kinds of rule. For each of them fails to satisfy two *desiderata* of an Aristotelian theory of rule. First, an account of Aristotle's view about the kinds of rule should allow us to draw meaningful distinctions among *at least three kinds of correct rule*. As we have seen, Aristotle stresses this point. Nature, he says, doesn't make people like the multipurpose delphic knife, suited to perform many tasks and receive many kinds of treatment: a man's wife should not be ruled in the same way as any of the other members of the household— she should be treated differently than the slaves *and* differently again than the man's sons, while the sons and the slaves must be treated differently than each other.⁵¹ Since the correct/deviant dichotomy is merely twofold, it cannot illuminate all these distinctions, and it's of little help in satisfying the *desideratum*.

Second, a theory of rule should treat different kinds of rule as *different kinds of activity* in a suitably strong sense. To see this, imagine that Aristotle promised to explain that there are several εἴδη of sculpture. It would be disappointing if he pointed to "carving maple" and "carving oak" as two of them and then simply ended the account. Nothing about that distinction explains why we should take the two activities to differ in kind or to require different accounts. While an explanation of the differences between kinds of sculpture might well *begin* with the difference between materials worked on, it would be much more satisfying if these were related to substantive differences in the activity itself. For example, carving wood is indeed different—and even different in kind—than casting bronze. But the difference is not constituted by the material difference between bronze and wood. Rather, that difference is a *cause* of a further difference—the difference between additive and subtractive sculpture. And those seem like honest-to-goodness different kinds of sculpture because they are substantively different kinds of activity. A satisfactory theory of the kinds of rule should be like that: the famous differences between the deliberative faculties of women, children, natural slaves and the free should help to *explain* it, but they should not *exhaust* it.

Thus the natural differences between subjects don't satisfy the second *desideratum*. And the temporal distinctions have the same problem. Aristotle does indeed think that women should be ruled permanently, children temporarily, and free men intermittently. This provides grounds for saying that each is ruled differently in *some* sense, but here too it would be disappointing if this exhausted the claim that they differ from each other in form. We are looking for an account according to which when a *kurios* turns from ruling his slave to ruling his wife, he stops doing one sort of thing and starts doing another, as when he stops shaping clay and starts carving wood.

Happily, the discussion of household friendships in *EN* VIII provides an account of rule that satisfies the two *desiderata*. When the time comes to explain why each kind of household rule resembles one of the constitutions, Aristotle gives a series of γάρ clauses providing reasons for the various parts of the analogy. At first glance, they are not very illuminating. He writes, for example, that fatherhood resembles monarchy because good fathers care for their sons, while the rule over slaves is tyrannical because it is in the interest of the master.⁵² Brotherhood, on the other hand, resembles timocracy because (and only so long as) the brothers are equal and therefore must take turns ruling.⁵³ This gives us two seemingly unrelated, even arbitrary, ways of linking household relationships to constitutions: via the altruism of the ruler or the lack thereof and via the friends' equality or inequality; in one case, Aristotle appeals to the benevolent/altruistic distinction and in the other to the temporal distinction, and he gives no indication of how these ideas are supposed to be related.

Husbands, Wives, and Aristocratic Rule

More helpful, though, is Aristotle's treatment of the "aristocratic" rule of husband over wife and of the "oligarchic" relationship that results when marriages go wrong.

> The association of husband and wife seems aristocratic in character, because it according to his worth (κατ' ἀξίαν) that the husband rules, and over those things that he should. Whatever is appropriate for a wife (ὅσα δὲ γυναικὶ ἁρμόζει) he hands over (ἀποδίδωσιν) to her. But if a husband dominates (κυριεύων) in everything, he converts it into an oligarchy, since it is not in virtue of his worth that he does so and not as the better person. Sometimes wives rule, because they are heiresses, and so their rule is not based on virtue but is a consequence of wealth and power—just as in oligarchies.⁵⁴

Aristotle here describes good marriages as "aristocratic" and bad marriages as "oligarchical," exploiting the distinction between correct and deviant constitutions. But notice that he has abandoned the usual associations with that distinction. The bad marriages Aristotle calls "oligarchical" need not be ruled selfishly rather than benevolently. Rather, the problem is with *how* the ruling of the husband interacts with the being-ruled of the wife. They may be oligarchical when the wrong person is in charge (and for the wrong reasons) as when an heiress's wealth make her sovereign.⁵⁵

For a husband to rule "according to his worth"—his *ethical* worth and in particular in virtue of the authoritative deliberative faculty he has but she lacks—it is necessary that he be in charge. But, Aristotle says, that is not sufficient, for he is not ruling according to his worth if he has *too much power*.

In such cases he "dominates in everything" rather than merely "ruling over those things he should."

Recall the definition of *politeia* we considered earlier, according to which a constitution is a τάξις of ἀρχαί—a power structure—including but not limited to the determination of who is κυριώτατος. Notice that on this definition, the structure falls naturally into two parts—(i) the simple question of who rules, and (ii) the lesser "offices" that contribute to shared activity and perhaps constrain or inform the actions of the ruler. This same division underlies the two kinds of oligarchic marriage. When a woman takes charge of a marriage, Aristotle thinks that the wrong person is in charge; if a husband rules in everything (rather than handing over to his wife responsibility for "preservation" within the household), the remaining powers and responsibilities are incorrectly assigned. This analysis presupposes a more complex picture of rule than we find in *Politics* I, where Aristotle often talks as if everyone is either straightforwardly a ruler or a subject. Aristotle's treatment of bad marriage makes it clear that there are in fact *three* sorts of station people may occupy in a community's power structure. People may have no power at all, they may be κυριώτατος, *most* or perhaps better *ultimately* in charge, or they may occupy an intermediate position, granting them some limited set of powers and responsibilities.

Again, Aristotle's discussions of political institutions in the *Politics* provide a suggestive model for thinking about the personal cases. It is useful to distinguish at least two sorts of lesser contributors.

First, there are people we might call "subordinate officials." Aristotle generally describes officials or magistrates, ἀρχαί or ἄρχοντες, using cognates of κύριος, as sovereign over some domain or other. And we may imagine such people making decisions shaping the lives of their subordinates, along the lines of our general account of rule in Chapter 2. Among Aristotle's examples of magistrates are the people in control of revenues and of the guard, and those who distribute grain in times of scarcity.[56] To do their jobs well, these people must exercise technical expertise and bring their moral orientations to bear on the variable situations in front of them. Indeed they must use some *telos* to provide meaning to the various activities of people under their purview, just as the master-builder does to his subordinates, and (if they are good citizens of a good city) they therefore contribute to the highest end. But it does not follow that they are sovereign. Quite the opposite—as the image of the *architektôn* reminds us, the general's military deliberations are pointless or perverse unless they are informed and animated by the one highest end, the common good of the city. Aristotle points out the variety and heterogeneity of these positions: the general is one sort of person, the grain measurer is another, and priests and heralds fall under the same general heading, although they would normally be considered officers at all.[57]

Aristotle discusses a second, still more limited, position in a power structure in *Pol.* III.1, where he weighs in on a debate about whether judges and assembly members should be called *archontes*.[58] Elsewhere, he often speaks as if they do not, strictly speaking, hold office. His reason is clear enough: voting in a criminal trial does not indicate that you are in charge of anything, and neither does voting in the assessment of a magistrate, giving speeches in the assembly, or performing other such tasks. Yet Aristotle here says that it would be absurd to deny that these people rule in any sense, especially considering that in cities like Athens the judges and assemblymen are *collectively* sovereign. He stipulates that while such people do not count as *archontes* in an unqualified sense, it's fair enough to say that their role is to participate (μετέχειν) in rule and that we may label their judgment and civic deliberation as "indefinite office" (ἀόριστος ἀρχή).[59]

There are ready analogies between women, as Aristotle sees them, and officials in both "subordinate" and "indefinite" offices. Just as Aristotle thinks that women should have only limited power in the household, so too does he think that the masses in normal Greek cities should not be allowed to hold "the greatest offices" (ἀρχῶν τῶν μεγίστων), since they have neither justice nor practical wisdom. In both cases, the challenge is to acknowledge a limited but real claim to power without giving away too much.

As he considers the various kinds of magistrate and their roles in the city, Aristotle writes the following:

> Generally speaking, those should be most particularly spoken of as offices to which are assigned deliberation and judging and command (ὅσαις ἀποδέδοται βουλεύσασθαί τε περί τινῶν καὶ κρῖναι καὶ ἐπιτάξαι) concerning certain matters, and especially the latter, for command is more characteristic of ruling.[60]

Here civic judgment and deliberation function in a similar way to the deliberation of individuals. As we saw in Chapter 2, deliberation contributes to action but is not on its own sufficient to make us do anything. People and cities only perform actions if, in addition to deliberating, they make a decision—or if a ruler makes a decision on their behalf. Yet there is a whole range of other things they may do to shape any eventual action.

Such considerations help to explain why Aristotle takes such pains to stress the difference between the kinds of rule suitable to slaves and to women. *Kurioi* will of course *rely* on their slaves as they do their tools and animals. But, again, men must "give over" to women "that which is fit to them."

What exactly does Aristotle think husbands ought to give over to their wives? The civic examples suggest a number of possible answers. It may be that Aristotle thinks that women should, like the grain measurer, just be left alone to perform certain tasks by their own lights, so long as they have in view the higher ends of the household. Perhaps, differently, we should imagine them doing things rather like "electing" or (especially) "examining" their husbands, thereby contributing to household judgment and deliberation in the manner of an assembly. Maybe Aristotle is suggesting that a woman discuss the good of the household with her husband in such a way that her virtue improves and informs his decisions or that she should have the opportunity to veto or criticize some decisions before he acts.

On the specifics of the relationship between men and women, I don't think that Aristotle's text allows us to go much beyond these sorts of speculation.[61] But any plausible interpretation of Aristotle's comments in *EN* VIII will suggest that men ought to *trust* their wives (as they must not trust their slaves or their children). They must somehow limit their deliberations and actions or make themselves vulnerable to the contributions of others to household activity.[62]

As we have seen, Aristotle writes in the *Politics* that this sort of rule is made appropriate by the "unauthoritative" deliberative faculties of women. The claim is notoriously difficult, resting as it does on a single word that Aristotle does not use frequently, and it has by now been the subject of very many interpretations. Some think that the female deliberative faculty lacks authority over the nonrational parts of the woman's soul because women (like other female animals) are disposed to excessive uncontrolled *thumos*; others think that it lacks authority over *men*, so that rule of men over women is in some sense ultimately social.[63] Without getting drawn too far into this debate, we may say that the *Nicomachean* account tells in favor of the former, "social" interpretation. The heart of Aristotle's counsel to husbands is that they give or concede something to women, whose distinctive feature is that they ought to contribute something to the household. That sort of argument fits ill with interpretations according to which their defining characteristic is uncontrolled, excessive emotion.

It is, in any case, the qualified and complex kind of rule Greek husbands exercise over their wives that Aristotle calls "aristocratic."

This, at least, is his account in the *Nicomachean Ethics*, which contains his longest (and I think best-worked-out) discussion of the kinds of rule. Aristotle complicates the story in *Politics* I. There, in a briefer and more schematic discussion than the one we have been considering, he writes that a husband's rule is not aristocratic but "political."[64] Some scholars have treated these two claims as contradictory, and it may well be that Aristotle changed his mind about how to think about the rule of men over women. But I think it's just possible to see the two discussions as compatible. For one thing there is no formal contradiction in comparing marriage to *both* aristocratic and political government. Marriage may of course be akin to a political regime in some respects and to an aristocracy in others. And Aristotle says nothing in the *Politics* that conflicts with the substance of the account he gives in the *Ethics*.

My view is that his main goal in the *Politics* is not to give a full account of the kinds of rule but to indicate how rule over women is different from rule over children and slaves. A comparison with political rule is perfectly well suited to this job—and it allows marriage to occupy an analytic slot that is otherwise unoccupied in *Politics* I, which does not discuss the relationship between brothers. The features of marriage that Aristotle describes as "political" are just the same as the ones I've discussed here—the idea is that women are different kinds of people than children, and different in a way that requires and entitles them to contribute moral judgment to the activities they share with their husbands.

When, in the *Politics*, he calls the rule over women "political," then, he is emphatically not saying that women are equal to men—on the contrary, as he begins the discussion, he restates his conviction that men are naturally "fitter for command" (ἡγεμονικώτερον) than women and points out that marriage does not involve the arbitrary measures (specifically, alternation of rule) that characterize the relationship between people between whom there are no differences to prevent them from treating each other as equals.[65] His position in the *Politics* accords to women only a very mixed compliment: that they can and should contribute to the household in a manner analogous to the contributions of the masses to the political process of democracies. The natures of husbands and wives are, on Aristotle's view, such that both can and should contribute morally and deliberatively to the household. But they are not so similar that they make it necessary to introduce the exchange of responsibility, grounded in convention and artifice rather than nature, that would make their relationship political.[66]

Fathers, Sons, and Kingly Rule

There is further support for this interpretation in Aristotle's comments about the rule of fathers and kings in the *EN*. When he first introduces monarchy to the discussion, he claims that its distinguishing features are the king's self-sufficiency and his thoroughgoing superiority over all his subjects ("οὐ γάρ ἐστι βασιλεὺς," he writes, "ὁ μὴ αὐτάρκης καὶ πᾶσι τοῖς ἀγαθοῖς ὑπερέχων"— "no one is a king who is not self-sufficient and superior in all good things").[67] The superiority of kings and fathers (which Aristotle presumably thinks is particularly evident in contrast with the dependence and inferiority of children) is such that the person suited to be κύριος is also suited to take responsibility for *all* the actions of the collective—he need not and should not "hand over" anything to those in his charge.[68] Fatherly or kingly rule is thus the simple case in which the nature of partners dictates that one party should get complete control, encompassing both levels of authority.

The reason for this is given in a passage in *Politics* I that we saw briefly in Chapter 1, in which Aristotle writes that what separates slaves, children, women, and Greek men are the various natures of their capacity to deliberate. Children, he says there, have only an immature capacity to deliberate. This presumably means that they have the properties of the not-yet-virtuous people that Aristotle describes in *EN* II. They cannot perform virtuous actions "as the virtuous do them"—knowingly, from a settled disposition and from their own decision—yet they can nevertheless perform virtuous actions either by chance or according to the directions or the example of another (ἄλλου ὑποθεμένου).[69] Slaves, who lack the capacity altogether, are certainly equipped to perform technical tasks or to overcome obstacles that complicate their daily lives— there is no reason to think that Aristotle doubts that they can judge when the ox needs extra food, for example.[70] What they cannot do independently, on his view, is form moral judgments that express practical wisdom in a way that will restrict and influence the master's capacity to set morally informed ends for the household. Ruling over slaves and children, on this account, is distinctive because the ruler must make all truly practical decisions (rather than merely technical ones) on their behalf.

This, I think, gives us a satisfactory account of the difference between two of the three kinds of "correct" rule as they appear in household relationships, one that fares better than the standard answers in the literature. Just as the difference between clay and wood helps to explain the difference between additive and subtractive sculpture without constituting that difference, so too does the difference between kingly/fatherly rule and marital/aristocratic rule respond to alleged natural differences between women and children. But as with the difference between additive and subtractive sculpture, the story does not end there. Paternal and marital rule are substantively different kinds of activity, not just because one is permanent and the other is temporary but because they amount to distinct modes of cooperation; one calls for moral trust and delegation, and the other does not. And they both differ from the domination of slaves, because that is not strictly speaking cooperation at all.

Brothers, Political Rule, and Democratic Rule

In political/fraternal communities, Aristotle says that everyone is "equal, and of the same age, and such persons are mostly similar in their feelings and character" (ἴσοι γὰρ καὶ ἡλικιῶται, οἱ τοιοῦτοι δ' ὁμοπαθεῖς καὶ ὁμοήθεις ὡς ἐπὶ τὸ πολύ).[71] In such relationships, unlike those of a father to his wife, his child, and his natural slave, there are no natural grounds for putting one person in charge rather than the other or more generally for assigning responsibilities in any particular way at all. Thus some further principle must enter the picture. This principle will distribute authority in a way that is arbitrary from the standpoint of justice but at least not completely unfair. That principle, Aristotle repeatedly says, is ruling and being ruled "κατὰ μέρος." The phrase can sometimes mean "in part," just as we have seen that some magistrates rule over a part of the city. In central cases, though, it means "in alternation," taking turns in and out of rule.[72]

The Athenian political model here is the one-year term during which a citizen would be elected or chosen at random to hold office. After the term was done, the officeholder would step aside to make room for someone else. In smaller-scale relationships, we might imagine that community members alternate and adjust their roles without the institutions and formal practices needed for the *polis*, instead passing around control situationally.[73] Perhaps one friend defers to the other based on each person's expertise in the matter at hand. Maybe they deliberate together, but with the understanding that one person is more invested and will ultimately make the decision. It's not hard to dream up other possibilities. And when equal partners act together, they will presumably *also* frequently allow subordinates to occupy the middle position that characterizes aristocratic rule: whoever is being ruled for the moment will have opportunities to evaluate and contribute to the ruler's decisions. I submit that these sorts of relationships, characterized by shifting roles for each party and especially by alternation in ultimate ethical outlook, are what Aristotle means by political rule.

When no such measures are instituted at all, and everyone "has license to do what he or she wants," then the relationship crumbles and becomes "democratic."[74] This, we may note in passing, is yet another new way of describing "deviant" rule relations without appealing to benevolence and exploitation. And it is also, like the relationship between master and slave, a kind of human interaction that is by Aristotle's lights barely a community at all. A chaotic democracy of this kind presumably stretches the limits of mereology—it will be more like a heap than a composite whole.

VII. Conclusion

All told, the discussion of household relationships in Book VIII of the *Nicomachean Ethics* gives Aristotle's students the means to distinguish among quite a wide variety of forms of rule: (i) "despotic" rule, which is simple exploitation; (ii) "royal" or "paternal" rule, in which the ruler has complete, benevolent control over shared activities; (iii) "aristocratic" or "marital" rule, in which the ruled party limits and shapes the decisions of the person in charge; two kinds of "oligarchic" rule, one of which (iv) involves someone who should merely be trusted but instead takes charge of shared action, while the other (v) involves a leader who fails to delegate and trust as much as he should; and finally (vi) "political" rule, in which natural differences do not dictate who should occupy what position, and human institutions must therefore take their place. To this list we might add (vii) the special case of "democratic" rule. This does not quite belong on the list since it involves clusters of people who are strictly speaking neither friends nor communities; they cannot cooperate because no one is in charge.

Aristotle does not say much about how political friendship is exercised among friends, perhaps because in those favorable circumstances it involves so much situational improvisation that there's nothing general that can be said. He does, however, have a good deal to say about equality, the relation that structures political rule, and about its operations in more institutional political contexts. Those are our topics in Chapters 4 and 5. We will see that in the communities Aristotle describes as political, actors need to exercise extensive judgment as they manage the economy of ruling and being ruled in the face of the many contingencies and difficulties of human life.

4

Political Rule, Equality, and Equalization

I've been arguing that one of the main innovations in Aristotle's theory of rule is its expansive pluralism, according to which there are some seven kinds of rule, including three "correct" kinds that are appropriate for free people. If, as I have argued, Aristotle's theory of rule is designed to sort all communities into kinds, we might expect the several of the kinds of rule to play important roles in the *Politics*. But in fact through much of *Politics* II to VIII, Aristotle turns his attention to one form in particular—namely political rule, which clearly plays a unique role in his ambiguous views about human community. The special features of political rule will occupy us throughout Chapters 4 and 5. Here I begin by considering the rhetorical force of the term *politikê* in two revealing passages. I then find my way to the all-important question of equality. We have seen that political rule is defined in terms of equality and that definition evidently somehow links political rule to justice. But we will see that the links among those concepts are complex. They are informed by Aristotle's views about the common sense of his contemporaries and expressed with language borrowed from mathematics. And they show that Aristotle is not the kind of egalitarian he has often seemed. Indeed he does not think that the members of political communities need be equal in value or in status one to another, or even that they need be very much alike.

I. Protreptic Uses of Political Rule

But before addressing equality directly, it will be useful to consider two passages that seem to revert from Aristotle's full theory to "rule dualism." The many kinds of rule we have been considering seem to drop away, leaving the older, simpler distinction between *politikê* and *despotikê*.

The first is in *Politics* III.4, in the middle of Aristotle's discussion of the virtues of citizens. As so often, Aristotle finds himself faced with an *aporia*. Should promising citizens devote all their energy to learning to rule well, he asks, at least in the realm of personal relationships? On the one hand (this is the first horn of the *aporia*) it would seem that they should. We know from the *Ethics* that there is a special connection between *phronêsis* and politics. Aristotle has just argued that the rulers are the only people who need human (rather than merely civic) virtue in order to play their role in the city correctly. So all those concerned with developing and exercising virtue seems to have some justification for devoting themselves exclusively to rule.[1] But then again (this is the second horn of the *aporia*) people are sometimes praised for learning the "political" virtue that involves not just ruling but being ruled by others (this position is especially well attested in the Laconizing literature of the time, which recommends subjecting young men to severe discipline in order to prepare them for their turn at power).[2] Aristotle lingers on the problems with this alternative. It's not just that learning to be ruled takes time and energy that might be better spent elsewhere. More worryingly, submitting to rule might seem like something a free person should actively *avoid* doing, since it is widely thought to be abject and servile (ἀνδραποδώδης).[3] If the *endoxa* are right, then however impressive the results of Spartan-style discipline and the modesty and obedience it demands from the young, it's hard to avoid thinking that the practice imposes de facto slavery on free people.

To solve the problem, Aristotle turns to the binary analysis of rule that I now want to consider: *politikê* on the one hand and *despotikê* on the other. Despotism, he says, is a kind of rule directed toward mere necessities (περὶ τὰ ἀναγκαῖα). Aristotle doesn't make it very clear what this expression means. Perhaps it's an empirical claim to the effect that in practice most real-life despotic rule amounts to getting enslaved people to take care of food, land, and so on—the stuff of mere life, not of living well. But whatever the exact nature of the link between despotism and necessity, Aristotle thinks it provides a reason for rulers to avoid learning to be ruled despotically. But this is not the end of the story. "There is," Aristotle continues, "also a kind of rule exercised over those who are similar in birth and free. This we call political rule."[4] Those who submit to political rule, Aristotle suggests, are not (or at least not necessarily) afflicted with the same indignity as those who submit to despotic rule. Indeed, Aristotle continues, in order to rule politically, we must first *be ruled* politically, just as the Spartanizing literature suggests. The *aporia* is solved: free people should avoid learning how to be ruled—despotically. But they should nevertheless seek out a dual education involving both ruling and being ruled—politically.

Let's proceed to the second passage. In *Politics* VII.3, Aristotle is considering the value of the political life. Some people, he says, reject politics because they think it is an unimpressive business of bossing around inferiors. "Certainly," Aristotle concedes,

> there is nothing dignified about using a slave as a slave (οὐθὲν γὰρ τό γε δούλῳ ᾗ δοῦλος χρῆσθαι σεμνόν); giving commands concerning necessary things has nothing noble about it (οὐδενὸς μετέχει τῶν καλῶν). But to consider every sort of rule as despotism is not correct. There is no less distance between rule over free persons and rule over slaves than between what is by nature free and what is by nature slavish.[5]

In the first of our passages, Aristotle addresses people who are worried about *being ruled* because they are afraid of being treated like slaves. Here he is addressing people who object specifically to *ruling others*, or at least to dedicating one's life to doing so. Again Aristotle's interlocutors suppose that all rule shares objectionable properties with *despotikê*. And again, Aristotle concedes that one sort of rule, despotism, does indeed have the problems in question—*despotikê* is indeed altogether unsatisfactory as a life project—but then distinguishes despotism from political rule and says the latter is free from the problems that afflict the former.[6]

Now when people talk about protreptic in Aristotle's practical philosophy, they usually focus on the thorny question of how to fit together disengaged philosophical reflection on the one hand and active civic involvement on the other.[7] But however we solve that age-old problem (if indeed it can be solved), we should not forget that Aristotle also hopes to convince at least some of his politically minded students to abandon bad ways of living a *political* life in favor of better ones. That, I submit, is his project in both of the passages we are considering.

Perhaps his audience includes philosophers who will someday be invited to establish the law code for a new colony or to replace one that is failing; if so, the *Politics* may guide them.[8] Even if it does not, Aristotle's teachings will help young people to pursue justice and the fine within their existing cities, at least to the limited extent that arguments can make a difference for such matters of character.[9] His students, if they learn well, will deliberate about civic actions in the assembly and they will vote in the criminal courts; perhaps they will participate in other ways, for example as prosecutors.[10] And if the appropriate lotteries or elections go their way, they may hold office. If they pay attention to Aristotle's strictures all the while, it will help keep faction at bay and make it more likely that the city's children will grow up in an environment that encourages them to do the same when they're old enough. In both of the passages we have just looked at, in short, Aristotle uses the distinction between *despotikê* and *politikê* to push his students toward the right sort of political activities. When he invokes the distinction, he is encouraging his students to engage in politics in addition to the other kinds of rule that they exercise at home and even to consider dedicating their lives to it.

Aristotle's summons to *politikê* is evidently meant to appeal to a range of students and listeners. He hopes that his account of political rule will appeal to quietists disgusted with politics because they see it as unjust domination and also to opportunists attracted to rule because they think it will bring them profit and glory.[11] In both these cases, Aristotle contrasts *politikê* with *despotikê* in an attempt to persuade his listeners to involve themselves in a political practice consisting of both ruling and being ruled within a community of free, equal people, because he fears they won't have noticed its distinct nature.

The argument in our two passages, however, is negative: Aristotle points out that political rule does not (at least not necessarily) have the unappealing properties his audience might expect and so relieves it of guilt by association. We need to look elsewhere to see just how he expects them to think about whatever positive properties it might have.

II. Political Rule Revisited

I argued in Chapter 3 that Aristotle thinks that every community, association, and relationship (κοινωνία—that is, every group in which people cooperate to achieve some shared goal) has a structure (τάξις) that determines positions of authority (ἀρχαί), including one that is ultimately in charge (κυριώτατος). I argued that Aristotle understands political rule as one such power structure, allowing subordinates not only to contribute to decision making from below but also to make decisions of their own, shaping the actions of their neighbors from above. Political rule is constituted, in other words, (first) by rule-by-turns or some other mechanism guaranteeing everyone some opportunity to take charge of the aspects of life that they share and (second) by practices allowing subordinates to "participate" in rule by limiting or providing input into the decisions of the ruler. By contrast, Aristotle understands despotic rule as the crudest form of exploitation, where one person permanently uses another as a tool, with only an instrumental interest in his or her own good. Does he have these same definitions in mind in the two passages we have been considering, the ones where he praises political rule to his readers?

We might suppose that he does not, perhaps because the text precedes his full theory or because he has suspended or abandoned it. After all it was, as we have seen, common practice to discuss politics in terms of the simple distinction between altruistic rule ("correct" rule in Aristotle's jargon) on the one hand and violent or exploitative ("deviant") rule on the other.[12] If this were right, our passages would, by using *politikê* and *despotikê*, be lumping together political rule with paternal rule and marital rule, and abandoning distinctions that, as we've seen, he works hard to establish in *Politics* I and *EN* VIII.

But it is unlikely that Aristotle's apologetics for *politikê* are supposed to apply to those other kinds of rule too. In *Politics* I, for example, Aristotle associates rule over women with mere life rather than living well and so makes it clear that he agrees with most everyone in his circles that rule over women may be necessary but that it is trivial and insufficient for happiness, in much the same way as ruling over slaves. When he recommends political rule in *Politics* III and VII, he is evidently aiming at something he holds in much higher regard, a noble activity that could constitute a good life. And dialectically speaking, a defense of *politikê* that included the rule of women and children would be a tough row to hoe. The audience members who turn up their noses at *any* kind of rule will likely think of ruling women and children as a case in point— they will be more easily moved by a narrower conception of *politikê* than a broader one.

Moreover, in both of the passages we just considered Aristotle is concerned precisely with the feature that distinguishes political rule from the other kinds of "correct" rule according to the fuller theory developed in *EN* VIII. That feature is the practice of ruling and being ruled in turn or in part, thus allowing all parties to contribute in differentiated ways to their shared activities. The other nonpolitical forms of benevolent rule don't involve that. So when Aristotle invites his listeners to commit themselves to *politikê*, it seems that he is still thinking of political rule in its narrow sense. Indeed, the advantages and disadvantages of turn-taking and shared rule are a consistent focus of the *Politics* as a whole, which we can see in large part precisely as an extended assessment of the value of political rule.

Does he intend "*despotikê*" in a similarly narrow sense, according to which the subject's soul is completely subordinated to the interests of the ruler? The texts aren't explicit one way or the other, but it seems most likely that Aristotle is indicating a broader range of power relations. In the passage from *Politics* III discussed earlier, he takes the time to discuss the many kinds of necessary work (he calls them "kinds of slavery") with which despotism is concerned. These include not just household slavery but also rule over poor people and manual laborers—people who are treated as free citizens in some cities, even if they would not be so treated under the best constitution.[13] And so although he doesn't quite say so, Aristotle seems to be thinking of any kind of rule that isn't political—that is, everything that we might call "hierarchical rule." The distinction between *politikê* and *despotikê* indicates that political rule stands apart, not just from deviant kinds of rule like despotism and oligarchy but also from the other kinds of "correct" rule.

In the remainder of this book I will use the word "politics" to render *politikê*. Likewise I will refer variously to Aristotle's views about "political practices," "the value of politics," and so on. Such uses of the word "politics" and its cognates seem to me to capture an important aspect of Aristotle's thought, according to which the give-and-take required by dealing with people similar to oneself is a central aspect of human life, distinct from the rest.

But it also highlights an important area of possible misunderstanding. *Politikê* and its cognates refer to a wide range of different concepts in Aristotle himself, and modern commentators have piled on various anachronistic abuses of the concept of "politics" besides. So before launching into my argument proper, I'd like to take a moment to note explicitly some of the things that I will *not* be addressing when I discuss Aristotle's conception of political rule. For one thing, I exclude the much broader concepts of (i) the science of politics and (ii) human activity that takes the *polis* as its end. On Aristotle's view, politics in those senses cover pretty much all of human life. After all, Aristotle famously writes that human beings are political animals, that all communities exist for the sake of the political community, that the actions of individuals are at their best when they take the *polis* as a whole as their end, and so on.[14] These are certainly crucial tenets in Aristotle's practical philosophy, and they give us some reason to say that *everything* is "political" in Aristotle's account of human affairs. But they should not distract us from the fact that political *rule* is just one kind of social relation among others.

Perhaps more subtly, we should not confuse the distinction between political and other kinds of rule with any version of the distinction between household and city or worse yet between public and private.[15] Of course, Aristotle does think there is a crucial difference between households and cities. Most notably, the ones merely keep us alive while the others let us live *well* and thereby attain the human end. But, as we have seen, the distinction between political rule and the other kinds cuts across this distinction between household and *polis*. Not all *poleis* are ruled politically (not, for example, those ruled by godlike kings or tyrants); nor, as we will see in more detail later, do all of the smaller institutions governing the *polis*—assemblies, councils, and courts, as well as individual rulers and magistrates—necessarily use political rule, even in regimes that are by and large political. Indeed, Aristotle notes that the various organs of government may use different kinds of rule, as when deliberation and magistracy are oligarchic but the courts are aristocratic.[16]

By the same token, some communities only distantly related to the official organs of government provide paradigm cases of political rule. Interactions between equals in the marketplace, the gymnasium, and the battlefield are cases in point, even if they take place in oligarchies, and so too is the friendship of brothers similar in age, even though it is within the household.

When Aristotle suggests that his readers stop identifying rule with domination and exploitation, and instead invites them to learn both how to rule and how to be ruled, he is not just inviting them to live in *poleis*, as they certainly do already, or to participate more enthusiastically in any given political institution, which may or may not advance the cause of political rule and may or may not be a good idea under particular circumstances. Moreover, he is not asking a question that occupies him elsewhere, of what kind of *polis* is best. Rather, he is inviting the people in his audience to cooperate with their neighbors in a particular way, namely by passing back and forth the opportunity to make decisions establishing the goals of shared activity. In so doing, they forge a certain kind of community (again: a political community but not necessarily a *polis*).[17] Our question is why Aristotle thinks that this kind of cooperation—that of people who take turns ruling and being ruled by people they regard as their equals—is a good thing (if he does indeed think so) and more precisely whether he thinks political communities are better than the more hierarchical ones where some people permanently rule their inferiors.

III. Equality of Value

When Aristotle distinguishes political rule from the other kinds, he usually mentions not only rule by turns, the practice that I have argued partly constitutes political rule, but two *properties enjoyed by the members of political communities*: freedom and equality. Aristotle associates these very closely with political rule; indeed, he sometimes uses them to provide something like a definition, as when, early in the *Politics*, he distinguishes *politikê* from both δεποστεία and οἰκονομική by stating that it is "rule over people who are free and equal" (ἡ δὲ πολιτικὴ ἐλευθέρων καὶ ἴσων ἀρχή).[18]

For Aristotle, as for his contemporaries, freedom is in the first instance a negative concept—you are treated as free whenever you are *not* treated as a slave.[19] And he thinks that slaves (at least when so by nature) are people whose good should not be pursued for its own sake but for the sake of their rulers—people, in other words, who deserve to be used as tools. When people are free, by contrast, this status is necessary and sufficient for them to be ruled in view of their own good. Since political rule is a form of benevolent rule, it's clear why the citizens suited to it must be free.

But freedom does not by itself entitle anyone to political rule—it is a necessary but not a sufficient condition for politics. Children are free, but they must be ruled monarchically rather than politically; women are free, but they must be ruled aristocratically.[20] To qualify for politics, you must not only be free but also *equal* to the other members of some community. Equality, then, is the mark that distinguishes political communities as special and distinct from all other relationships. I will spend the rest of this chapter considering how this concept illuminates Aristotle's views about political rule.

What does it mean for the members of some community to be ἴσοι, equals?[21] This may seem like a trivial question, one whose answer is part of the surface meaning of the text, as well as from political common sense and the bare meaning of the word, in both English and Greek. In its most basic sense, for Aristotle, equality is a relationship between quantities: if we double the length of a line two units long, then it's possible to "fit" (ἁρμόττειν) it to a line that is four units long—the length of the two lines will be equal; some analogous but more complex operation will allow us to say that the area of some squares is equal to the area of some circles. Surely, it would seem, it's perfectly obvious how to extend this to people. To say that some people are "equals" must simply mean that *each person's value is equal to the value of each other person*. Let's call this conception of equality "equality of value."

This is certainly how Aristotle's references to the equality of citizens are normally understood. And there's a reason for that—it's sometimes exactly what he means when he describes people as equals. Most prominently, Aristotle uses the concept in this way to establish common ground with his main political rivals, democrats and oligarchs of various descriptions. Thus at *Politics* III.9 he says:

> Justice seems to be equality, and it is, but not for everyone, only *for equals*. Justice also seems to be inequality, since indeed it is, but not for everyone, only *for unequals*. They [i.e. democrats and oligarchs, and maybe other partisans] disregard the "for whom," however, and judge badly. . . . So since what is just is just for certain people, and consists in dividing things and people in the same way (as we said earlier in the *Ethics*), they agree about what constitutes equality in the thing but disagree about it in the people. . . . For one lot thinks that if they are unequal in one respect (wealth, say) they are wholly unequal, whereas the other lot thinks that if they are equal in one respect (freedom, say) they are wholly equal. But about the most authoritative considerations they do not speak.[22]

We will return later to the parts of this quote that I've elided. But for now the important point is that it's perfectly obvious that when Aristotle describes people as "equals" here, he means "people of equal value, according to some standard."

Here as elsewhere, Aristotle commits himself to two basic claims connecting this kind of equality to just distributions. He takes one of them to be a matter of common sense and the other to be more philosophically difficult. The common-sense view is that if two or more people hold equal value according to some appropriate standard, justice requires that they be treated equally. That obviously invites the question of *what* standard is appropriate. As we saw, oligarchs think the relevant consideration is wealth and democrats think it is freedom. Clearly, other contexts would call for other standards: if you're choosing a doctor the relevant standard will be ability to produce health; if you're judging a footrace, it will be how quickly the competitors ran. But these sorts of considerations are "just only to a point." That is, they neglect the standard necessary to achieve *unqualified* justice (διὰ τὸ λέγειν μέχρι τινὸς ἑκατέρους δίκαιόν τι νομίζουσι δίκαιον λέγειν ἁπλῶς). The consideration necessary to establish unqualified justice, the "most authoritative" (κυριώτατον) one, is simply *virtue*.[23] At bottom and from the point of view of a philosopher, the members of a community are ἴσοι (and therefore suited to equal treatment) when each of them is equal in virtue to each of the others.

If this interpretation of Aristotle's conception of equality seems obvious and uncontroversial, it might seem also to lead to an easy answer to our question about the value of political rule. Since Aristotle thinks that the members of his audience do indeed live in communities with lots of others roughly equal to them, a simple principle of desert requires that they adopt political rule. For if everyone is the same or similar, then everyone deserves the same thing, and that includes both the honors associated with political office and the leisure associated with release from it, and thus everyone should spend some time at the helm and some away from it. We have, then, a simple and compelling story beginning with a pre-political equality, moving through the requirement that equals be treated equally, culminating in a distinctive set of procedures and practices, fit to be embodied in the institutions of government.[24]

IV. Equality and Equalization

You will have gathered, however, that I think there are problems with this story and the definition of equality that underlies it. One place where they show themselves is in the claim that the members of a political community can be equal in *several ways*. Aristotle makes this point at *Nicomachean Ethics* V.6, in a passage about political justice and the communities in which it is appropriate. "What we are looking for," he says,

> is both what is just without qualification and what is just in the context of the political community. This is found where people share their lives

together with a view to self-sufficiency: people who are free, and equal either proportionately or arithmetically (ἴσων ἢ κατ' ἀναλογίαν ἢ κατ' ἀριθμόν).²⁵

Aristotle is unquestionably thinking of the same kind of community as in the passages we have been considering all along, namely political communities made up of people who are free and equal. But here he specifies that the people can be equal either arithmetically, on the one hand, or proportionally, on the other. We should read this passage alongside another one from the *Politics* (which itself points backward to *EN* V), in which he names yet a third way of being equal that is involved in political community and the practice of rule by turns. "It is reciprocal equality [τὸ ἴσον τὸ ἀντιπεπονθὸς]," he says, "that preserves cities, as was said earlier in the *Ethics*; this is necessarily the case even among persons who are free and equal, for all cannot rule at the same time."²⁶

It's worth pausing to note that the bare idea that politics involves several ways of being equal is already enough to put some pressure on the conception of equality we just sketched, which I've been calling equality of value. The point of Aristotle's arbitration of the dispute between democrats and oligarchs is to identify the *one* standard for judging equality of value that is true ἁπλῶς and to show how democrats and oligarchs depart from it. So even if we didn't know what Aristotle meant by geometrical, arithmetical, and reciprocal equality, we would have reason to think that while some of them might amount to equality of value, the others might not. And it would follow that when Aristotle describes the parties to political rule as "equals," he likely doesn't *just* mean that that they are equal in value—for there are other kinds of equality at work as well.

But of course the tools to make sense of these three kinds of equality are near to hand. And I would like to argue that looking at them closely makes it still clearer that when Aristotle says that the members of political communities are "equals," he does not mean by any stretch of the imagination that they are equal in value. In fact, *none* of these three kinds of equality amounts to equality of value. All three are treated in a very well-known text: *EN* V (or *EE* IV), chapters 3–5.

Proportional Equality

The first kind of equality is "equality according to geometrical proportion." As with other species of equality, Aristotle introduces it in order to make sense of a particular kind of justice: the kind shown in "the distribution of honor, wealth, and the other divisible assets of the community" (τὸ ἐν ταῖς διανομαῖς τιμῆς ἢ χρημάτων ἢ τῶν ἄλλων ὅσα μεριστὰ τοῖς κοινωνοῦσι τῆς πολιτείας).²⁷ Now, Aristotle's conception of distributive justice is well known and easily understood. He states it clearly and simply midway through *EN* V.3. "Awards," he says,

> should be according to merit; for all men agree that what is just in distribution must be according to merit in some sense, though they do not all specify the same sort of merit, but democrats identify it with the status of freeman, supporters of oligarchy with wealth (or with noble birth), and supporters of aristocracy with excellence.²⁸

Aristotle thinks it obvious that desert is determined by a person's worth (although, as we've already seen, he treats the criterion by which we should judge worth as a matter of some controversy). And it follows easily that justice in distributions requires that more deserving people get more and that less deserving people get less. He himself stresses that there is nothing complicated or controversial about this.

What is harder to understand is why Aristotle buries this simple idea in a much longer argument that takes up all of *EN* V.3. That argument is so dense and jargon-laden, even by Aristotle's high standards, that at first it's tempting to imagine that he's trying to impress some mathematicians who stopped by his classroom. I'll quote it at length:

> (1) Since the unjust man is unequal and the unjust act unequal, it is clear that there is also an intermediate for the unequal. And this is the equal; for in any kind of action in which there is a more and a less there is also what is equal. If, then, the unjust be unequal, the just is equal, as all men suppose it to be, even apart from argument. And since the equal is intermediate, the just will be an intermediate. (2) Now equality implies at least two things. Necessarily, then, the just involves at least four terms: the persons with an interest are two, and the things in which they deal are two. (3) And there will be the same sort of equality between the people and between the things involved, in so far as the second pair, the things, stand to each other in the same relationship as the first; for if the persons are not equal to each other, they will not have equal shares. [Here I elide the discussion of distribution according to worth quoted just above.] (4) The just, then, represents a kind of proportion. For the proportionate is not just a property of numbers that

consist of abstract units, but of number in general; proportion is equality of ratios, and involves four terms at least (that discrete proportion involves four terms is plain, but so does continuous proportion, for it uses one term as two and mentions it twice; e.g. as the line A is to the line B, so is the line B to the line C; the line B, then, has been mentioned twice, so that if the line B be assumed twice, the proportional terms will be four); and the just, too, involves at least four terms, and the ratio is the same—for there is a similar distinction between the persons and between the things. As the term A, then, is to B, so will C be to D, and therefore, alternando, as A is to C, B will be to D. Therefore also the whole is in the same ratio to the whole; and this coupling the distribution effects, and, if the terms are so combined, effects justly. The conjunction, then, of the term A with C and of B with D is what is just in distribution, and this species of the just is intermediate, and the unjust is what violates the proportion; for the proportional is intermediate, and the just is proportional. (6) Mathematicians call this sort of proportion "geometrical"; for it is in geometrical proportion that one whole also stands to the other whole as each term stands to the other in a given pair.[29]

The argument's main conclusion appears at 1131a29, at the beginning of the section I've numbered (3): "the just, then, is a kind of proportion" (ἔστιν ἄρα τὸ δίκαιον ἀνάλογόν τι). The main support for this conclusion appears in (2), in the form of the claim that the just "involves at least four terms" (ἐν ἐλαχίστοις εἶναι τέτταρσιν). Aristotle supports this intermediate conclusion by arguing that there must be (in the first place) at least two *recipients* whenever goods are distributed (Aristotle refers to them as the οἷς, the "for whom" of justice), and these must, moreover, be considered in light of the *shares* each receives, the "of which," ἐν οἷς, or simply the "stuff," πράγματα. If we assign a value to each of these four items, Aristotle says at (4), we see that distributive justice turns out to be a proportion-of-proportions: the ratios created by the two pairs of values will be equal. For example, if I'm barely enkratic, and we represent that by saying that I have a value of 4, while you are moderately virtuous, so that you are a 6, and then we further suppose that I get some small pile of goods with a value of 2, then justice in distribution requires that you get goods worth 3. If you do, the ratio formed by me and my share, 4:2, is equal to the ratio formed by you and yours, 6:3. (Or, to put the same calculation differently, the ratio formed by the two of us, 4:6, is equal to the ratio formed by the shares, 2:3.)

As I've said more than once now, this is a complicated way to put a simple point, especially one that Aristotle thinks is obvious and one that he explains much more straightforwardly as an aside in the middle of this very stretch of text. Why does he even bother with the thesis that the just is a kind of proportion, with the highly artificial device of assigning numerical values to people, and with the mathematical rigors needed to show how everything fits together? One reason, stressed by several commentators, is that assigning numbers in this way makes it easier to see each share of goods as a mean between too much and too little, so that there is a connection, however tenuous, between his treatment of the virtue of justice and his definition of virtue as a mean state.[30] This is indeed one preoccupation of *EN* V, and Aristotle does gesture at it in the introduction to the argument, section (1).

But it is less important than another point, also stressed (and with greater emphasis) in that same section: that the discussion of proportions illuminates the role of equality (here τὸ ἴσον) in just distributions. Aristotle thinks we need to get clear about proportions precisely in order to solve an *aporia* about justice and equality. We've seen the first of the conflicting *endoxa* already: that desert determines justice in distribution, so that if some parties to a distribution are better than others, they will get appropriately bigger shares. An obvious consequence, on the assumption that some people are better than others, is that in many cases just distribution will involve unequal people and unequal shares. But this conflicts with the second *endoxon*, which is the main point of our section (1), namely that everyone thinks prephilosophically (ἄνευ λόγου) that justice, both as a virtue and as a state of affairs, is grounded in, or even identical with, equality. Thus, unjust people are thought to be unequal (or "unfair"—ἄνισοι) and so are unjust acts and situations.

So the problem is that while most everyone thinks that justice must secure some sort of equality, everyone *also* takes it for granted that just distributions often require inequality—that is, inequality of goods, corresponding to inequality of persons. Aristotle's solution, which justifies the seemingly unnecessary excursion into mathematics, is to show that even when people are unequal in virtue (or according to some other standard), and even when they are therefore treated differently, *some* two parts of the picture really are equal to each other. To wit, as Aristotle says in (4), "proportion is equality of ratios."[31] If we endorse the second *endoxon*, he is saying, we are right to think that equality has an important role to play in just distributions and even that justice is identical with or constituted by equality. But we would be wrong to imagine that it follows that *people* are necessarily equal or suited to equal treatment. That may sometimes be the case, but the things that *must* be equal are rather the ratios they form with each other and with the things distributed. Thus when Aristotle says that the members of a political community may be "geometrically equal," he does not mean that every citizen will be equal to every other citizen. Instead, he is willing to describe them collectively as "equals" (in the sense that suits them to political rule) whether or not they are equal in value to each other, provided equality enters into their relationships in the oblique way we've just described.[32]

Arithmetic Equality

In *Politics* V, Aristotle seems simply to identify arithmetic equality with what I've been calling equality of value.[33] But when he gives arithmetic equality a fuller treatment in *EN* V, the story is rather different. There he uses arithmetic equality not to indicate the democratic ideal of equal people treated equally but to explain how justice works in a particular subsection of social life—"in personal interactions" (συναλλάγμασι), by which he mainly means cases where one person injures another in such a way that some sort of retribution is needed. In such cases, he writes,

> the law pays attention solely to the difference created by the damage done, and where one person is committing an injustice, another suffering it, or one person inflicted damage and another has been damaged, it treats them as equal. So what is unjust in this sense the judge tries to equalize, because it is a matter of inequality; for in fact when one person is struck and another does the striking, or if one person actually kills and the other is killed, the effect of the action and the doing of it constitute unequal parts of a division—and the aim of imposing a loss on the doer is to equalize things, taking away from the gain realized.[34]

Once again, the idea is simple, and it is neither a matter of recognizing people's equality nor of treating them alike. Whenever one person wrongs another, he or she can be represented as gaining something at the other's expense. The amounts gained and lost are not obvious. Transactions bring about highly abstract social and ethical gains and losses, in particular of honor, and even with material goods the amount gained needn't be equal to the amount lost, since a possession can be more valuable to one person than another. This is presumably why a judge is needed to determine how much has been gained and lost, and to use that assessment to assign punishments, or presumably compensation, that undo both the gain and loss. If justice is served, then insofar as possible neither party ultimately benefits or suffers as a result of the exchange (though of course there are complications—an injury may, for example, be severe enough that the person who imposed it cannot give a large enough compensation).

What is just in these cases, Aristotle says, is "having the equal before and after" (τὸ ἴσον ἔχειν καὶ πρότερον καὶ ὕστερον).[35] That is, the quantity of goods that I have before our transaction must be equal, insofar as possible, to the quantity I have after justice has been done. The dialectic here is the same as with geometrical equality. Aristotle is bound by received opinion to give equality some role in justice; and he obliges but in a way that does not preserve the idea that citizens are equal *to each other*, as democrats suppose. Like geometrical equality, arithmetic equality as it is defined here does not require that I be equal to you in worth, nor that I have the same amount of goods as you, nor again that we be treated in the same way.

Reciprocal Equality

Reciprocal equality is the most obscure of the three kinds of equality in *EN* V. It might roughly be characterized as equality of exchange. Aristotle's first example of ἀντιπεπονθός is *lex talionis*, which requires straightforwardly giving what one has received or taking what one has had taken. But Aristotle quickly moves on to commercial transactions, where reciprocity is necessary for a fair exchange of *unlike* goods: one house is to be exchanged for a great many shoes or the equivalent in currency. When, in *Politics* II, he writes that reciprocity preserves the political community, he seems to have two sorts of exchange in mind: on the one hand, the ruler provides benefits to the people he rules, and they repay him with honor; on the other hand, those who are ruled repay their rulers by taking a turn in command, and vice versa.[36]

It's less than perfectly clear how reciprocity is supposed to fit into Aristotle's typology of justice. On the one hand, it might seem to be a part of corrective justice. He says that this concerns two kinds of transactions: some are voluntary, like buying, selling, and lending, while the others are involuntary, like theft and poisoning.[37] Since his main treatment of corrective justice concerns the involuntary cases, it seems natural to suppose that the treatment of commercial justice will cover the voluntary part. But then again when he introduces commercial justice, he immediately says it "is not compatible" or "cannot be harmonized" (οὐκ ἐφαρμόττει) with either distributive or arithmetic justice.[38] To make matters worse, he also says that reciprocity has a place in communities of exchange (ἐν ταῖς κοινωνίαις ταῖς ἀλλακτικαῖς), only if it is "proportionate rather than equal" (κατ᾽ ἀναλογίαν καὶ μὴ κατ᾽ ἰσότητα).[39]

I frankly don't think Aristotle gives an entirely clear or consistent picture of how reciprocal equality is related to the other two kinds. But the crucial point for our purposes is conveyed by the last of the claims I've just cited: however reciprocal equality fits into his larger scheme, it does *not* presuppose the equality of the parties, either in virtue or according to any other standard of value. Aristotle's main concern in *EN* V.5 is to make sense of justice in the exchange of unlike goods (shoes for a house, in his favorite example) and of the role that need and currency play in mediating between them. And so we might expect that reciprocal justice is the kind most inclined to treat people as equals—after all, the worth of the people making an exchange has nothing to do with the value of the items traded. This interpretation would imply that communities governed by reciprocal equality need not be composed of people equal to each other in value. But that is not what Aristotle says—he says that reciprocal commercial transactions presuppose the *inequality* of the exchange partners. Here is the text:

> No community is formed from two doctors. It is formed *from a doctor and a farmer, and, in general, from people who are unequal and need to be equalized.* This is why all items for exchange must be comparable in some way. Currency came along to do exactly this, and in a way becomes an intermediate, since it measures everything, and so measures excess and deficiency—for instance how many shoes are equal to a house. Hence *as builder is to shoemaker, so must the number of shoes be to a house;* for if this does not happen there will be no exchange and no community.[40]

Scholars have tried in vain to explain or to explain away the idea that the relative value of a builder and a shoemaker will somehow enter into the price the one pays for the other's product.[41] But Aristotle leaves no reasonable room for doubt that on his view reciprocal equality presupposes not just a difference between goods to be exchanged but also an inequality between parties to the exchange. Far from presupposing the equality of the parties, commercial transactions presuppose their *in*equality, and correct for it in some obscure way, equalizing not just goods but people. Thus Aristotle does not think equality of value is necessary for reciprocity, any more than for proportional and arithmetic equality.

Equalization

One remarkable feature of this account is that Aristotle takes it for granted in all kinds of equality that some political actor (either a distributor or a judge) must *do something* to make the relevant values come out equal. Equality of value is a simple relational property, antecedent to what anyone does. Geometrical, arithmetic, and reciprocal equality are relational properties that are partly constituted by *social practices*, things that people may or may not do to others. Thus Aristotle speaks throughout the discussion not only of "equality" (ἰσότης) but also of "equalizing" (ἰσάζειν). Currency and need equalize people and products. A judge "equalizes" the unfair situations created by unjust transactions (τὸ ἄδικον τοῦτο ἄνισον ὂν ἰσάζειν πειρᾶται ὁ δικαστής).

Elsewhere in the *Ethics* he returns to the idea that *people* can be "equalized" through proportional distribution. When a better person is friends with a worse one, Aristotle writes, the superior should love less and the inferior should love more, so that the one who deserves more gets more love. "For when the loving is distributed according to merit," he says, "that produces equality of a sort" (ὅταν γὰρ κατ' ἀξίαν ἡ φίλησις γίνηται, τότε γίνεταί πως ἰσότης).[42] He returns to this point a couple of pages later: "It is most of all in this way that unequal people can be friends—for it equalizes them" (οὕτω δ' ἂν καὶ οἱ ἄνισοι μάλιστ' εἶεν φίλοι: ἰσάζοιντο γὰρ ἄν).[43] When he says, then, that the members of a political community are geometrically, arithmetically, or reciprocally equal, he means not that that they are equal in value, but rather that someone has, wherever necessary, given them things or taken them away, incorporating equality into their relationships in a way that is very different from that standardly accepted by democratic champions of equality. Once the equalization is complete, they are ready for the give and take of political rule.

Isonomia?

At this point, someone may object that I'm overlooking a crucial part of Aristotle's conception of equality. All three forms of justice, the objector will say, presuppose a single, further kind of equality. Aristotle evidently thinks that criminal justice, fair distribution, and reasonable exchange all involve applying a single, consistent set of rules to every member of some group of people. And this recalls a conception of equality that certainly existed in Aristotle's time— indeed, one that was the main form of equality in Athenian political discourse and practice. The idea (often expressed with the word ἰσονομία, roughly "equality before the law") was that the law should treat all citizens without favoritism, and this was used variously by disenfranchised groups like the poor to claim a place in government. Aristotle too thinks that everyone should be treated equally so long as there is no relevant difference between them. So when he says that political communities are made up of equals (the objector will ask), doesn't it stand to reason that *this* must be what he has in mind: no one within such a community should be treated any better or worse than anyone unless the difference is justified by a fair, objectively determined inequality of merit?

It seems to me for several reasons that this cannot be the conception of equality underlying political rule. There is in the first place an argument from silence. Although Aristotle spends a lot of time explaining what it is for people to count as "equals" in various ways (as we've just seen at some length), equality of status never appears in this discussion, nor does he use the word ἰσονομία or otherwise signal any sympathy for that idea.

Second, *isonomia* is too broad to do the work Aristotle asks of it. Suppose, as the objector suggests, that Aristotle considered any two people as "equal" just when any difference in how they should be treated responds to some difference in their desert. It would follow that he thought free Athenians and natural slaves enjoyed equality of status. After all, Aristotle thinks that natural slaves should get worse treatment than the free because they are inferior in objective, morally relevant ways.[44] But the sense of equality that we're after is used precisely to signal a *difference* between the community formed by fellow citizens of cities like Athens and that formed by a master and his slaves. When Aristotle describes the members of political communities as equals, he must mean something more.

Finally, as Paul Cartledge has well argued, the standard Greek conception of equality was tied up with what (or rather who) the citizens were *not*. Political or civic equality, he says,

> meant equality of status and respect within the conceptual framework of the Greeks' normative socio-political system of polarized hierarchy. Insofar

as the Greek citizen was by definition male not female, free not slave, native insider not stranger or outsider, and adult not a child, he was equal to all other citizens, and deserving therefore of equal respect, privilege, consideration, and treatment.[45]

This conception of equal status is a version of equality of value: it treats any two people as equal just so long as they aren't marked out as inferior because of their foreign birth, sex, etc. But as we have seen, Aristotle argues against such standards for equal treatment, including notably the "democratic" conception that people should be treated alike if they are free. Equal freedom is not equality ἁπλῶς, and Aristotle argues emphatically that political thinkers must acknowledge the political significance of *other* kinds of similarity and difference, most notably in virtue. On the democratic view, all citizens come out as exactly equal because all of them are *entirely* or *perfectly* male, free, native, etc. But Aristotle thinks that the best standard for judging people's value is virtue, and this is a matter of degree. More generally, the considerations that matter to him for politics are differences of degree, not of kind, and he does not think that fellow citizens are *exactly* equal to each other in any sense that matters.

5

Political Rule and the Good

I. What Communities Should Be Ruled Politically?

So much, then, for our survey of the role of equality in political rule. We've seen that Aristotle does not think people must be equal to each in order to qualify for political rule. Rather, equality enters their relationships through institutions and practices that "equalize" them by responding in various ways to their similarities and differences. I would now like to consider how Aristotle thinks about those institutions and practices, and what he ultimately thinks is good about political rule and the various institutions through which it allows citizens to take turns ruling and being ruled and to participate in rule when they are out of power. We will see that just as his views on equality are qualified and ambivalent, so too is his approach to the institutions of politics.

The usual approach to these issues is to ask how to reconcile Aristotle's clear and consistent approval for political rule with his (less frequent but more explicit) ranking of kingship and aristocracy as the best of constitutions.[1] But we are now in a position to formulate the question in a different way.

We might start by pointing out that not only is political rule *compatible* with differences in value, as we saw in Chapter 4, but real-life political communities *reliably include* people of unequal worth, as a matter of empirical fact and conceptual necessity. Aristotle makes this point explicit at the level of the *polis* as a whole. He takes it to be obvious that "it is impossible for a city to consist entirely of good people,"[2] and he argues at various points in *Pol.* IV–VI that although under normal circumstances the unwashed poor—in particular, *banausoi* and *thêtes*, menial workers—must be granted some share in political rule, higher offices should be restricted to the rich.[3] Moreover, even among full-fledged citizens of the ideal city sketched in *Politics* VII, some citizens will be more deserving of rule than others at any given time: the young should be soldiers, and political rule is reserved for older people, who have a greater share of *phronêsis*. This arrangement, Aristotle says, "contains conformity with merit" (ἔχει γὰρ αὕτη ἡ διαίρεσις τὸ κατ' ἀξίαν).[4] Finally, the assumption that political communities contain better and worse members runs through even his more abstract formulations of the various kinds of justice. When he says that distributive justice treats equals equally *and* unequals unequally, this plausibly enough suggests that we can expect our communities (including our *political* communities, where we have seen distributive justice is most at home) to contain people both equal and unequal to ourselves. Some members of political communities will be better in morally significant ways than others.

If we take it as a given that all political communities include some people who are superior to others, just like households and other nonpolitical communities, then we may ask about the value of political rule this way: Why does Aristotle think that *some* communities of unequals—that is, communities some of whose members are better than others in morally significant ways—should be ruled by turn, rather than assigning permanent rule by merit, as distributive equality seems to require? That is, why does he think that some communities of unequals should be ruled politically, while others should not?

II. Similarity, Difference, Pretence, and Imitation

Before trying to answer, it's worth noting that Aristotle says quite explicitly that the principle of desert must sometimes be ignored in political communities. He makes this especially clear in a passage discussing the correct legal attitude to corrective justice. "It makes no difference [οὐδὲν γὰρ διαφέρει]," he says,

> whether a decent person has defrauded a worthless one, or a worthless person a decent one, or whether the adultery was committed by someone decent or someone worthless; the law pays attention solely to the difference created by the damage done, and where one person is committing an injustice, another suffering it, or one person inflicted damage and another has been damaged it treats them as if they were equal (χρῆται ὡς ἴσοις, εἰ ὁ μὲν ἀδικεῖ ὁ δ' ἀδικεῖται, καὶ εἰ ἔβλαψεν ὁ δὲ βέβλαπται).[5]

Since Aristotle thinks that corrective justice is essential in any well-run city, and thus in at least some communities structured by political rule, it follows that members of political communities should sometimes help and harm their fellows without regard to their worth—which is to say without regard to what they naturally deserve. This could hardly contrast more with justice according to desert, which requires that we recognize as fully as possible the facts about the people we interact with and, where they are relevant, allow those facts to determine how we treat them.

A passage in *Politics* II.2 (we have already seen it in part—it is about the connection between reciprocity and rule by turns) contains a further twist. Aristotle has been arguing that a city (unlike, say, a military alliance) is the sort of whole whose unity requires that some of its parts differ from each other. At 1261a30, he turns to political communities in which there *don't*, at first sight, seem to be any notable differences between people—communities in which everyone is free and equal. He writes that reciprocal equality—that is, the kind of equality achieved by the fair exchange of goods—is necessary to preserve these communities. In communities of equals, this takes the form of rule by turns: every citizen must sometimes rule but at other times obey, according to some regular rotation. This sort of exchange is necessary, Aristotle says, because everyone cannot rule at the same time (ἅμα γὰρ οὐχ οἷόν τε πάντας ἄρχειν).

But when this sort of arrangement is in place, it is "as if shoemakers and carpenters were to exchange places rather than the same people always being shoemakers and carpenters." The image of people switching jobs is used often enough in ancient texts (Isocrates makes it, for example, at *Busiris* 8), and it is not flattering. The principle of specialization is widely taken to be one of the greatest human political accomplishments. "It is clear," Aristotle writes, that "it is better that the same always rule, where this is possible." He continues:

> but in cases where it is not possible because all are equal in their nature (ἐν οἷς δὲ μὴ δυνατὸν διὰ τὸ τὴν φύσιν ἴσους εἶναι πάντας), and it is at the same time just for all to have a share in ruling (regardless of whether ruling is something good or something mean), there is at least an imitation of this (τοῦτο γε μιμεῖται). For some rule and some are ruled in turn, as if becoming other persons.[6]

What is being imitated here? Clearly it must be the practice that Aristotle has just claimed is best, although it is impossible in communities of equals: namely that there be specialist rulers who are qualitatively different than the people they rule.⁷ The practice of rule by turns allows communities of unequal people to "imitate" hierarchical communities in which some members are permanently in charge of others.⁸

We've seen that Aristotle thinks that the members of political communities reliably differ in value. And we've seen further that Aristotle thinks we should sometimes ignore those differences. But this passage marks an even greater departure from the principle of desert. In the cases Aristotle has in mind, instituting political rule is not a matter of responding to the facts about people. It isn't even a matter of selecting a narrow range of facts to respond to, as in corrective justice. Rather, Aristotle is saying that we should sometimes imitate difference, creating a kind of ersatz inequality.

In Book I, Aristotle describes the same process, of creating virtual differences between otherwise equal people. "It is true," he says,

> that in most cases of political rule people take turns at ruling and being ruled, because they tend by nature to be on an equal footing and to differ in nothing (ἐξ ἴσου γὰρ εἶναι βούλεται τὴν φύσιν καὶ διαφέρειν μηδέν). Nevertheless, whenever one person is ruling and another being ruled, they try to create a difference (ζητεῖ διαφορὰν εἶναι) by means of appearances, words, and honors (καὶ σχήμασι καὶ λόγοις καὶ τιμαῖς). Witness what Amasis said about his footbath.⁹

The bit about Amasis is a reference to a passage in Herodotus where a king who was once a commoner refashions a golden footbath "in which Egyptians had once vomited and urinated and cleaned their feet" into a statue of a god.¹⁰ In this story, Herodotus highlights the ways that a thing's history (i.e., being urinated in, etc.) can suggest that we should evaluate it in one way, while its matter and form (a golden statue of a god) suggest another evaluation. In Herodotus' account, Amasis persuades his Egyptian subjects that the considerations about matter and form outweigh those about history (the footbath's ascent from filth to nobility is supposed to represent Amasis' own biography), but it's not clear whether Herodotus expects his readers to find this convincing. When Aristotle appropriates the story, though, it seems clear that he uses it to represent a kind of transformation that is superficial and even misleading in one way, but that really does matter politically: the appearances, words, and honors that distinguish rulers from the people they rule are not natural differences, but they amount to something like a virtual transformation of ordinary citizens into superior people, worthy of obedience. When the natural facts don't otherwise meet our political needs, Aristotle claims, we can make do by instead changing social facts.

What emerges when we bring these points together is that Aristotle thinks that (i) political rule is appropriate for people who are equal or similar in virtue; yet (ii) there are probably significant differences in virtue between any two members of the communities where political rule is found, which means they deserve to be treated unequally; but (iii) we must *also* sometimes ignore those differences, treating people as equal even when they are not; and in still *other* cases (iv) we must act as though some people are better than others, even though they are, as a matter of natural fact, equal. That's a lot. To see how it can all be so, we need to get still clearer about what Aristotle means when he says the members of political communities are equal to each other and about when he thinks people's natural differences should and should not determine their treatment. More broadly, all this pretense and imitation lends new urgency to the question of how he can recommend life in a political community to his students at all.

III. Equal Enough for Politics

Aristotle sheds some light on these questions in a passage in *Politics* VII, as he lays out the foundations of his discussion of education in the best regime.

> (1) Since every political community is constituted of rulers and ruled, this must then be investigated—if the rulers and the ruled should be different or the same throughout life (εἰ ἑτέρους εἶναι δεῖ τοὺς ἄρχοντας καὶ τοὺς ἀρχομένους ἢ τοὺς αὐτοὺς διὰ βίου); for it is clear that education too will have to follow in accordance with this distinction. (2) Now if the ones were as different from the others as we believe gods and heroes differ from human beings (ὥστε ἀναμφισβήτητον εἶναι καὶ φανερὰν τὴν ὑπεροχὴν τοῖς ἀρχομένοις τὴν τῶν ἀρχόντων)—much exceeding them in the first place in body, and then in soul, so that the pre-eminence of the rulers is indisputable and evident to the ruled—it is clear that it would always be better for the same persons to rule and the same to be ruled once and for all. (3) But since this is not easy to assume, there being none so different from the ruled as Scylax says the kings in India are, (4) it is evident that for many reasons (φανερὸν ὅτι διὰ πολλὰς αἰτίας) it is necessary for all in a similar fashion to

share in ruling and being ruled in turn (ἀναγκαῖον πάντας ὁμοίως κοινωνεῖν τοῦ κατὰ μέρος ἄρχειν καὶ ἄρχεσθαι). (5) For equality consists in giving the same to those who are alike, and it is difficult for a constitution to last if its organization is contrary to justice (τό τε γὰρ ἴσον ταὐτὸν τοῖς ὁμοίοις, καὶ χαλεπὸν μένειν τὴν πολιτείαν τὴν συνεστηκυῖαν παρὰ τὸ δίκαιον).[11]

The last sentence here, the one I've marked as (5), might seem to support the "desert interpretation" that I've been criticizing. After all, it says that equality (τὸ ἴσον) calls for a single kind of treatment "for similar people" (τοῖς ὁμοίοις), and it offers this principle as logical support (with "γάρ") for the practice of sharing in rule, recommended in (4). But this is a misunderstanding, based on a misconception of the rather vague expression "similar people."

So far, I have followed standard practice by focusing on the roles of freedom and especially equality in Aristotle's conception of politics. But in fact, this doesn't quite capture Aristotle's language. There is a third term that is in fact just as prominent: *similarity* very often replaces or accompanies equality in Aristotle's discussions of political rule. *Politics* III.4, to take one of several examples, describes *politikê* without mentioning equality, as the kind of rule "exercised over those who are similar in kind [τῶν ὁμοίων τῷ γένει] and free."[12] Locutions like this confirm that, as we've seen, Aristotle doesn't think everyone involved in political rule has to be *exactly* as virtuous as everyone else. Whether by nature, luck, or their own initiative, Aristotle takes it for granted that some citizens in any city will outshine others, at least a little. Commentators, however, typically take this as a trivial qualification, a gesture at differences too small to mention or irrelevant for the purposes of politics. In this vein, they often speak—as I too have done earlier in this chapter—in terms of Aristotle's commitment to political rule for people who are "equal or nearly equal" in value.[13]

But when Aristotle talks about similar and equal people, he often reaches for examples that fit poorly with this interpretation. For example, in section (2) of our passage, he writes that political rule would not be appropriate for a community including both normal people and gods or heroes. These examples are obviously not designed to evoke just any differences between people. Rather, Aristotle is trying to bring to his readers' minds the very largest differences in value available to the Greek imagination. This is a pattern. Again and again, when he wants to explain the role of equality of value in human life, Aristotle indicates not that we are all essentially the same, but quite differently that none of us towers over anyone else as much as a god. When in Book III he sketches what a person would have to be like to deserve to be a king, for example, he says such a person "would reasonably be regarded as a god among human beings."[14] Again, to highlight the role of value equality in friendship, he points out that no one could be friends with a god (and that kings are not friends with those who are "much their inferiors").[15] These passages about equality are not designed to contrast equal-or-nearly-equal people with unequal ones but to distinguish everyday inequalities from truly enormous ones. They suggest that when Aristotle says that the members of political communities are "similar or equal," he does not mean that they must be identical or nearly so, but only that their inequality must not be extraordinarily vast.

And if this is so, then the problems start to dissolve. When Aristotle says that people are suited to politics when they are equal in value, he means that they must meet some minimum standard of similarity. The bar is set low enough to leave lots of room for inequalities that will need to be addressed within the community, so that the various kinds of justice, including those presupposing inequality, will still have a place. To be suited for politics, people need not be exactly equal, very nearly equal, or even approximately equal to each other—they need only be equal enough for politics. The practices of equalization take over from there.

In section (2) of our passage, Aristotle leaves the mythical examples behind and suggests where the dividing line between the two degrees of inequality—normal inequality appropriate for political rule versus extreme inequality inappropriate for it—might lie.[16] Hierarchical rule is best, he says, just when the person ruled finds the superiority of the ruler "to be evident and indisputable" (ἀναμφισβήτητον εἶναι καὶ φανεράν). How difficult does Aristotle think it is for people to meet this standard? When it comes to free adult men in the Greece of his time, Aristotle is clear that hardly anyone can be expected to agree with his neighbors about who is better than whom.[17] In fact, this kind of disagreement is the underlying cause of the debate between democrats and oligarchs that we touched on earlier. Aristotle, as we have already seen, thinks that these partisans disagree with each other because they "strip away" or "abstract" (ἀφαιροῦσι) considerations about the value of those they compare themselves to and therefore come up with wrongheaded standards of human value. That is, these people focus on some narrow human quality like wealth and free birth. Aristotle thinks such features have some political importance—and in the middle books of the *Politics*, he shows how they may enter into various kinds of political thought. But to focus on any one of them not only overlooks the others but, more crucially, overlooks the "most authoritative consideration," virtue, which determines justice in its unqualified sense. Human beings are prone to make this mistake, as Aristotle explains, because of a deeper problem, a widespread weakness in human judgment. "The judgment" these partisans make, he says, "concerns themselves [περὶ αὑτῶν ἡ κρίσις], and most people [οἱ πλεῖστοι] are pretty poor judges about matters close to them [φαῦλοι κριταὶ περὶ τῶν οἰκείων]."[18] Even doctors, as he says later, tend to consult other doctors when they get sick, "their assumption being that they are unable to judge truly because they are judging about their own cases, and while in pain."[19] The implication of this passage seems to be that in order to avoid the political conflicts that arise from our inability to judge our own worth, we would need to find gods and heroes to rule us. But as Aristotle says in part (3) of our passage, it is "not easy" to find people who surpass normal Greek men that much; indeed, there "are not" kings who are like that, notwithstanding the tall tales of explorers like Scylax.[20] This means that in normal communities, we must decide who rules on some basis other than worth.[21]

I've restricted this analysis to free men because, notwithstanding the talk about gods and heroes, Aristotle certainly doesn't think that it's impossible to find *human beings* who differ from each other this much. For a start, he surely assumes (as perhaps many people still do) that children will recognize themselves as vastly inferior to adults and therefore find it appropriate to submit to their authority. Likely, he thinks that the same thing goes for women and natural slaves: not only that they are inferior to free Greek men but that the inferiority is so obvious that under normal circumstances they will themselves recognize it and accept their subordination without much fuss.[22] And just a few lines after our passage, Aristotle argues that in the city of our prayers—where, of course, he assumes against reasonable expectation that all citizens will be virtuous—young men in military duty will not chafe at being ruled, nor think themselves better than their rulers, at least not when they know they will get their chance to rule over the next round of young soldiers when they are older (ἀγανακτεῖ δὲ οὐδεὶς καθ' ἡλικίαν ἀρχόμενος, οὐδὲ νομίζει εἶναι κρείττων, ἄλλως τε καὶ μέλλων ἀντιλαμβάνειν τοῦτον τὸν ἔρανον ὅταν τύχῃ τῆς ἱκνουμένης ἡλικίας).[23]

The key phenomenon that defines this approach to equality—that is, the approach contrasting "normal" inequality to "clear, indisputable" inequality—is *dispute* about people's worth. By his own lights, Aristotle has good reason to make this central to his political theory. For he thinks the disagreements that proliferate in the absence of any clear differences in value are among the greatest political evils.[24] The *Politics* returns again and again to the importance of civic harmony and stability, the preservation of which is worthwhile even in very flawed regimes. And it returns again and again to the ways that disaster follows when people think themselves equal to their neighbors but get worse treatment than they do—or think themselves superior to their neighbors but get treated equally.[25] Cities whose members cannot agree about each other's worth are powder kegs, prone first to faction and then collapse, and Aristotle assumes this is disastrous for everyone, even people who would in principle have been better off under some other regime. This is the danger Aristotle has in mind in section (4) of our passage, where he repeats that rule by turns is necessary precisely because it is "difficult for a constitution to last" (χαλεπὸν μένειν) if it is not founded on the principle of like treatment for similar people. It is primarily to avert the danger of faction, rather than to achieve anything intrinsically valuable, that Aristotle thinks we should rule and be ruled by turns; and this is itself appropriate not because of the equality or near equality we all enjoy but rather because most everyone has lousy judgment.

IV. Sameness, Difference, and *Phronêsis*

Suppose that you and I are extremely virtuous (though not, alas, as outstanding as gods and heroes), and we find ourselves in a political community, alongside decent people we know perfectly well to be our inferiors. The *Politics* is directed in large part to people like us.[26] What does its treatment of political rule mean for our actions and deliberations?

On Aristotle's view, excellent people like us belong to the group most justified in trying to overthrow the existing regime—but least likely to do so.[27] He indicates quite clearly how we must understand our situation. Since you and I are just, we aim to make sure that everyone gets whatever they deserve, and we have excellent judgment about who deserves what. So we recognize that that we ourselves deserve to be honored by being put permanently in charge of our less-virtuous neighbors. We also wish for those neighbors to receive the benefits we would secure for them if we were in charge. So we have good reasons to regret that we are not kings.

Nevertheless, we will not try to seize power. The main thing holding us back is that we recognize the evils of faction. If we formed an aristocratic faction and fought to wrest power from our inferior neighbors, that would condemn everyone involved to many misfortunes (including of course the misfortune of unjust distribution, since factional conflict would cause many people to take losses they don't deserve). And Aristotle emphasizes that since we can count on being outnumbered by our inferiors (who will not recognize our superiority), our takeover is bound to fail anyway.[28]

Alongside these reasons not to revolt, we also have positive reasons to embrace the existing egalitarian political order. One is that just as it is better to use better rather than worse tools, so too it is better to rule over better rather than worse subjects (ἀεὶ βελτίων ἡ ἀρχὴ ἡ τῶν βελτιόνων ἀρχομένων).[29] Better subordinates, as Aristotle explains, contribute to better shared actions (that is the point that underlies the idea we saw at the beginning of Chapter 4, namely that even *ruling* over slaves is tainted with slavishness). And contributing to our political regime will give us at least some chance to rule over free, moderately virtuous people. Another reason to support egalitarian politics is to restrict the malign influence of various inferiors. In the Assembly and when they are selected for office, those people will be prone to bad decisions. Political institutions will give us a chance to limit the damage they can do.[30] But perhaps the most important reason is that a stable political regime provides a context in which political animals like us can realize our potential as human beings. Political activity gives us and our neighbors the opportunity to exercise the ethical virtues to the varying extents that we have them. Moreover, many of those virtues take their fullest form when they are directed toward others (or toward the city as a whole) and guided by *nomos*. Likewise, the citizens of a political community may grant themselves and each other some leisure to reflect philosophically and so take steps toward wisdom. This is to say that supporting and participating in political rule is a tolerably good way to pursue happiness—our own and also the happiness of our friends and the city as a whole. And that, as we learn in the famous opening arguments of the *Nicomachean Ethics*, is the ultimate goal of everything we do: every art, inquiry, action, and pursuit. Finally, even though preserving political rule means that people will not get exactly what they deserve, we can console ourselves with the fact that we have at least applied a rough approximation of the principle of desert. For in political rule, similar treatment is accorded to "similar" people, in a legitimate if qualified sense of the term. In particular, people with a moderate share of virtue get a moderate share of power and honor, as they would not if they were permanently ruled by their superiors.[31] Thus if we support an existing political regime, we will prevent bad things from happening, contribute to the conditions necessary for good ones, and achieve at least a rough approximation (Aristotle might call it a *mimêsis*) of just distribution.

The line of thought I have just sketched comes together into a messy, qualified, and perfectly intelligible set of reasons for Aristotle to recommend political rule to his audience. His students will emerge from Aristotle's lectures with a good reason to support the institutions that help equalize the citizens in the various ways we considered earlier.

Let us return for a moment to the two rival species of equality, proportional and geometrical. At the beginning of his discussion of faction, Aristotle says explicitly that no community can last if it doesn't involve both. "It is a bad thing" (φαῦλον), he says, for a constitution to be organized "unqualifiedly and entirely" according to either arithmetic equality or equality according to worth.

> This is evident from what actually happens (ἐκ τοῦ συμβαίνοντος), since no constitution of this kind is stable (οὐδεμία γὰρ μόνιμος ἐκ τῶν τοιούτων πολιτειῶν). The reason is that when one is in error from the beginning and in one's principles (ἀπὸ τοῦ πρώτου καὶ τοῦ ἐν ἀρχῇ ἡμαρτημένου), it is impossible to avoid encountering something bad in the end (μὴ ἀπαντᾶν εἰς τὸ τέλος κακόν τι). Hence arithmetic equality should be used in some cases, and equality according to merit in others.[32]

Aristotle is thinking of "mixed" *politeiai* incorporating both democratic institutions and oligarchic ones, for example by restricting civic participation with a minimum property qualification but also increasing it by paying qualified farmers to participate.[33] But the point is broader. Aristotle's point is that there is no solution to the bad ideas endemic to political life (i.e., identifying worth with mere freedom or wealth) except the piecemeal, situational work of *phronêsis*. Political skill, Aristotle says, is a matter of prudently picking and choosing among the various kinds of equality based on circumstance.

Good political actors introduce equality into their neighbors' relationships in a variety of ways, sometimes directly and sometimes obliquely. In the first instance, they do it to avoid conflict. But they also do it for any number of other reasons. On the one hand, they accord the highest honors only to the best people (so that not just anyone can be selected as general). Not only is this what those people deserve, but it is necessary to keep them from getting too resentful and to make sure truly important decisions are in the right hands. On the other hand, when they serve as judges, skilled politicians will not have the time or insight to fully and correctly evaluate everything relevant to a case. So they make do with a rough and ready practice of seeing how much each of two parties has lost and gained in a single transaction. And in still other cases, they give someone undeserved special treatment, as when they honor and obey some undistinguished official during his randomly assigned tenure. All these practices are required both by the metaphysical fact that rulers must be different from their subjects and by the psychological fact that rulers and subjects hew better to their roles when those differences are visible. Taken together, such practices ensure that few citizens' pride is wounded so deeply that they give up on cooperation altogether, but that merit and competence nevertheless direct public life as much as possible. And insofar as we are imperfectly virtuous, Aristotle's philosophy will remind us of the considerations that matter when *pleonexia* might otherwise drive us to seek out too much power over others, or (supposing we think ruling is a hardship) to give up on politics altogether, handing it over to people who don't deserve it and cannot be trusted.

Such considerations are typical of Aristotle's approach to practical wisdom, where we must as a matter of course adjust our actions to conflicting considerations and adapt ourselves to imperfect circumstances of various kinds. And they are necessary to explain why Aristotle endorses both the exchange of power between similar people and the variety of forms of justice that he recommends within political communities. Distribution according to desert plays a role here, but it is only a small one—and that is why the standard interpretation of political rule is so misleading.

We have, then, one answer—indeed, the main one—to the question I asked at the beginning of this chapter, about what is good about political rule. We can now see that although Aristotle does give his students reasons to support and engage in political rule, those reasons are qualified in two important ways. First, from the point of view of a virtuous agent, political rule is (at best) *contingently* valuable. If you live in a normal city, you will have a reason to support egalitarian political practices and institutions. But you will have no such reason if you have the bad luck to find yourself surrounded only by grossly inferior people, the good luck of living with someone of godlike virtue, or the superlative good luck of being divinely virtuous yourself. Second, when political rule is appropriate, it is in large part *instrumentally* good, especially because of how effective it is in staving off disaster and making room for happiness. Yet for all that, under normal circumstances engaging in political rule expresses the virtues, particularly justice and practical wisdom. And that means that it can be partly constitutive of happiness.

V. Ruling, Holding Office, and Controlling the City

This line of reasoning, on Aristotle's view, will in all likelihood give most of his readers sufficient grounds to participate in political rule and to protect the institutions that advance it. In other words, it will give them reasons to pursue a professional political life, involving themselves in the institutions shaping their cities' collective actions.

It is worth pausing to return once more to the political institution most tightly connected to the activity of rule in cities like Athens: the ἀρχαί, "offices" or "magistracies." For Aristotle's readers that institution had an especially tight relationship with ruling, since "to rule" and "to hold office" are both expressed by the Greek verb ἄρχειν, and similar relationships obtain between words like "ruler" and "office-holder." Early political thinkers took it for granted that the doubles in question were not mere homonyms but rather that holding office amounts, ipso facto, to ruling the city. Melissa Lane has dubbed this assumption the "standard equation."[34] It provides an easy way to think about the constitutions ending in -archy, like "oligarchy" and "monarchy." You may, for example, gloss "oligarchy" more or less indifferently as (i) the constitution in which few people hold office or (ii) the constitution in which few people rule.[35]

Now if one of Aristotle's Athenian readers holds office—suppose that he is elected general, to pick an important if atypical case—he will have the opportunity to deliberate about important affairs and to see his decisions (indeed his own moral perspective) come alive in the actions of many other subordinates. As long as his term lasts, the fellow citizens under his command will defer to him and act within the *telos* set by his decisions. Everyone will defer to him as if he deserved rule more than anyone else, even though that is unlikely to be the case. His tenure as general will give him an opportunity to realize his potential for human virtue more fully than his tenure as a soldier. Meanwhile, he will continue to defer to other officials on non-military matters. In these ways, the institutional sense of the word ἀρχή, according to which it means "office," often does indeed indicate the ways it empowers people to rule.

But as Lane argues, one of Aristotle's goals in the *Politics* is precisely to complicate the equation between the two senses of *archein*. In particular, Aristotle aims to show how someone can hold office without thereby ruling, and that the *demos* can be in charge of a city even though only a few people can hold office at a given time. The decoupling of the standard equation has implications for individual officeholders too. Recall, for example, that there were in Athens several generals at any given time and that they sometimes worked together on a single campaign. They must have sometimes had conversations as equals, engaging with each other in the sort of political rule that Aristotle imagines among brothers. Then again, history records some leading others, with and without legal direction for doing so. In some favorable cases, perhaps the subordinate generals fell into line, being ruled in a kingly or aristocratic manner. And it would not be surprising if in other cases one general bossed the others around as if they were children or slaves.

Such examples make it clear why, even *qua* officeholder and with regard to the performance of official duties, no one should imagine that holding office is identical with (or even sufficient for) ruling. Although holding office provides unique opportunities to rule, it also typically involves being ruled, participating in rule, and so on. There is indeed no strict or necessary relation between holding office and ruling. And the point should be generalized to other political formations. In an oligarchy, for example, a small group of the rich rule jointly over a larger group of the poor (oligarchically, of course, since they rule based on wealth not virtue, and they do not take turns ruling and being ruled). But in *Politics* V.1, Aristotle considers the conflicts that naturally arise *within* groups of oligarchs. Since oligarchs rule on the principle that wealth entitles some people to rule over others, it should come as no surprise that the wealthier oligarchs try to lord it over the poorer oligarchs.[36] This is just one instance of Aristotle's general view that within any group of people, faction is imminent. "Just as in war," he writes, "the crossing of ditches, even if they are small, splits apart the ranks, so every difference appears to split a group into factions."[37] And so however helpful it may be at one level of analysis to treat a social class or a clique as a whole, there remain questions about the relations—which necessarily involve ruling and being ruled—among its parts. And so where Aristotle describes a social group as ruling a city, he often goes on to discuss which individuals rule *within* that group, as, for example, when he discusses the rise of demagogues within democratic masses.[38] The lesson for our purposes is that although rule of some individuals over others is highly important to what we might call "institutional" or "professional" politics, there are no simple connections between the overall power structure of a city and the ways its citizens rule each other in their plural and overlapping interactions.

There is another gap between personal rule and institutional politics. The former is a teleological relationship linking the activities of both the rational and affective parts of people's souls; the latter often involves thinner, more mechanistic processes. I have already argued (in the section on impersonal rulers in Chapter 3) that the rule of the law is too general and restrictive to provide proper decisions. The law cannot rule the way a person does; rather it limits the actions of people who rule. The same goes for the work—as decisive as it sometimes is—of the courts and the assembly. According to the democratic ideal, as we have seen, the *demos* controls officers by electing and by inspecting them, and perhaps also by speaking in the Assembly. A member of the *demos* may thereby make it more likely that some people rule rather than others. He may introduce considerations that shape the decisions of people in power. But none of that counts as *ruling* in the teleological sense we have explored in this book. Nor do the actions of the *demos* as a whole, even in the famous cases of *Politics* III.11 where the combined virtue of the people qualifies them to be sovereign over the city. Although Aristotle does not help us out by using this terminology perfectly consistently, we may conceive of the κράτος (power) in δημοκρατιά as distinct from *archein*. It involves providing *efficient* causes for the actions of people who rule, and doing so from a subordinate position.

VI. Politics and Choosing the Bad

That's about as much as we can say about how political rule looks from the perspective of political actors. But although that point of view is fundamental to Aristotle's practical philosophy, by no means can all the evaluative claims in the *Ethics* and *Politics* be reduced to advice. Indeed many important doctrines are only distantly related to anything anyone can do. Consider, for example, this explanation of the two ways virtue can be used, from *Politics* VII.13:

> By "conditional" (ἐξ ὑποθέσεως) I mean those that are necessary; by "unqualified" (ἁπλῶς), I mean those that are noble. For example, in the case of just actions, just retributions and punishments (αἱ δίκαιαι τιμωρίαι καὶ κολάσεις) spring from virtue, but are necessary uses of it (ἀναγκαῖαι δέ), and are noble only in a necessary way (τὸ καλῶς ἀναγκαίως ἔχουσιν), since it would be preferable if neither a man nor a state needed these things (αἱρετώτερον μὲν γὰρ μηδενὸς δεῖσθαι τῶν τοιούτων μήτε τὸν ἄνδρα μήτε τὴν πόλιν).[39]

In the last sentence here, Aristotle is imagining something that's effectively impossible for human beings: cities and individuals with no need for punitive justice. At first sight, it may seem strange that he should say this kind of virtue-free situation would be preferable to our present condition. Virtuous actions (which certainly include the administration of just punishment) constitute our *telos*, they are noble, and they should be done for their own sake. Still, immediately after expressing this point, Aristotle digs in his heels. The problem with punitive justice, he continues, is that dishing out punishment and just retribution (unlike honors and resources) involves "the choice of something bad" (κακοῦ τινὸς αἵρεσις). Ross and other editors strike this phrase from their editions. Aristotle, they suppose, most likely meant not that punitive justice involves the *choice* of something bad but rather its "destruction" (ἀναίρεσις). But perhaps this emendation is unnecessary. For it is a general feature of Aristotle's treatment of life in the sublunar realm that things may be legitimately described as both bad and good, albeit from different perspectives. Aristotle suggests this point, for example, at *EN* X.8 1178b15, as he considers the activities suited to gods. It would clearly be ridiculous, he says, to imagine (as the epic poets do) that the gods can be brave, moderate, and so on. For the gods, there are no threats to be afraid of, no base appetites to domesticate, and so on. "Everything about practical doings," Aristotle says, "if one looks through all the kinds, will obviously turn out to be petty and unworthy [μικρὰ καὶ ἀνάξια] of gods."

We may better grasp the point of claims like this if we compare them to ideas in Aristotle's metaphysics and natural philosophy. The closing pages of Book I of the *Parts of Animals*, for example, are usually remembered as a celebration of biology: the study of perishable sublunar things, like the study of the heavens, has its distinctive charms (χάριν), since as Heraclitus said, there are gods in the humblest places. But we should not forget that, in the same breath, Aristotle takes pains to reassert the inferiority of perishable things to their heavenly counterparts. A faint glimpse of the latter, he says, greatly outweighs even precise knowledge of the former, and the study of biology involves things that are not only "ignoble" (ἀτιμότερον), but that no one can look at without "much repugnance" (πολλῆς δυσχερείας).[40]

The religious language here is no accident. This passage draws on a core piece of Aristotelian doctrine: that attributes and activities are good when they contribute to the goals built into an organism, but that these kinds of good are distinct from (though grounded in) the goodness of the divine beings in and beyond the heavens. This doctrine gives a philosophical point to saying that things may be good and bad simultaneously. We can evaluate things both from the point of view of an animal species and from a cosmic or divine point of view. So, for example, if we study the basset hound according to the canons of Aristotelian biology, we will notice the ways that its long ears and its shuffling gait contribute to its distinctive way of life, and we will therefore see how each of those things is good. But the evaluative story doesn't end there. The organs and activities of basset hounds allow them to survive and reproduce, which allows their kind to live forever even though the individuals cannot.[41] And this clears the way for a second evaluation. For the highest end of any mortal animal can only be a pale imitation of the unqualified good of divine immortality. From the point of view of a basset hound, saliva and runny eyes are good, for they clear away the dust it is exposed to in its life close to the ground. But the gods have no need for such things—they are good only because of the dog's circumstances are less than ideal. The goodness of the gods is not relative to a species but absolute. So while philosophers can learn to see traces of the divine in the lowliest creatures, when they return from the menagerie, they will also (and without contradiction) see as clearly as anyone that those creatures can be rather disgusting.[42]

This approach allows Aristotle to incorporate the Greek opposition between the toil and hardship of human life and the blissful leisure of the immortals into his scientific program, and to reconcile it with his teleology.[43] Sometimes, as in the discussion with which we started this section, he talks in terms of things that are good "by hypothesis." In the same passage, he also spells this out in terms of "necessity," along the lines of the two definitions of that concept in *Metaphysics* Δ:

> We call "necessary" that without which, as a condition, a thing cannot live; as breathing and food are necessary for an animal; and the conditions without which good cannot be or come to be, or without which we cannot get rid or be freed of an evil; e.g. drinking the medicine is necessary in order that we may be cured of disease, and a man's sailing to Aegina is necessary in order that he may get his money.[44]

This, I want to suggest, is ultimately the perspective we need to understand the value of political rule and especially the practices that we have lingered on in this chapter, involving disregarding or falsifying differences in value between people.

It belongs to an approach to politics that Aristotle describes at the beginning of *Politics* IV. The philosopher, he says there, must be able to determine not only what constitution we would pray for, provided there were no external impediments (μηδενὸς ἐμποδίζοντος τῶν ἐκτός) but also what is best under certain conditions (ἐκ τῶν ὑποκειμένων) and based on certain presuppositions (ὑποθέσεως).[45] He returns to this project at IV.11, where he finally settles on the best constitution and way of life "for most cities, and for most people," based on the levels of virtue and education they are liable to share.[46] It is in this melancholy context that he writes that the city "wishes to be made up of equal and similar persons as far as possible."[47] With this claim in mind, let's return to a passage we saw earlier, in which Aristotle insists very explicitly that ruling by turns is this kind of second-best option, a practice to which we resort because the option we might hope for is not available. Citizens, as you will recall,

> cannot all rule together, but must change at the end of the year or some other period of time or in some order of succession. The result is that upon this plan they all govern; just as if shoemakers and carpenters were to exchange their occupations, and the same persons did not always continue shoemakers and carpenters. And since it is better that this should be so in politics as well, it is clear that while there should be continuance of power where this is possible, yet where this is not possible by reason of the natural equality of the citizens, and at the same time it is just that all should share in government (whether to govern be a good thing or a bad), and for equals thus to submit to authority in turn imitates their being originally dissimilar;

for some govern and others are governed by turn, as though becoming other persons.[48]

Aristotle here emphasizes the contrast between the arrangement that would be best if we could achieve it—uninterrupted rule by political experts—and the alternative practice that we must fall back on, granted our imperfect conditions.

I've already argued that when Aristotle describes the citizens of political communities as naturally equal (as he does here), he doesn't mean that everyone is as good as everyone else, but that they're similar enough to disagree about who should rule. We may now add to that argument that the cognitive features that make political rule necessary for normal Greek men—in particular, bad judgment with regard to one's own worth—force human beings to fall away from the kinds of rule more suitable to gods.

Granted that Aristotle says political rule "imitates" permanent, hierarchical rule, we might expect that if it is conditionally good, then hierarchy will be absolutely good, associated with the divine. We've seen that he certainly does make this association to some extent, since gods and kings are both immeasurably superior to run-of-the-mill human beings. But it also seems likely that the connection runs deeper, and that Aristotle accepts a tradition, passed down by Plato, where perfect hierarchy is associated with the divine, while the rule of near equals over one another is an all-too-human falling away from that ideal. Plato famously introduces that distinction in the myth of the *Statesman*, where he contrasts the perfect stewardship of Cronos with the more stopgap stewardship of human rulers in our own age, when πολιτικοί "are much more like their subjects in nature."[49] But the most telling passage in Plato is not from the *Statesman* but from the *Laws*, where Plato identifies the very practice of geometrical, as opposed to arithmetic, equality with divine rule. "The two kinds of equality," he says,

> are called by the same name, but are in reality in many ways almost the opposite of one another; one of them may be introduced without difficulty by any state or any legislator in the distribution of honors; namely, that of measure, weight, and number, which he ensures by lot. But there is another equality, of a better and higher kind, which is not so easily recognized. This is the judgment of God; among men it avails but little; that little, however, is the source of the greatest good to individuals and states. For it gives to the greater more and to the inferior less, and in proportion to the nature of

each; and above all, greater honor always to the greater virtue, and to the less less; and to either in proportion to their respective measure of virtue and education.[50]

The basic complaint here, about the blindness of the law to specificity, and the contrast of such unfair systems with the rulings of a judge who, like Zeus, uses his discretion to settle each case according to its merits, is of course not at all foreign to Aristotle. On the contrary, he complains that the law, since it is necessarily universal, cannot correctly apply to all relevant cases and insists that we must correct it with appropriate amendments and with judicial decrees whenever exceptional cases arise.[51]

This passage helps to explain why, as we have seen, Aristotle emphasizes the ways that corrective justice ignores desert. There is every reason to think that for Aristotle as for Plato, a perfect judge would not, as in his account of corrective justice, treat a "decent adulterer" (whatever exactly he has in mind when he says this) in just the same way as a wicked one. Rather, he thinks that we resort to arithmetical equality only when circumstances force us to fall short of the divine because of the complexity of life in the *polis* (the difficulty of finding consistently excellent judges, the prohibitive number of adultery cases to get through in a week) or the unlikelihood, given human weaknesses, that a society relying on the discretion of judges will tend to get things right. And this may be the reason that Aristotle says, without further explanation, that geometrical equality is the "primary kind" of equality when it comes to justice.[52]

I opened this chapter with the question whether political rule is good. I've now answered that from the perspective of the virtuous agent, political rule is indeed good (some of the time and assuming certain widespread conditions), because in passing back and forth the capacity to establish communal goals, it allows human beings to achieve the higher ends constitutive of their species. If we shift to the perspective of the human species, we still find that political rule is good—although again in a qualified sense, for although political rule benefits us, few human beings come close to achieving the human ideal while they are engaged in politics. And if we shift again to the perspective of the cosmos, we find that political rule is really not very good at all, since it falls far short of the perfect kingship of a god and because it means ignoring differences in value that a god would recognize.

If this is so, then Aristotle's position is something of a mirror image to much later political thought. Many thinkers have suggested that if human nature were better than it is, there would be no need for states, which, however legitimate they might be, empower some people to coerce others. On this view, anarchy is as it were the constitution of our prayers. But, so the story goes, human beings are flawed and prone to violence, and we are forced, contrary to an idealized vision of justice, to put some people in power over others. We must then regretfully do what we can to mitigate the injustice inherent in that practice. This is for example just what Kant says in the lines immediately preceding his famous quote about the crooked timber of humanity.

> Man is an animal which, if it lives among others of its kind, requires a master. For he certainly abuses his freedom with respect to other men, and although as a reasonable being he wishes to have a law which limits the freedom of all, his selfish animal impulses tempt him, where possible, to exempt himself from them. He thus requires a master, who will break his will and force him to obey a will that is universally valid, under which each can be free.[53]

Aristotle too believes that we are cobbled together from crooked timber. But for him the ideal and the stopgap are reversed. If we were blessed with perfect judgment of our own and each other's worth, and if we were surrounded by the best neighbors we could hope for, we would naturally fall out into permanent, unchanging hierarchy. It is only because we fall short of this ideal that we must resort—alas—to treating each other as equals.

Conclusion

I. Review of the Argument

"The sage," Aristotle liked to say, "falls in love and takes part in politics; he gets married and he spends his life with the king." He also said that "friendship is a single soul living in two bodies."[1] Or that's what Diogenes Laetritus reports. It's doubtful that these *bon mots* are Aristotle's words, and they may sound more like the ideas of Stoics than Aristotle. But if the argument I've just finished making is right, they capture something important about his ideas. For Aristotle, I've argued, much of what is most important in human action belongs to close, hierarchical relationships. And when two people cooperate, this knits together the activities of their souls.

I've tried to show that this adds up to a substantive and philosophically rich theory—Aristotle has a general account of what rule is, he divides it into well-articulated smaller types, and he connects it with his broader views about *phronêsis* and the good. This theory is grounded in his philosophical commitments about action, community, and value, and it ties together parts of the corpus that we too often read in isolation. Rule, for Aristotle, is not just at home in the *Politics* but also in the *Ethics* and even the *Rhetoric*; it isn't just about the domination of slaves and women but also about the interactions of virtue friends and fellow citizens; and it's not just about the fixed institutions of the household and the city but rather about the countless ways one human being can cooperate with another.

We saw in Chapter 1 that Aristotle positions his theory of rule in a broader discussion connecting the status of *douloi*, enslaved or slavish people, to *logos*, persuasive speech. Aristotle, I suggested, draws on a minority view in this position, holding that *logos* provides the right way to rule over slaves as well as free people. We should not, however, take this doctrine as a gesture of respect for the equal dignity of rational beings. Quite differently, for Aristotle as for Xenophon, *logos* provides the best way to rule over slaves because it is the most efficacious tool for controlling their souls. In Chapter 2, we considered Aristotle's generic definition of rule. In all cases of interpersonal rule, one person rules another when goals established in the first person's soul provide an end for the activities of the second. This sort of interaction leaves a lot of room for the people who are ruled to think for themselves and to make contributions of their own to shared action. But it also means that, for Aristotle, whenever one person rules another (at least at any given time, in respect of any given dimension of their interactions) one person's thoughts establish the teleological horizon for the other's actions. In Chapter 3, I argued that Aristotle thinks rule is coextensive with cooperation, and that he uses the concept of rule to divide communities and relationships into species, based not only on who is ultimately in charge but also on how powers and responsibilities are entrusted to people lower on the hierarchy. In Chapter 4, we saw that in spite of the verbal importance of equality to the concept of political rule, the connections between equality and politics are more distant than is often recognized. Political rule is better seen as recognizing similarity and difference and responding to it (as Aristotle misleadingly says, "equalizing" people) than in recognizing any antecedent equality. And in Chapter 5, we saw that Aristotle encourages the ambitious young men in his audience to pursue one sort of rule in particular: political rule, which requires that citizens treat each other as free and equal, ruling and being ruled by turns. But we saw that while Aristotle thinks this kind of cooperation has much to recommend it, he looks on it with real ambivalence. In most situations, he thinks political rule is good for human beings, but only because, alas, we are flawed animals forced to pursue justice in communities in which it's hard to agree about who is better than whom.

II. Liberalism and the Motley Reception of Aristotle's Theory of Rule

Perhaps it's already clear that I think that one of the main lessons of Aristotle's theory of rule is that he's less of a liberal (or perhaps I should say *even* less of a liberal) than Aristotle scholars often think.[2] In Chapters 1 and 2, I argue that Aristotle advises masters to persuade their slaves with rational arguments because this helps to dominate them more effectively and completely—

not because he thinks we should do right by them as rational beings. In Chapter 3, I argue that he says that rule comes in several kinds largely in order to encourage rulers to recognize differences in the *ways* their subordinates are inferior to them—not to distinguish a good egalitarian kind of rule from a bad hierarchical one. And in Chapters 4 and 5, I argue that when he recommends political rule, and thereby gives freedom and equality important places in his political philosophy, he does it, in a certain sense, with a heavy heart.

In this respect, I've been stressing what scholars inevitably call Aristotle's "strangeness" or his "distance from us." Now, it's become a commonplace in some parts of the academic world that these characteristics provide the best reasons to study historical texts. On this view, historical distance is particularly useful in illuminating our own unquestioned assumptions, making available to us ideas that we wouldn't otherwise have thought of, and shedding light on the contingency of modern-day thought. Commonplace or not, I pretty well agree with it.

But I'd now like to briefly consider some of the ways that the distance between Aristotle and his present-day successors goes beyond mere disagreement. Two thinkers can have very different doctrines but be closely related dialectically. After all, when one thinker develops the ideas of another, the new ideas may go so far beyond the original that they differ from their source in almost every respect. And one thinker can develop a position by rejecting another's ideas, sometimes pretty well point-by-point. In both sorts of cases, there is plenty of disagreement in substance, but clear and direct connections remain. I think that one lesson that we stand to learn from Aristotle's theory of rule is that his political philosophy is different from its modern successors in this way as well as in its content.

The point isn't just relevant to those who think of Aristotle as a proto-liberal. In fact, one of the reasons Aristotle scholars sometimes exaggerate his continuities with liberalism is to answer another influential group of people who distort him by exaggerating his *disagreements* with it, for example by treating him as the father of an anti-liberal communitarianism. Although I haven't lingered on them, I think such overstatements of Aristotle's difference from liberalism are mistakes too.[3] There are twin tendencies to exaggerate *both* similarities *and* differences between Aristotle's political thought and liberalism, and both are misleading. In fact, I think both are symptoms of exaggerating the kind of direct, dialectical relationship between Aristotle and modern political thought that I was just describing.

One crude version of this error springs from a certain way of thinking about the history of Western political thought. The story I have in mind begins with the hierarchy and paternalism of the Homeric world, which supposedly survives more or less intact, if heavily intellectualized, in Plato's *Republic*. But, the story continues, Athenian democrats soon started to overturn this sort of politics. Under their influence, political thinkers started to realize the political importance of freedom and equality. In this story, Aristotle took an important early step on a path that—after being interrupted by the Middle Ages, through much of which the *Politics* was not in circulation—was taken progressively further by Hobbes (who, notwithstanding his authoritarianism, makes human equality the fundamental precondition of politics), by Locke, and by Kant. According to this story, to quote a widely used political philosophy textbook, "every plausible political theory has the same ultimate value, which is equality."[4]

The history of Western political thought that I've just given is of course a cartoon, and it has been under heavy fire for decades. But in some form it is certainly implied by the tables of contents of many survey books and the reading lists of many introductory courses. I'm frankly not sure how many scholars in the history of philosophy would nowadays accept a suitably elaborated and qualified version of it. But even those who wholly reject it might still think that there are direct ties between Aristotle and liberalism. After all, they might point out, the founders of modern political thought almost always had well-thumbed copies of the *Politics* in their libraries, and their work is full of technical language and fragments of arguments that indisputably originate with Aristotle.[5] Surely (so goes the argument), this shows that much modern philosophy is to some great extent made up of extensions of Aristotle on the one hand and responses to him on the other.

There are certainly many resemblances and connections between Aristotle's *Politics* and various founding liberal texts. But they often conceal not just disagreements in doctrine but systems that scarcely have anything to do with each other. Perhaps just one example (particularly relevant to the argument I'm bringing to a close) will suffice to illustrate the dangers. In Locke's *Two Treatises of Government*, he writes the following:

> The Power of a *Magistrate* over a Subject may be distinguished from that of a *Father* over his Children, a *Master* over his Servant, a *Husband* over his Wife, and a *Lord* over his Slave. All which distinct Powers happening

sometimes together in the same Man, if he be considered under these different Relations, it may help us to distinguish these Powers one from another, and show the difference betwixt a Ruler of a Common-wealth, a Father of a Family, and a Captain of a Galley.[6]

Obviously, this passage looks a lot like a passage from the *Politics* that is one of the main subjects of this book. J.S. Maloy makes the case that in writing the *Two Treatises*, Locke intentionally aligned himself with Aristotle, against the quasi-Platonic project of modeling the power of the king on that of a father, a project that follows naturally from the analogy between family relationships and the relationships within the guardian class in the *Republic*.[7] Now it scarcely needs to be said (and Maloy acknowledges) that Locke's political philosophy departs radically from Aristotle. But this isn't just because, as everyone will agree, other aspects of Locke's philosophy are incompatible with Aristotle's basic commitments (Locke, for example, thinks that people may or may not consent to being ruled by others, that the best reason to submit to political rule is to protect one's property rights, etc.). Nor is it just that the idea he is purportedly taking from Aristotle—political rule—is stripped of crucial associations with the political life in ancient Greece, including especially the practice of rule by turns. Rather, Locke's supposedly Aristotelian conception of political rule is itself defined in terms of a sort of equality that—as I argued in Chapter 4—had no place at all in Aristotle's thought. If Locke is inspired in some sense by Aristotle, this doesn't mean that he adopts, develops, modifies, or even understands his ideas. I submit (though I won't make the argument) that *many* of the Aristotelian echoes in liberal thought, from the seventeenth century onward, are rather like this passage from Locke.

And this is what we might expect considering the period between Aristotle and Hobbes, missing from the cartoonish narrative I just gave. Not only did political thought continue through late antiquity and the middle ages, but it continued along lines that do not fit comfortably into the narrative. Among other things, the long period between Aristotle and Hobbes testifies neither to the collapse of hierarchical political philosophy nor to the rise of equality in its place. We've seen that Aristotle's political philosophy is in large part a counsel of *noblesse oblige* that justifies his students' claim to rule the people around them even as it limits and redirects it. This kind of thought continued in several forms through the Hellenistic period and the Renaissance. There was, for one thing, the tradition of mirrors to princes, running from Xenophon and Isocrates through the Hellenistic period to Machiavelli and beyond.[8] Likewise, neo-Platonists and their students elaborated on the theme of the philosopher king, exploring the connection between philosophical knowledge and political expertise.[9]

And insofar as Aristotle's views soon came to be challenged or eclipsed by various rivals, these weren't only or primarily egalitarian, nor were they based on the ideal of freedom. One prominent strand of social thought running from late antiquity to the modern period, for example, turned from the question of *how to rule* to a question Socrates stresses in Plato's *Apology* and *Crito*: *how to obey*. Obedience to God and obedience to his human representatives are, for example, recurring themes in Augustine, as is the view that docility is an essential aspect of human development.[10] Others continued to emphasize this question through to the beginning of the modern period. Thus Francis Bacon opens his essay "Of Great Place" by appealing to a long tradition of literature about the ways that service shapes all human life. Even the most powerful people, he says, "are thrice servants—servants of the sovereign or State, servants of fame, and servants of business; so as they have no freedom, neither in their person nor in their actions, nor in their times."[11]

In short, if Aristotle's political philosophy contains the seeds of liberalism, not only did they take a long time to sprout, but they have no special priority over any number of other Aristotelian ideas that could have developed (and sometimes did develop) into a wide variety of unfamiliar, non-liberal forms. Thus, attending to the ideas in Aristotle might help to shed light on a number of issues in the subsequent history of political thought that have not, so far as I know, gotten much attention. For example, it might also be useful to consider whether what I have called "rule pluralism" has analogues or descendants in the centuries that followed. Similarly, we might try to trace the fortunes of the idea that human social relationships inevitably involve some people acting as final causes on the souls of others.

I think, for similar reasons, that attention to Aristotle's theory of rule might also provide tools for thinking about politics in the present. Although much neo-Aristotelianism is less Aristotelian (and more neo) than we might think, there are likenesses of Aristotle's theory of rule in several places where they have seldom been noticed, and the concepts and associations in Aristotle's theory of rule might well help us understand them more clearly. We might, for example, point to the typologies of power developed by Max Weber and Robert Dahl, and to Michel Foucault's thesis that there is no avoiding power relationships. Or we might turn to the topic—now central to popular left-wing thought—of privilege, which, like Aristotle, takes it as a given that some people have power over others and then asks what they should do about it.

Beyond the academy, there is the familiar idea in popular discussion of sports and business that something called "leadership" is essential for effective cooperation, and some kinds of leadership (kinds, perhaps, that executives might learn at expensive seminars) are better than others. If the story I've told here is correct, these strands of thought share certain concerns with Aristotle. But it seems to me that many of them might also benefit from engaging more closely with the claims that we've seen here: that the thoughts and actions of some are yoked to values and projects of others; and that when we confront power (both when others wield it over us and when we wield it over them) we should keep an eye on its variety, on its complexity, and on the difficulty of negotiating it appropriately in a world that is further from the ideal than we might wish.

Notes

Introduction

1. *Lys.* 207d–10b.
2. *Lys.* 209a4.
3. *Lys.* 210b1–c3.
4. *Lys.* 210a1–7.
5. *Pol.* I.1, 1252a8–16.
6. *Pol.* I.1, 1252a20–26. See also *Pol.* I.3, 1253b18.
7. *Pol.* I.7, 1255b16–19.
8. This tactic—of motivating his positions by distancing himself from the radicalism of the Academy—is a mainstay of Aristotle's pedagogy and rhetoric. See Stephen Menn, "Aristotle," in *Encyclopedia of Philosophy*, ed. Donald Borchert, Vol. 1, 2nd ed. (Detroit: Macmillan, 2006), 267.
9. See Jaqueline Bordes, *Politeia dans la pensée grecque jusqu'à Aristote* (Paris: Belles Lettres, 1982).
10. For one example of this kind of talk, see *Laws* IV, 712e9–10, where the Athenian stranger says that none of the city-types normally called πολιτεῖαι deserve the name, since they are organized despotically in the interest of some ruling group, but that Crete and Sparta both do, since they aim at the good for the city as a whole. See also Josiah Ober's *Political Dissent in Democratic Athens* (Princeton: Princeton University Press, 1998).
11. This point is complicated by the fact that although rule over women seems like it should count as a subspecies of οἰκονομική, Aristotle (just once) says that it is "political." See the section "Kinds of Rule" in Chapter 3.
12. Paul Moraux has argued that the dialogue *On Justice*, listed in ancient catalogues of Aristotle's work, must contain the story that he neglects to develop in his surviving work. *A la recherche de l'Aristote perdu: Le dialogue "Sur la justice"* (Louvain: Publications Universitaires de Louvain, 1957).
13. I build on a recent body of work recognizing the importance of rule to Aristotle's thought. Malcolm Schofield was among the first contemporary scholars to insist (against a tradition that took the main topic of *Politics* I to be the claim that the

polis is natural) that the distinction between kinds of rule is the book's main idea (Malcolm Schofield, "Ideology and Philosophy in Aristotle's Theory of Natural Slavery," in *Saving the City* [New York: Routledge, 1999], 101–23). Marguerite Deslauriers develops that insight in "The Argument of Aristotle's *Politics* I," *Phoenix* 60:1 (2006), 48–69. Notable recent monographs giving the topic of rule sustained attention include David Riesbeck, *Aristotle on Political Community* (Cambridge: Cambridge University Press, 2016), Andrés Rosler, *Political Authority and Obligation in Aristotle* (Oxford: Clarendon Press, 2005), and Adriel M. Trott, *Aristotle on the Nature of Community* (Cambridge: Cambridge University Press, 2014). Recent essay-length discussions include Thornton Lockwood, "Justice in Aristotle's Household and City," *Polis* 20:1/2 (2003), 1–21, Robert Mayhew, "Rulers and Ruled," in *A Companion to Aristotle*, ed. G. Anagnostopoulos (Oxford: Blackwell, 2009), and Fred D. Miller Jr., "The Rule of Reason," in *The Cambridge Companion to Aristotle's Politics*, ed. Marguerite Deslauriers and Pierre Destrée (Cambridge: Cambridge University Press, 2013), 38–66.

14 *Politics* I.5, 1254a26–33. ὅσα γὰρ ἐκ πλειόνων συνέστηκε καὶ γίνεται ἕν τι κοινόν, εἴτε ἐκ συνεχῶν εἴτε ἐκ διῃρημένων, ἐν ἅπασιν ἐμφαίνεται τὸ ἄρχον καὶ τὸ ἀρχόμενον, καὶ τοῦτο ἐκ τῆς ἁπάσης φύσεως ἐνυπάρχει τοῖς ἐμψύχοις· καὶ γὰρ ἐν τοῖς μὴ μετέχουσι ζωῆς ἔστι τις ἀρχή, οἷον ἁρμονίας. Fred Miller treats it under the heading the "Principle of Rulership" (*Nature, Justice, and Rights in Aristotle's Politics*. [Oxford: Clarendon Press, 1995], 20–1). For a useful analysis, see page 342ff of Joseph Karbowski, "Aristotle's Scientific Inquiry into Natural Slavery," *Journal of the History of Philosophy* 51:3 (2013), 331–53.

15 It therefore excludes some things that English speakers might call "relationships," such as the relationship between enemies, and some groups that English speakers might call "communities," such as military leagues.

16 *Politics* I.5, 1254a19-21.

17 Saunders reacts with appropriate astonishment: "Are there no *purely* co-operative enterprises, no associations, in which no one rules?" *Aristotle: Politics I*, Clarendon Aristotle Series (Oxford: Oxford University Press, 1996), 77. Like most scholars I have found, he takes it as obvious that the principle applies at a minimum to the *polis*.

18 Newman and Riesbeck deny that the principle can apply to all κοινωνίαι, pointing to commercial relationships where buyer and seller seem to act separately and independently, yet neither commands the other to do anything. Their arguments depend on premises that I reject over the course of this book, notably that rule is defined by command. Riesbeck also assumes that Aristotle

intends to apply the principle only to substances—yet that cannot be what Aristotle has in mind, since the case he has in mind is the union of master and slave. Riesbeck, *Aristotle on Political Community*, 139n10, W.L. Newman, *The Politics of Aristotle* (Cambridge: Cambridge University Press, 2010 [reprint of 1884 edition]), i: 42. See further the sections "Do Friendships Always Involve Rule?" in Chapter 3 and "Reciprocal Equality" in Chapter 4.

19 ἀλλὰ μὴν καὶ ἐν τοῖς τέτταρσι καὶ τοῖς ὁποσοισοῦν κοινωνοῖς ἀναγκαῖον εἶναί τινα τὸν ἀποδώσοντα καὶ κρινοῦντα τὸ δίκαιον (*Pol.* IV.4, 1291a21–24). We will see in Chapter 2 that for Aristotle a ruler is defined precisely as a person positioned to make decisions for another, especially about justice.

20 The dominant strand of interpretations along these lines is broadly liberal. See for example Miller, *Natural Rights* and Rosler, *Political Authority*. But I have tried to describe the position in a way that also captures Arendtian readings like Trott, *Aristotle on the Nature of Political Community*.

21 He does on the other hand say on a few occasions that it is just for the law to rule rather than any human being. The problem, however, is that he thinks the law must always be applied by a person's decision. I discuss this point further in Chapter 3.

22 *EN* I.1, 1094a11–13.

23 On the relationship between ruling and holding office, see the section "Ruling, Holding Office, and Controlling the City" in Chapter 5.

24 *Pol.* III.1, 1275a32.

25 Plato develops this paradigm in *Philebus* (16b5–18d2): The Egyptian god Theuth confronted the infinite range (ἄπειρον) of human speech (φωνή). He brought together various vocal sounds, for example connecting βα with γα, seeking out both principles that they shared (α, for example, is common to both syllables) and principles that constitute their difference (β and γ). He emerged with the alphabet, the complete but minimal toolkit necessary to represent anything anyone might ever say. See Stephen Menn, "Collecting the Letters," *Phronesis* 43:4 (1998), 291–305.

26 *EN* VIII.10, 1160b9.

27 "Equality and Hierarchy in Aristotle's Political Thought," in *Saving the City: Philosopher-Kings and Other Classical Paradigms* (London: Routledge, 1999), 101.

28 The best overall account of these issues in Aristotle's practical philosophy is Gauthier's new introduction to the 2002 edition of his classic translation and commentary with J.Y. Jolif of the *Nicomachean Ethics* (*L'Éthique à Nicomaque*, 2 vols. Louvain: Éditions Peeters, 1970 [2002]). I owe this reference and an improved overall sense of the textual status of the *EN* to an unpublished

manuscript by Samuel Baker, "Aristotelian Revision and Editorial Error in *Nicomachean Ethics* VI.2," presented at the Central Meeting of the American Philosophical Association in 2020.

29 See especially *EN* X.9, where Aristotle concludes the argument of the *Ethics* and argues that it suggests that "we must next" turn to the study of the constitutions found in the *Politics*.

30 Malcolm Schofield, "Aristotle's Political Ethics," in *The Blackwell Guide to Aristotle's Nicomachean Ethics*, ed. Richard Kraut (Oxford: Blackwell, 2006), 305–22, 305.

31 For example, Aristotle repeatedly classifies the kinds of rule in the household by comparing them to different constitutions—but at *Politics* I.13, he describes the rule of husbands over wives as "political" and in *Nicomachean Ethics* VIII, he says it is "aristocratic." I have not found a better way to address such problems than to proceed case by case. Thus, since the *Nicomachean* passage contains a fuller explanation of Aristotle's reasoning and chimes better with his reasoning elsewhere, I treat it as my central source and I present Aristotle's theory as saying that husbands rule over their wives "aristocratically." But I acknowledge the contradiction and point to reasons Aristotle may have put his position differently in the *Politics*.

32 See Marguerite Deslauriers, *Aristotle on Sexual Difference* (Oxford: Oxford University Press, forthcoming), Sophia M. Connell, *Aristotle on Female Animals* (Cambridge: Cambridge University Press, 2016), and Mariska Leunissen, *From Natural Character to Moral Virtue in Aristotle* (Oxford: Oxford University Press, 2017).

33 See Deslauriers, *Aristotle on Sexual Difference*, and my review of Leunissen's *From Natural Character to Moral Virtue* in *The Philosophical Review* 128:2 (2019): 224–28.

34 Josiah Ober defends a similar method in *Political Dissent in Democratic Athens*, 7–8.

35 Some scholars try to soften the Greek by translating ἄρχειν with expressions like "leadership" or even "mode of decision making" (Vivienne Gray, *Xenophon's Mirror of Princes: Reading the Reflections* [Oxford: Oxford University Press, 2011]; Howard Curzer, *Aristotle and the Virtues* [Oxford: Oxford University Press, 2012]). Such expressions do capture some important aspects of Aristotle's view, but I think they obscure others. Needless to say, I have needed to make related decisions throughout the book, such as whether to use male pronouns to refer to people, such as philosophers, who Aristotle would have assumed to be men, and how to convey Aristotle's degrading discussions of slavery. I sometimes

speak in one, more objectionable, way when I try to represent Aristotle's voice and another when I step back into my own. For a brief, helpful discussion of how these issues apply to scholarship on slavery, see P. Gabrielle Foreman et al., "Writing About/Teaching About Slavery: This Might Help" (Community sourced document, June 17, 2020, 12:37 PM https://naacpculpeper.org/resources/writing-about-slavery-this-might-help/).

36 See, for example, Johanna Hanink, *The Classical Debt: Greek Antiquity in an Era of Austerity* (Cambridge: Harvard University Press, 2017), Denise McCoskey, *Race: Antiquity and Its Legacy* (Oxford: Oxford University Press, 2012), and (for a Roman case) Jan Nelis, "Constructing Fascist Identity: Benito Mussolini and the Myth of the 'Romanità,'" *The Classical World* 100:4 (2007), 391–415. Rebecca Futo Kennedy discusses these issues in a series of articles for the online magazines *Eidolon* and *Medium*. See also "On the History of Western Civilization, Part 1," *Medium*, last modified Apr 2, 2019. https://medium.com/@rfutokennedy/on-the-history-of-western-civilization-part-1-3c7d6f3ebb10. Kennedy is working on a monograph on race in classical antiquity that I expect to contribute further to this body of work.

37 Malcolm Schofield gives an illuminating survey of the main strands of these interpretations in "Equality and Hierarchy in Aristotle's Political Thought."

38 The most important sources for this methodology are Quentin Skinner and the so-called Cambridge School in the history of ideas (see especially Quentin Skinner, "Meaning and Understanding in the History of Ideas," *History and Theory* 8:1 [1969], 3–53). See also Michel Foucault's Nietzschean genealogy ("Nietzsche, la généalogie, l'histoire," *Hommage à Jean Hyppolite* [Paris: P.U.F. 1971]). For several illuminating discussions of these traditions and related questions, see *Philosophy and Its History*, ed. Mogens Laerke, Justin E. H. Smith, and Eric Schliesser (Oxford and New York: Oxford University Press, 2013). I return to the purpose and method of this style of history in the Conclusion.

Chapter 1

1 *Pol.* I.1, 1252a7–9 and I.3, 1253b18–20. Many of the authors who take Aristotle's rule pluralism seriously also stress his opposition to rule monism. See, for example, Riesbeck, *Aristotle on Political Community* and Schofield, "Ideology and Philosophy," 115–40.

2 *Pol.* I.7, 1255b20.

3 See the "Prelude" in the Introduction.

4 Aristides, *In Defense of the Four*, 348. This is probably an excerpt from Aeschines' *Alcibiades*.
5 *Mem.* III.4, 6–11. Cf. *Oec.* XIII.5: "Whoever can make people skilled in ruling human beings," he says elsewhere, "can clearly make them skilled slave-masters; and whoever can make people skilled slave-masters can make people skilled to be kings."
6 *Pol.* VII.2, 1324b32–35.
7 Annas and Waterfield, for example, write that Aristotle's discussion is written "clearly with the present passage in mind" (Plato: *Statesman*, ed. Julia Annas and Robin Waterfield [Cambridge: Cambridge University Press, 1995], 5n8). Paul Moraux says that "on a noté depuis longtemps qu'Aristote critique directement les vues exposées par Platon dans le *Politique*" (Moraux, *A la recherche*, 26). See also Robert Mayhew, "Rulers and Ruled" and Victor Goldschmidt, "La théorie Aristotélicienne de l'esclavage et sa methode," in *Zetesis: Album amicorum* (Antwerp: De Nederlandsche Boekhandel, 1973), 153–8.
8 *Stat.* 259c1–5, trans. Rowe.
9 *Stat.* 274e1–4. In the end, there does turn out to be a well-defined science of rule—but it is an architectonic matter of determining when other, more contentful crafts should be practiced and weaving together the courageous and moderate parts of the city.
10 *Pol.* I.13, 1260b5–8.
11 *Laws* VI, 777e. According to Glenn Morrow, Aristotle misunderstands this passage. On his account, Plato is making a narrow legal distinction, where "νουθέτησις" refers not generally to admonishment but more specifically to a verbal penalty—that is, a warning—in the place of corporal punishment (*Plato's Law of Slavery in Its Relation to Greek Law* [New York: Arno Press, 1976], 44–5). I will follow Aristotle's interpretation of Plato here. It is, as we will see, plausible in light of other aspects of Plato's thought.
12 *Soph.* 229e5–230a2, trans. White modified. The passage may be contrasting a negative stage in the educational process, like the Socratic *elenchus*, with a more positive one.
13 *Apol.* 26a.
14 William Fortenbaugh, "Aristotle on Slaves and Women," in *Articles on Aristotle 2*, ed. Jonathan Barnes, Malcolm Schofield, and Richard Sorabji (London: Duckworth, 1975), 135–9.
15 For recent discussion, see Karbowski, "Aristotle's Scientific Inquiry." Karbowski is helpful on the connection between the preliminary definition of the slave as a living tool and the later statement that slaves lack the deliberative capacity.

16 One dramatic piece of evidence is Aristotle's comfort with using wars of aggression to enslave people who would otherwise resist taking up the yoke assigned to them by nature (*Pol.* I.8, 1256b26).

17 Trott takes the problems to be intentional; on her view Aristotle is describing a station that cannot be occupied by any human being (*Aristotle on the Nature of Community*, 175–92).

18 For example, if slaves are living tools by nature, how can Aristotle recommend manumission as a reward for good behavior? And if they have no deliberative capacity, then how can they be human beings, granted that reason is the essential human property? For a discussion of many claims to this effect, and a detailed argument that Fortenbaugh can't rescue Aristotle from contradiction, see Nicholas D. Smith, "Aristotle's Theory of Natural Slavery," *Phoenix* 37:2 (1983), 109–22. See also Bernard Williams, *Shame and Necessity* (Berkeley: University of California Press, 1993), 110–15. This consensus has recently come under fire from scholars who argue that Aristotle's account *is* philosophically coherent. Such scholars tend to follow Fortenbaugh's lead, arguing that Aristotle's treatment of slaves is much more liberal than it appears. See, for example, Richard Bodéüs, "De l'âme servile affranchi de lois," in *Le veritable politique et ses vertues selon Aristote* (Louvain-la-Neuve; Dudley, MA : Peeters, 2004), 79–106, which argues that Aristotle thinks that even natural slaves are educable and that Aristotle hopes masters will educate their natural slaves in virtue and thereby free them.

19 See, for example, Marguerite Deslauriers, "Aristotle on the Virtues of Slaves and Women," *Oxford Studies in Ancient Philosophy* 25 [2003], 213–31. Malcolm Schofield, "Ideology and Philosophy in Aristotle's Theory of Slavery," in *Saving the City*, and Karbowski, "Aristotle's Scientific Inquiry."

20 Williams, *Shame and Necessity*, 107–8. Williams' sources are Demosthenes 22.3, Antiphon *I Tetral.* 2.7, and Lysias 4.10–17, along with Aristotle's *Rhet.* I.15, 1376b31. For fuller discussions of this material, see also Giuseppe Cambiano, "Aristotle and the Anonymous Opponents of Slavery," *Slavery and Abolition Studies* 8:1 (1987), 22–41; Kenneth Dover, *Greek Popular Morality in the Time of Plato and Aristotle* (Oxford: Basil Blackwell, 1974), 284–7; and Moses Finley, *Ancient Slavery and Modern Ideology*, expanded edition, ed. Brent Shaw (Princeton: Markus Wiener, 1998), 161–3.

21 See Michael Gagarin, "The Torture of Slaves in Athenian Law," *Classical Philology* 91:1 (1996), 1–18, which argues that βάσανος, the mandatory torture of slaves, rarely actually happened, even though orators constantly spoke as if it did.

22 These examples are collected and discussed in "Classical Athens," by T.E. Rihll in *The Cambridge World History of Slavery*, vol. 1, ed. Keith Bradley and Paul Cartledge (Cambridge: Cambridge University Press, 2011), 48–73.
23 For a thorough survey of later ancient texts critical of slavery, see Peter Garnsey, *Ideas of Slavery from Aristotle to Augustine* (Cambridge: Cambridge University Press, 1996).
24 For a useful survey of this material, see Peter Hunt, "Slaves in Greek Literary Culture," in *The Cambridge World History of Slavery*, vol. 1, ed. Keith Bradley and Paul Cartledge (Cambridge: Cambridge University Press, 2011), 22–47, esp. 23–5.
25 See Robert Schlaifer, "Greek Theories of Slavery from Homer to Aristotle," *Harvard Studies in Classical Philology* 47 (1936), 166–67. Early examples include Aeschylus, *Persians* 241–42, and Herodotus VII, 135.3. For related use of δεσποτεία, see *Laws* III, 697c–d.
26 Demosthenes 9.36.
27 *Const. Ath.* I.2 and I.5, trans. Rackham, modified
28 Thomas Wiedemann, *Slavery* (Oxford: Oxford University Press, 1987), 11 *apud* Peter Hunt, "Chapter 2: Slaves in Greek Literary Culture," in *The Cambridge World History of Slavery*, vol. 1, ed. Keith Bradley and Paul Cartledge (Cambridge: Cambridge University Press, 2011), 22–47. Hunt also provides a helpful bibliographical essay, as well as a survey of the main evidence about this kind of political ideology based on the language of slavery.
29 This is a variation on the commonplace that equality calls for better treatment for the good and worse treatment for the bad. See also F.D. Harvey, "Two Kinds of Equality," *Classica et Medievalia* 26 (1965), 101–46). On slaves as an inferior, essentially different kind of person, see Dover, *Greek Popular Morality*, and Finley, *Ancient Slavery*.
30 See the Demosthenes passages earlier, as well as the speech by Lysias discussed subsequently.
31 In some literary contexts (although not all, as we will see), including much chest-beating Athenian democratic rhetoric, this is a self-evident linguistic truism.
32 *Pol.* I.3, 1253b20–23 trans. Rackham.
33 Giuseppe Cambiano offers the fullest discussion of what the position might have amounted to in his "Aristotle and the Anonymous Opponents of Slavery," *Slavery and Abolition Studies* 8:1 (1987), 24–5. One possible source for this view is Alcidamas, a student of Gorgias, whom Aristotle (or at least a scholiast)

quotes in the *Rhetoric* as saying "god has left all men free; nature has made no man a slave" (*Rhet.* I.13, 1373b5–20).

34 Lysias, *Funeral Oration*, 18–19, trans. Lamb. For a useful discussion of this text and many others like it, see R.G.A. Buxton, *Persuasion in Greek Tragedy: A Study of Peitho* (Cambridge: Cambridge University Press, 1982).

35 For more examples of the general line of thought discussed in this paragraph, see also Demosthenes 10.4 and Isocrates 20.10. For discussion, see Mogens Hansen, "Democratic Freedom and the Concept of Freedom in Plato and Aristotle," *Greek, Roman and Byzantine Studies* 50 (2010), 1–27, 3–4l. And for a related discussion of Plato's use of the word δουλεία, see Glenn Morrow, "Plato and Greek Slavery," *Mind*, New Series, 48:190 (1939), 186–201, 187–88, and Dover, *Greek Popular Morality*. See also John T. Kirby, "The 'Great Triangle' in Early Greek Rhetoric and Poetics," *Rhetorica: A Journal of the History of Rhetoric*, 8:3 (Summer 1990), 213–28. In a footnote to a paper on persuasion in Plato's *Laws*, Christopher Bobonich briefly mentions the idea that "free people deserve persuasion and slaves deserve compulsion" ("Persuasion, Compulsion, and Freedom in Plato's *Laws*," *Classical Quarterly*, New Series 41:2 [1991], 386n80).

36 This was, however, one meaning of the word ἐλευθερία. See Hansen's "Democratic Freedom," 9.

37 Compare the description of Sparta attributed by Herodotus to Demaratus (VII.104.4): "They are free, yet not wholly free: law is their master, whom they fear much more than your men fear you." For an argument that this discussion of Sparta is run through with democratic Athenian ideology (and a discussion generally related to these questions), see Sara Forsdyke, "Athenian Democratic Ideology and Herodotus' Histories," *American Journal of Philology* 122:3 (2001), 329–58.

38 On the importance of this claim to Aristotle's political philosophy, see Melissa Lane, "Popular Sovereignty as Control of Office-Holders: Aristotle on Greek Democracy," in *Popular Sovereignty in Historical Perspective*, ed. Richard Bourke and Quentin Skinner (Cambridge: Cambridge University Press, 2016).

39 See the section "Ruling, Holding Office, and Controlling the City" in Chapter 5.

40 KRS 291.3–4: The Goddess announces that there are two paths, and that the first one ("that it is") "is the path of persuasion (for she attends upon Truth)"— πειθοῦς ἐστι κέλευθος (Ἀληθείῃ γὰρ ὀπηδεῖ).

41 Josiah Ober has very helpfully developed the idea that these figures represent a tradition of dissent against a democratic consensus (*Political Dissent in Democratic Athens*).

42 *Helen* 8–14.
43 *Helen* 11: "If all men on all subjects had both memory of things past and awareness of things present and foreknowledge of the future, speech would be similarly similar, since as things are now, it is not easy for them to recall the past, nor to consider the present, nor to define the future; so that on most subjects most men take opinion as counsellor to their soul." Trans. Dillon and Gergel.
44 *Helen* 12. Translation Gagarin and Woodruff.
45 See Buxton, *Persuasion in Greek Tragedy*, and (in a discussion that itself draws extensively on Buxton) Christopher Bobonich, "Persuasion, Compulsion, and Freedom in Plato's *Laws*," *Classical Quarterly*, New Series 41:2 (1991), 365–88. The Goddess Peitho seems to have predated πειθώ as a social concept, and she was much more associated with sexuality and seduction than, say, persuasion in the political arena.
46 *Helen* 12. In Aeschylus' *Agamemnon* (385), the chorus uses similar language. It describes the personified figure Persuasion as an overwhelming force that can't be resisted ("βιᾶται δ'ἁ τάλαινα Πειθώ"). This passage is highlighted and discussed in Kirby, "The Great Triangle."
47 It's not clear that this is Gorgias' settled view. At the end of the *Palamedes*, he exploits the same attitude as Lysias: "Pity and entreaties and the intercession of friends are useful when judgement takes place before a mob. But among you, who are the foremost of the Greeks in fact and in reputation, I should not persuade you with the aid of friends or entreaties of pity. I must escape this charge by making justice very clear and showing you the truth, not deceiving you. You must not pay more attention to words than to deeds, or prefer accusations to proofs, or consider a short time to be a wiser judge than a long time, or think slander more credible than experience" (33–34).
48 Plato attributes just this view to Gorgias at *Phlb.* 58a-b: "Many times, Socrates, I have heard Gorgias maintain that the art of persuasion far surpasses all others and is far and away the best, for it makes all things its slaves by willing submission, not by violence."
49 *Helen* 9, 14. Trans. Gagarin and Woodruff.
50 *Helen* 9. Trans. Gagarin and Woodruff.
51 The text here is jumbled, although the meaning is not in question. D.M. MacDowell, following Diel, has "τὸ γὰρ τῆς πειθοῦς ἐξῆν ὁ δέ νοῦς καίτοι εἰ ἀνάγκη ὁ εἰδώς ἕξει μὲν οὖν, τὴν δὲ δύναμιν τὴν αὐτὴν ἔχει," (which he translates "for persuasion expelled sense; and indeed persuasion, though not having the appearance of compulsion, has the same power") (*Gorgias:*

Encomium of Helen [Bristol: Bristol Classical Press, 1982]). Daniel Graham has "τὸ γὰρ τῆς πειθοῦς ἐξῆν <ἰδεῖν ὡς κρατεῖ>, ἣ ἀνάγκης εἶδος ἔχει μὲν οὔ, τὴν δὲ δύναμιν τὴν αὐτὴν ἔχει" ("it is possible <to see how> the faculty of persuasion <rules>, which does not indeed have the form of necessity, but does have its power") (*The Texts of Early Greek Philosophy*, vol. II [Cambridge: Cambridge University Press, 2010]). "Form" is a contentious translation of εἶδος here. Other possibilities include "appearance" or even "mode." For the classic discussion of early uses of the word εἶδος, see A.E. Taylor, "The Words Εἶδος, Ἰδέα in Pre-Socratic Literature," *Varia Socratica* (Oxford: James Barker, 1911). For a longer, more recent discussion, see André Motte et al. (eds), *Philosophie de la forme: Eidos, Idea, Morphe dans la philosophie Grecque des origines à Aristote* (Liège: Peeters, 2003).

52 For a closely related point—that for Gorgias the soul can be described with the same physical language as the body—see Charles Segal, "Gorgias and the Psychology of Logos," *Harvard Studies in Classical Philology* 66 (1962), 99–155. He points out the similarities between Gorgias' view here and Democritus: "Medicine cures the diseases of the body, but wisdom takes away the soul from sufferings."

53 *Gorg.* 452d, trans. Jowett.

54 B112, B114. Trans. Inwood.

55 B31.

56 Of course, this is not necessarily to say that he got them directly, or even indirectly, from Gorgias himself. There is, however, reason to think that Plato was an attentive reader of Gorgias' speeches: the *Apology* seems to be closely modeled on Gorgias' *Palamedes*. See Guido Calogero, "Gorgias and the Socratic Principle *Nemo Sua Sponte Peccat*," *Journal of Hellenistic Studies* 77:1 [1957], 12–17.

57 *Soph.* 235b7. Likewise in the *Phaedrus* (268d1), he describes an orator (apparently Thrasymachus) as magically charming (ἐπᾴδων κηλεῖν) audiences.

58 *Men.* 80a2–b3. In the *Symposium* (218a), Alcibiades also complains about the dazzling, paralyzing effects of Socratic discourse.

59 Plato is also emphatic that speech often fails to have much effect at all. Indeed, in the dialogue named after Gorgias, Socrates argues that the apparent power of orators is deceptive. The orator needs to flatter the people he persuades and to give them pleasure, and this puts him—the orator—under the control of the mob, not the other way around. See also *Rep.* VI, 493a–d an I, 327c–28a, and *Phaed.* 261a7–b2 and 271c10.

60 The concept of dialectic preserves the conception of *logos* as argumentative conversation between people rather than merely as individual reflection.

61 *Rep.* VI, 493c–d. For an interesting discussion of how the orator affects and (especially) is affected by the character and values of the masses in his audience, see Rachana Kamtekar, "The Profession of Friendship," *Ancient Philosophy* 25:2 (2005), 319–39.

62 Plato marks his distinction between two kinds of persuasive speech by insisting on a distinction between πειθώ and λόγος, which Gorgias uses almost interchangeably. Plato almost always treats πειθώ as something negative, something to be *prevented* or held off by learning philosophy. Indeed one benefit of a philosophical education seems to be that it makes you unpersuadable. See *Tim.* 51e, where we learn that knowledge and true belief are distinct because "one of them arises in us by teaching, the other by persuasion; and the one is always in company with true reasoning, whereas the other is irrational; and the one is immovable by persuasion, whereas the other is alterable by persuasion" (trans. Lamb). Thanks to Calvin Normore for emphasizing this point to me.

63 *Rep.* VII, 519e3.

64 This is not to deny that Plato also sometimes endorses a more straightforward kind of paternalism, where the ruler uses force on subjects simply because he or she understands their good better than they do.

65 E.g., *Rep.* IV, 431c2, where he mocks the supposed freedom of the pleasure-loves in the *demos.*

66 *Soph.* 253c. Plato here seems to be borrowing from an aristocratic tradition that aimed to narrow the definition of freedom (see Kurt Raaflaub, "Democracy, Oligarchy, and the Concept of the 'Free Citizen' in Late Fifth Century Athens," *Political Theory* 11:4 [1983], 517–44). In this tradition, "free is not applied to every person who is not a slave but only to the truly free—the members of the noble and wealthy upper class." It refers to "those pursuits that are removed from the immediate and base necessities of life and, therefore, suitable for the truly free person." The tradition would culminate in the Stoic doctrine that only the sage is free.

67 "Slavery in Plato's Thought," in *Platonic Studies* (Princeton: Princeton University Press, 1973), 150.

68 *Laws* IV, 722b5–c4 (trans. Pangle).

69 *Laws* IV, 723a7.

70 Quoted in Bobonich, "Persuasion, Compulsion, and Freedom," 368. Bobonich's paper gives a useful overview of this debate, arguing forcefully that the preludes

are meant to give citizens an epistemically solid rational basis for accepting the laws. In the final paragraphs of his paper, Bobonich briefly suggests that Plato thinks free citizens deserve persuasion just because they are free, much as I am proposing.

71 *Rep.* IX, 590d3–5.
72 For a detailed account of the treatment of slaves in the *Laws*, see Morrow's *Plato's Law of Slavery* and "Plato and Greek Slavery." Morrow contrasts Plato's proposed legislation with the law of slavery in Athens and finds Plato's proposals more severe.
73 Morrow, ibid., 195. The unlimited punishment of slaves guilty of assault is endorsed at 879a. Here Plato seems to be following the Spartan rather than the Athenian model.
74 This is not to say that Plato thinks masters may never talk to their slaves, even about moral matters—he says, for example, that masters should tell their slaves about the evils of incest. *Laws* VIII, 838d–e.
75 *Laws* VI, 777a.
76 Perhaps I should not attribute these views directly to Xenophon. No one can deny that they appear in his texts, but there is a lively tradition of "ironic" readings of Xenophon according to which Xenophon offers up the theory I am sketching in a critical or satirical spirit. For my part, I think wholly Straussian readings cannot succeed, for largely the reasons in Gray, *Xenophon's Mirror of Princes*. Those arguments do not exclude, however, that his dialogues and narratives include a range of subtler forms of irony and authorial distance, as Melina Tamiolaki has argued ("Virtue and Leadership in Xenophon: Ideal Leaders or Ideal Losers?," in *Xenophon: Ethical Principles and Historical Enquiry*, ed. Fiona Hobden and Christopher Tuplin [Leiden: Brill 2012], 563–89). But none of this matters much for my argument here. Whether Xenophon is endorsing this view or skewering it, it is precisely the sort of view Aristotle has in mind in *Politics* I and which he develops and transforms throughout his practical philosophy.
77 Although I find it convenient to group together Xenophon, Gorgias, and Aristotle in a "countertradition," it is difficult to establish influence among the thinkers I discuss in this chapter. I do not, for example, mean to suggest that Xenophon styled himself a disciple of Gorgias, nor that Aristotle styled himself a disciple of Xenophon. Louis-André Dorion has argued persuasively that Aristotle read at least Xenophon's *Memorabilia*. My goal, more modestly, is to demonstrate ideas that Aristotle might have encountered and which help to explain otherwise surprising features of his thought.

78 Xen *Mem.* II.1.8, trans. Marchant.
79 Xen. *Mem* II.1.11, trans. Marchant modified: οὐδὲ εἰς τὴν δουλείαν ἐμαυτὸν τάττω, ἀλλ᾽ εἶναί τίς μοι δοκεῖ μέση τούτων ὁδός, ἣν πειρῶμαι βαδίζειν, οὔτε δι᾽ ἀρχῆς οὔτε διὰ δουλείας, ἀλλὰ δι᾽ ἐλευθερίας, ἥπερ μάλιστα πρὸς εὐδαιμον ίαν ἄγει. This is of course similar to a Platonic position that we should remove ourselves from interactions with others, the better to pursue philosophical contemplation. Aristotle considers such claims at *Pol.* VII.2, 1324a39-40.
80 Xen. *Mem* II.1.13, trans. Marchant. Notice, however, that although Xenophon denies that it's possible *neither* to rule nor to be ruled, he thinks that many people occupy both stations simultaneously.
81 Indeed, he is quite interested in people like Ischomachus' foreman in the *Oeconomicus*, who rule some people as a way of serving others.
82 Louis-André Dorion, "Socrate et la basiklikê tekhnê: Essai d'exegèse comparative," in *Socrates: 2400 Years Since His Death (399 BC - 2001 AD)* (Athens: European Cultural Centre of Delphi, 2004), Donald Morrison, "Tyrannie et royauté selon le Socrate de Xénophon," *Les études philosophiques* 69:2 (2004), 177–92. Carol Atack, *The Discourse of Kingship in Classical Greece* (New York: Routledge, 2020).
83 *Mem* III.4.6, I link this aspect of Xenophon's thought with a nascent style of universalism in "Social Science and Universalism in Xenophon's *Oeconomicus* IV," in *Foreign Influences. The Circulation of Knowledge in Antiquity*, ed. B. Castelnérac, L. Gili and L. Monteils-Laeng (Turnhout: Brepols, forthcoming).
84 Compare Meno's proposed definition of virtue and Socrates' response at *Meno* 77b2–78c.
85 Xen. *Oec.* I. See Louis-André Dorion, "Socrate οἰκονομικός," in *Xénophon et Socrate: Actes du colloque d'Aix-en-Provence*, ed. Michel Narcy and Alonzo Tordesillas (Paris: Vrin, 2008), 253–82.
86 This doctrine is particularly pronounced in the *Memorabilia*. See, for example, Xen. *Mem.* IV.2.11. The point about self-control has been most fully developed by Louis-André Dorion, in the essays throughout *L'autre Socrate: Études sur les écrits socratiques de Xénophon* (Paris: Belles Lettres, 2013).
87 *Mem.* III.2.4: καὶ οὕτως ἐπισκοπῶν τίς εἴη ἀγαθοῦ ἡγεμόνος ἀρετὴ τὰ μὲν ἄλλα περιῄρει, κατέλιπε δὲ τὸ εὐδαίμονας ποιεῖν ὧν ἂν ἡγῆται. Compare also *Cyr.* VIII.8.5: "Whatever the ruler is like the followers tend to become the same" (ὁποῖοί τινες γὰρ ἂν οἱ προστάται ὦσι, τοιοῦτοι καὶ οἱ ὑπ᾽ αὐτοὺς ὡς ἐπὶ τὸ πολὺ γίγνονται).
88 Xen. *Oec.* XIII.6–9.
89 *Mem.* III.3.8.

90 *Oec.* IX.11.
91 *Oec.* XXI.5-6.
92 Throughout his corpus, Xenophon deploys a wide range of metaphors of looking, seeing, and watching as keys to learning. See Emily Baragwanath, "The Wonder of Freedom: Xenophon on Slavery," in *Xenophon: Ethical Principles and Historical Enquiry*, ed. Fiona Hobden and Christopher Tuplin (Leiden: Brill, 2012), 631-3.
93 *Mem.* III.3.7.
94 *Mem.* III.3.8.
95 *Mem.* III.3.11.
96 Xen. *Oec.* VII.26, trans. Pomeroy.
97 *Mem.* I.2.10. τῇ μὲν βίᾳ πρόσεισιν ἔχθραι καὶ κίνδυνοι, διὰ δὲ τοῦ πείθειν ἀκινδύνως τε καὶ μετὰ φιλίας ταὐτὰ γίγνεται.
98 Xen. *Oec.* XIV.9-10.
99 Sarah Pomeroy, *Xenophon Oeconomicus: A Social and Historical Commentary* (Oxford: Clarendon Press, 1994), 66; Sarah Pomeroy, "Slavery in the Greek Domestic Economy in Light of Xenophon's *Oeconomicus*," *Index* 17 (1989), reprinted in *Oxford Readings in Classical Studies: Xenophon*, ed. Vivienne Gray (Oxford: Oxford University Press, 2010), 31-40. See also Baragwanath ("Wonder of Freedom," 659), who is well aware of Xenophon's support for slavery but nevertheless concludes that he "should be given credit" for his kindness.
100 See especially Baragwanath, "Wonder of Freedom."
101 Before recounting the extensive conversations Ischomachus used to train his wife, Xenophon has Critobulus, the dialogue's everyman, admit that although he entrusts more important things to his wife than to almost anyone else, there is hardly anyone he has spoken to less than her. Xen. *Oec.* III.12-13.
102 This issue has gotten a lot of attention. Compare, for example, Pierre Pellegrin, "Natural Slavery," trans. Zoli Filotas in *The Cambridge Companion to Aristotle's Politics*, ed. Marguerite Deslauriers (Cambridge: Cambridge University Press, 2013) with Trott, *Aristotle on the Nature of Community*.
103 Xen. *Oec.* IV.2. On the distinction between honorable toil and degraded gruntwork, see Steven Johnstone, "Virtuous Toil, Vicious Work: Xenophon on Aristocratic Style," *Classical Philology* 89 (1994), 219-40.
104 Xen. *Mem.* II.1.16-17, trans. Marchant.
105 I exclude from this argument the nominally free people who Xenophon says at *Oec.* I.17 and X.10 make themselves slaves through lack of self-control. It's not clear what treatment by others he thinks is suitable for them, but it's doubtful

that he thinks they should be enslaved and punished by the likes of Socrates and Ischomachus.
106 Xen. *Mem.* XII.19.
107 Julia Annas, "Plato's *Republic* and Feminism," *Philosophy* 51:197 (1976), 307–21, 311.
108 *EN* X.9, 1179b25.
109 On "using" friends, see Gray, *Xenophon's Mirror of Princes*, 298–304. She recommends translating εὖ χρῆσθαι as "treating well." Gray is correct that Xenophon sometimes describes rulers and subjects as using each other *mutually*, and that he always stresses that rulers should use their subjects *well*, namely in a way that benefits everyone, as described earlier. But in my view, something important is nevertheless lost by her proposed translation.

Chapter 2

1 *Pol.* I.13, 1259b37.
2 *Meno* 72c. Of course Aristotle had the resources to duck this request. He might have said, for example, that ἄρχειν and its cognates are used equivocally or that some uses are derived accidentally from marginal properties of another.
3 I wrote the original draft of this book before reading David Riesbeck's *Aristotle on Political Community*. I have since benefited a great deal from reading it. Riesbeck's book covers many of the same themes as mine; in many ways it is also similar in its interpretive approach. Page by page and passage by passage I am often in agreement with his readings, and his discussion complements mine at more points than I can track in the notes. Our interpretations of Aristotle, however, end up looking very different; he comes much closer to the sorts of egalitarian or proto-liberal reading that I seek to call into question.

   Riesbeck's general definition of rule is a case in point. Where I define rule in terms of *logos* and decision, Riesbeck frames his account in terms of "verbal commands" given by rulers. Thus his discussion of rule often defaults to a model of efficient causation rather than the teleological account I give here. Downstream from that definition, Riesbeck correctly notes the variety of ways that subordinates may actively contribute to rule, and I agree with much of what he says in his nuanced account of the ways people can do that. Yet he ends up treating participation in the assembly and even consenting to a king as ways of ruling. That is incompatible with the understanding I defend here, for reasons I give throughout this chapter and the next.

4   It is not obvious what kinds of "things" the πίστεις are; this makes the word hard both to interpret and to translate. One interesting rendering is John M. Cooper's "persuaders"; see "Ethical-Political Theory in Aristotle's *Rhetoric*," in *Aristotle's* Rhetoric: *Philosophical Essays*, ed. David Furley and Alexander Nehamas (Princeton: Princeton University Press, 1994), 193–210. It's probably best, however, just to use "proofs." For an argument to that effect, see Myles Burnyeat, "Enthymeme: Aristotle on the Logic of Persuasion," in *Aristotle's* Rhetoric: *Philosophical Essays*, ed. David Furley and Alexander Nehamas (Princeton: Princeton University Press, 1994), 3–56.
5   *Rhet*, I.2, 1356a1.
6   *Rhet*. I.2, 1356a1–12. This kind of support must be "through *logos*" in the case of character, and it must "result from the *logos*" in the case of emotion. See Jacques Brunschwig, "Rhétorique et dialectique, *Rhétorique* et *Topiques*," in *Aristotle's* Rhetoric: *Philosophical Essays*, ed. David Furley and Alexander Nehamas (Princeton: Princeton University Press, 1994), 57–96; and John M. Cooper, "Ethical-Political Theory in Aristotle's *Rhetoric*," in *Aristotle's* Rhetoric: *Philosophical Essays*, ed. David Furley and Alexander Nehamas (Princeton: Princeton University Press, 1994), 193–210.
7   This is a central question for Jamie Dow, *Passions & Persuasion in Aristotle's* Rhetoric (Oxford: Oxford University Press, 2015). I am in substantial agreement with his treatment of emotions ("passions" in his translation), though I disagree with his treatment of persuasion through character. In particular, Dow overlooks the connections between souls that Aristotle takes for granted, in favor of an anachronistic picture of consent.
8   *EN* II.5, 1105b26. See Aryeh Kosman, "Being Properly Affected: Virtues and Feelings in Aristotle's Ethics," in *Essays on Aristotle's Ethics*, ed. A. O. Rorty (Berkeley: University of California Press, 1980), 103–16.
9   It's uncontroversial that Aristotle accepts some version of the thesis that emotions (as well as desires and other things belonging to the ἄλογον) can be rational, though different people work out the position in different ways. See, for example, Martha Nussbaum, *The Therapy of Desire* (Princeton: Princeton University Press, 1994), 81–8; and John M. Cooper, "Some Remarks on Aristotle's Moral Psychology," *The Southern Journal of Philosophy* 27 (1988), 25–42.
10 Some caution is in order in drawing psychological conclusions from the *Rhetoric*, since the discussion of emotion there is not a scientific exposition of Aristotle's views on emotions, and it is made up of *endoxa* that Aristotle may not endorse. But however exactly these contested issues shake out, pretty much everyone agrees that Aristotle would see the views on the emotions that he discusses as at

least respectable. For more discussion, see Gisela Striker, "Emotions in Context: Aristotle's Treatment of the Passions in the *Rhetoric* and His Moral Psychology," in *Essays on Aristotle's* Rhetoric, ed. Amélie Rorty (Berkeley: University of California Press, 1980), 286–302.

11 *Rhet.* I.2, 1356a13–14.
12 There is an important set of cases where the speaker's character happens to be an important part of his subject matter: those where he is defending *himself* against prosecution in court. But from the perspective of the art of rhetoric, the role of the speaker's character in these speeches is no different from whatever else he happens to talk about: military strategy, the achievements of the Athenians, or whatever.
13 *Rhet.* II.1, 1378a9–10.
14 *Rhet.* I.3, 1358a37–8.
15 *Rhet.* II.1, 1378a8.
16 *Rhet.* I.2, 1356a7. The account fits well with Aristotle's claim that character persuasion is most applicable in situations where the truth is doubtful—for in those cases where listeners will be least able to sort things out for themselves, it stands to reason that they will be especially inclined to let someone else do it for them.
17 *Pol.* I.2, 1253a9–18. Trans. Lord, modified.
18 *EN* I.13, 1102b33–1103a3, trans. Rowe.
19 Sarah Broadie, *Ethics with Aristotle* (New York: Oxford University Press, 1991), 63–5.
20 As I noted earlier, Plato says something similar in the *Republic:* that if the best part of a person is weak, so that the person cannot be ruled by the divine and the intelligent, then that person should be ruled by someone who can make that happen (*Rep.* IX, 590c–d). The difference is that Plato thinks that this must be done by force or by deception, whereas Aristotle thinks it can be done by a certain kind of λόγος.
21 *EN* III.3, 1112b28, trans. Taylor, modified.
22 *EN* III.3, 1112b30–1, trans. Taylor: ὁτὲ μὲν δι' οὗ ὁτὲ δὲ πῶς ἢ διὰ τίνος. Most translators (e.g., Irwin and Crisp) render διὰ τίνος as "by means of what." But, as Taylor argues, this means that the reader has to supply some substantive difference between the "by-means-of-*what*" of a decision and the "by-means-of-*which*" of that same decision. Taylor plausibly suggests the translation, which as he notes fits nicely with the reference to things done through one's friends. See C. C. W. Taylor, *Aristotle: Nicomachean Ethics II–IV,* Clarendon Aristotle Series (Oxford: Oxford University Press, 2006), 157.

23 *EN* III.3, 1113a8-9.
24 Broadie, Taylor, and Irwin all ignore these passages, for example.
25 *EN* VI.10, 1143a7.
26 *EN* VI.10, 1143a14-16.
27 *Pol.* I.13, 1260a7-14.
28 *Pol.* I.13, 1260a31-3.
29 Deslauriers, "Aristotle on the Virtues of Slaves and Women," 213-31.
30 Division of the city into rulers and subjects: *Pol.* II.2, 1261a25-35; subjects need not use *phronêsis*: *Pol.* III.4, 1277a15 and 1277b25-30; citizenship defined in terms of judgment and deliberation: *Pol.* III.1, 1275b19.
31 For an illuminating comparison of personal and political deliberation and its connection to ruling and being ruled, see Bryan Garsten, "Deliberating and Acting Together," in *The Cambridge Companion to Aristotle's* Politics, ed. Marguerite Deslauriers and Pierre Destrée (Cambridge: Cambridge University Press, 2013).
32 Christopher Kirwan, *Aristotle: Metaphysics Books Γ, Δ, and E*, 2nd ed. Clarendon Aristotle Series (Oxford: Clarendon, 1993).
33 Met. Δ.1, 1013a10-11, ἡ δὲ οὗ κατὰ προαίρεσιν κινεῖται τὰ κινούμενα καὶ μεταβάλλει τὰ μεταβάλλοντα, ὥσπερ αἵ τε κατὰ πόλεις ἀρχαὶ καὶ αἱ δυναστεῖαι καὶ αἱ βασιλεῖαι καὶ τυραννίδες. ἀρχαὶ λέγονται καὶ αἱ τέχναι, καὶ τούτων αἱ ἀρχιτεκτονικαὶ μάλιστα (trans. Reeve, lightly modified).
34 *EN* VI.2, 1139a23.
35 *EN* III.3, 1112b24.
36 As John McDowell famously argues, the language of "seeing" in practical reasoning captures an important element of Aristotle's practical reasoning. See especially "Some Issues in Aristotle's Moral Psychology," in his *Mind, Value and Reality* (Cambridge: Cambridge University Press, 1998), 23-40.
37 *EN* III.2, 1112a16-18.
38 *EN* III.2, 1112a16-18; *EE* III.5, 1230a27-29. The literature on προαίρεσίς is vast, and I am sidestepping various controversies. My account here is especially indebted to Jessica Moss, "Virtue Makes the Goal Right," *Phronesis* 56:3 (2011), 204-61, and Agnes Callard, "Aristotle on Deliberation," forthcoming in the *Routledge Handbook of Practical Reason*, ed. Ruth Chang and Kurt Sylvan.
39 Characteristic product of the virtues: *EN* VI.1, 1139a22; indication of the agent's character: *EN* III.2, 1111b5.
40 Compare to the writing teacher at *Nicomachean Ethics* II.4, 1105a24.
41 *Pol.* I.7, 1255b19-36.
42 *Pol.* III.4, 1277b28-9.

43 *EN* VI.5, 1140a25-8.
44 For further discussion of ἀρχιτεκτονικαί and rule, see Joseph Karbowski, "Aristotle on the Deliberative Abilities of Women," *Apeiron* 47:4 (2014), 435–60. Karbowski notes that "Aristotle goes so far as to treat the master craftsman as the proper agent of the relevant activities because they are guided by means of his thought" (*Pol.* 7.3 1325b21-3). For a general account of architectonic craft, especially in Plato, see C. D. C. Reeve, "Platonic Politics and the Good," *Political Theory* 23:3 [1995], 413.
45 See, for example, *EN* VI.5, 1140b10, *EN* VI.5, 1140a26, and *Rhet.* I.9, 1366b20.
46 The claim that good rulers must have *phronêsis* while this is not important for the people they rule is at *Pol.* III.4, 1277a15–17 and *Pol.* III.4, 1277b26–29. The identification of political rule and *phronêsis* is at *EN* VI.8, 1141b23–24.
47 *Pol.* III.4, 1277a15–20.
48 *Pol.* 1.13, 1260a7–14.
49 *EN* III.3, 1112b11–16; cf. 1112b33–34, *EE* II.10, 1226b9–10, 1227a7–8. For a thorough examination of all the relevant texts, see Moss, *Aristotle on the Apparent Good*, 155–63.
50 *EN* VI.3, 1139a31–34.
51 Hans Beck suggests that ἄρχεσθαι, ἀρχόμενος, and related words might be conceived in the middle rather than the passive voice, "so that the act of 'being ruled' might be conceived of here as something that is performed by the citizens upon themselves and for their own benefit" ("Introduction," in *A Companion to Ancient Greek Government* [Malden: Blackwell, 2013], 2–6). It is certainly true that Aristotle doesn't conceive of submitting to rule simply as passive, but we should resist the idea that anyone can do it without a ruler. See especially the section "Kinds of Rule" in Chapter 3.
52 *DM* 8, 702a15–17.
53 *DA* III.10, 433a10–16. For a helpful recent discussion, see chapters 8–11 of Hendrik Lorenz, *The Brute Within: Appetitive Desire in Plato and Aristotle* (Oxford: Oxford University Press, 2006). See also Deslauriers and Filotas, "Aristotle's Human Beings."
54 *DA* III.3, 429a4–8. See Lorenz, *The Brute Within*, chapter 13.
55 *DA* III.7, 431a7–10.
56 *Phileb.* 39a-b.
57 *Pol.* I.13, 1260a12.
58 The quotation is from Curzer, *Aristotle and the Virtues*, 379. See also Martha Nussbaum, "Aristotle on Human Nature and the Foundations of Ethics," in

World, Mind, and Ethics: Essays on the Philosophy of Bernard Williams, ed. J. E. J. Altham and Ross Harrisson (Cambridge: Cambridge University Press, 1995), 86–131.

59 *Pol.* I.2, 1252b5-9, *Pol.* III.14, 1285a19–21. See Richard Kraut, *Aristotle: Political Philosophy* (Oxford: Oxford University Press, 2002), 277–305. For an argument against this reading, see Julie Ward, "*Ethnos* in the *Politics:* Aristotle on Race," in *Philosophers on Race*, ed. Julie Ward and Tommy Lott (Oxford: Blackwell, 2002), 14–37.

60 Heath, "Aristotle on Natural Slavery," 3.

61 It is relevant here that Aristotle thinks both that plants and animals are "self-movers" *and* that their motions are initiated by objects in their environments. See David Furley, "Self-Movers," in *Self-Motion: From Aristotle to Newton*, ed. James Lennox and Mary Louise Gill (Princeton: Princeton University Press, 1994), 3–14.

62 See, for example, *EN* VIII.1, 1155b5–14.

63 We have already considered the basic evidence, including the famous passage about how *logos* makes the human being the most political of all animals (*Pol.* I.2, 1253a7–15), and Aristotle's discussions of how the *alogon* is "obedient," it is "ready to listen," and it "chimes with" reason; it is "capable of listening and obeying" (*EN* I.13, 1102b26–33). We might also note the claim that the semi-rational part "speaks" with the same "voice" as reason (*EN* I.13, 1102b28).

64 Riesbeck, *Aristotle on Political Community*, 134–41.

65 Bernard Williams, "The Actus Reus of Dr. Caligari," *University of Pennsylvania Law Review* 142:5 (1994): 1661–73.

66 Ibid., 1672.

67 In other words, almost all of us engage in political rule. See Chapters 4 and 5.

68 In particular persuasion with *logos* is usually different than applying force or making people act under duress or ignorance. See *EN* III.11, 109b30–1111a4.

69 *Pol.* VII.2, 1324b30–32. οὔτε γὰρ τοῦ ἰατροῦ οὔτε τοῦ κυβερνήτου ἔργον ἐστὶ τὸ ἢ πεῖσαι ἢ βιάσασθαι τοῦ μὲν τοὺς θεραπευομένους τοῦ δὲ τοὺς πλωτῆρας.

70 Compare Riesbeck, *Aristotle on Political Community*, 243–4.

Chapter 3

1 Monographs devoted to the topic include A.W. Price, *Love and Friendship in Plato and Aristotle* (Oxford: Oxford University Press, 1989), Suzanne Stern-Gillet, *Aristotle's Philosophy of Friendship* (New York: State University of New

York Press, 1995), and Paul Schollmeier, *Other Selves: Aristotle on Personal and Political Friendship* (New York: State University of New York Press, 1994); see also Michael Pakaluk's commentary in the Clarendon Aristotle Series, *Aristotle: Nicomachean Ethics VIII and IX* (Oxford: Oxford University Press, 1998). For discussions that attend to the issues and passages I do (and that overlap in significant ways with my discussion), see chapter 2 of Riesbeck's *Aristotle on Political Community*, chapter 12 of Adam Curzer's *Aristotle and the Virtues*, and chapter 1 of Bernard Yack, *The Problems of a Political Animal* (Berkeley and Los Angeles: University of California Press, 1993). For a useful summary of other literature on friendship until 1999, see Heather Devere, "Reviving Greco-Roman Friendship: A Bibliographical Review," *Critical Review of International Social and Political Philosophy* 2:4 (1999), 149–87. Thornton Lockwood provides an extensive and more recent list of essays in "A Topical Bibliography of Scholarship on Aristotle's *Nicomachean Ethics*: 1880 to 2004," *Journal of Philosophical Research* 30 (2005), 78–85.

2 John M. Cooper, "Aristotle on the Forms of Friendship," *Review of Metaphysics* 30:4 (1977), 619.

3 Aristotle encourages this last thought by introducing the analogy with the claim that household relationships are "likenesses" (ὁμοιώματα) and "models, roughly" (οἷον παραδείγματα) of the *politeiai* (*EN* VIII.10, 1160b23–24). In the parallel passage from the *Eudemian Ethics* he calls them the "springs and origins" of friendship, justice, and politics: ἀρχαὶ καὶ πηγαὶ φιλίας καὶ πολιτείας καὶ δικαίου (*EE* VII.10, 1242b1–2).

4 See especially *EN* X.9, where Aristotle concludes the argument of the *Ethics* and argues that it suggests that "we must next" turn to the study of the constitutions found in the *Politics*.

5 The version of the analogy that appears in *Politics* I does indeed seem to be meant to help us understand the causal relationship between the household and the city. For a study of what Aristotle probably means by ὁμοιώματα and οἷον παραδείγματα, see Claudio William Veloso, "La relation entre les liens familiaux et les constitutions politiques," in *Politique d'Aristote: Famille, régimes, education*, ed. Emmanuel Bermon, Valéry Laurand, and Jean Terrel (Bordeaux: Presses Universitaires de Bordeaux, 2011), 23–40.

6 There he says that while a study of ethics must address the soul, it needn't study it with the depth appropriate to natural philosophy, as he does elsewhere, that is, in the *De Anima*.

7 The references to the "exoteric *logoi*" are at *Pol.* III.6, 1278b31–32; and *EN* I.13, 1102a27–33. For more, see Moraux, *A la recherche*, 14–22.

8   For an illuminating example of this style of interpretation, see Elizabeth Belfiore, "Family Friendship in Aristotle's Ethics," *Ancient Philosophy* 21:1 (2001), 113–32. She writes that "complete friendship and family friendship represent two different paradigms of the 'other self' relationship. In the complete friendship of unrelated people, similarly virtuous others become 'other selves' because of a deliberate choice, based on virtue. In contrast, family friends, especially in the paradigmatic family friendship, that between parents and children, are natural 'other selves' who share a biological and ethical sameness and who become 'other by being separated.'"

9   The sharp contrast between a domestic and public sphere in Aristotle risks anachronism, though it has some grounding in the distinction of *Politics* I between pursuing mere life and living well. For a compelling (and suitably qualified and complex) discussion of the different aims housed in the household and the *polis*, see Riesbeck, *Aristotle on Political Community*, chapter 3. Riesbeck, however, focuses on the *polis* as a whole to the exclusion of political dimensions in smaller-scale relationships.

10 *EN* VIII.7, 1158b12–19, trans. Pakaluk.

11 *EN* VIII.1, 1155a4, 1155b9–10.

12 *EN* VIII.5, 1157b7.

13 *Pol.* I.2, 1252a25–31. Note, however, that while the whole constituted by husband and wife is a community, the units "father-and-child" and "master-and-slave" are *too* unified to be κοινωνίαι strictly speaking, since in both cases the subordinate member is "as it were" or "in a way" a part of the ruler.

14 This is related to my central disagreement with Michael Pakaluk's stimulating analysis of the constitutional analogy. Pakaluk notes that chapter 9 introduces the concept of κοινωνία to the essay on friendship, and that it remains central until the end of chapter 13. But he argues that Aristotle uses this new focus to move from one kind of friendship to another—from "the informal relationships between pairs of friends that were ostensibly the topic of VIII.3-7" on the one hand to friendships "in associations" on the other. On Pakaluk's view, the latter contrasts with the former insofar as they "must involve law, or at least the assignment of duties and obligations to members as holding specified offices."

But as Pakaluk recognizes, Aristotle introduces the concept of κοινωνία by arguing that friendship and community are *coextensive* (with each other and with justice). If association and friendship are found "among the same people and concerning the same things," it seems all but incoherent to inquire about a subset of friendships found "in associations." Moreover, Aristotle believes that *all* friendships involve an exchange of benefits, honors, and friendly affection. They must, in other words, be governed by justice and something like law, written or unwritten. And as we will see, Aristotle is even committed to the view that all friendship involves something rather like "office." The distinction between formality and informality ultimately has little warrant in Aristotle's thought.

15 As I argue in Chapter 2, the reductionism-antireductionism distinction is misleading, since Aristotle thinks both that cognitive and rational process flow readily between souls *and* that goals have to originate in one individual or another. For a wide-ranging and useful discussion of the ways Aristotle is and (especially) isn't an individualist, see Dorothea Frede, "The Social Aspects of Aristotle's Theory of Action," *Philosophical Topics* 44:1 (2016), 39–57.

16 For characteristic examples, see Yack, *The Problems of a Political Animal*, 25–43, as well as Moses Finley, "Aristotle on Economic Analysis," *Past and Present* 47:1 (1970), 7–8.

17 *EN* VIII.8, 1159b20–24. Compare *EN* VIII.1, 1155a34–b9.

18 *EN* VIII.9, 1159b25–28, trans. Pakaluk. ἐν ἁπάσῃ γὰρ κοινωνίᾳ δοκεῖ τι δίκαιον εἶναι, καὶ φιλία δέ.

19 *EN* V.3, 1131a18–24. See Chapter 4 for much more on Aristotle's account of justice.

20 See Pakaluk, *Nicomachean Ethics*, 111; Riesbeck, *Aristotle on Political Community*, 47–9; and Yack, *Problems of a Political Animal*, chapter 1.

21 *EN* VIII.9, 1159b25–28.

22 *Rhet.* II.4, 1380b34–81a1. For treatments of the very difficult argument about community, see Riesbeck, *Aristotle on Political Community*, chapter 2, Michael Pakaluk, *Aristotle: Nicomachean Ethics VIII and IX* (Clarendon Aristotle Series, Oxford: Oxford University Press, 1998), 111–14, and Yack, *The Problems of a Political Animal*. For the importance of the *Rhetoric*'s definition of friendship, see Cooper, "Aristotle on the Forms of Friendship," 619–48. It is not entirely clear how to square the discussion in *EN* VIII.9 with an *endoxon* (or series of interrelated *endoxa*) that Aristotle seems to endorse at the beginning of *EN* VIII: "Those who are friends have no need of justice, but just people do need friendship as well; and the greatest form of justice seems to be friendly" (φίλων μὲν ὄντων οὐδὲν δεῖ δικαιοσύνης, δίκαιοι δ᾽ ὄντες προσδέονται φιλίας καὶ τῶν δικαίων τὸ μάλιστα φιλικὸν εἶναι δοκεῖ.) (*EN* VIII.1, 1155a29). I think the three views in question are (i) that if you regard someone as a friend, you won't, in addition, need the virtue of justice to keep you from taking more than your share from that person; that (ii) if you are fair-minded about giving people what they deserve, this still falls short of having the relationships necessary to be happy; and (iii) that the fullest commitment to giving people what they deserve will involve pursuing their good for its own sake. If so, there is no conflict

with chapter 9 as I interpret it. But in any case, if there is a contradiction, then chapter 9, which is intended as rigorous philosophy, should take precedence over chapter 1, which is a broad rhetorical prolegomenon, appealing to the importance of studying friendship.

23 *EN* VIII.9, 1160a27–30.
24 *EE* VII.9, 1241b12–17. Trans. Rackham, modified.
25 The various kinds of rule, as Aristotle says, have been "often defined" by his predecessors (*Pol.* III.6, 1278b32). At least as early as Herodotus, Greek thinkers distinguish between three kinds of constitution; Plato introduces the sixfold distinction that is Aristotle's starting point in his *Statesman*. For much more on this background, see Bordes, *Politeia dans la pensée grecque jusqu'à Aristote*. Also very useful on the ancient Athenian discussion of the constitution is Ober, *Political Dissent in Democratic Athens*.
26 *Pol.* III.6–7. Aristotle sometimes also writes that in nondeviant constitutions, the ruler rules in the interest of the whole rather than the interest of the ruled. The point is that in looking out for his subjects, the ruler also (accidentally) benefits himself and so ends up acting for in the interest of the whole (*Pol.* III.6, 1278b35).
27 For the claim that friends always seek the other's good for its own sake, see *Rhet.* II.4, 1380b35–81a2 and *EN* VIII.1, 1155b23–31. For an argument that this definition applies not just to virtue friends but also to the other two kinds, see Cooper, "Aristotle on the Forms of Friendship." Cooper argues that Aristotle is happy to define friendship as wishing others well for their own sake in general and that there is no reason to think that this definition applies only to virtue friendship; he also offers examples and arguments meant to make it plausible that even the distant relationships between partners to exchange and fellow citizens typically involve some small measure of mutual well-wishing.
28 Note, however, that at *Pol.* I.6, 1255b11–14, Aristotle says that "There is a certain advantage—and even a friendship of slave and master for one another—for those slaves who merit being such by nature." This outright contradicts what he says about slaves in the *Ethics*—that there can be no friendship between master and slave *qua* master and slave. The latter position coheres better with other claims in Aristotle's treatment of slavery and of friendship. Notably, the slave's status as a tool and as part of oneself is hard square with the claim that friends pursue each other's good for its own sake. Perhaps the claim in the *Politics* is meant to emphasize the idea that master and slave each benefit from the arrangement.
29 *EN* VIII.11, 1161a30–34.
30 Compare Curzer, who argues that Aristotle introduces the *politeiai* because he understands friendships as paradigmatically multilateral (*Aristotle and*

the Virtues, 252). It's true, as he notes, that Aristotle writes of the relationship between master (singular) and "slaves" (plural), as well as between father (singular) and "children" (plural). But I do not think this language has any philosophical importance. As far as I have been able to find, not once does Aristotle suggest that the ruler should treat such groups of subordinates differently than if there were just one slave or child. Curzer's overall treatment of friendship is illuminating, and I applaud how well he avoids undue fixation on the three kinds of friendship listed at the beginning of Book VIII—indeed he enumerates an amazing seventy-two distinct kinds of friendship.

31 *Pol.* III.6, 1278b9–10.
32 Mogens Hansen, "Seven Hundred *Archai* in Classical Athens," *Greek, Roman and Byzantine Studies 21* (1980), 151–73.
33 See the section "Ruling, Holding Office, and Controlling the City" in Chapter 5.
34 *Pol.* III.6, 1278b15.
35 Some scholars (often of a broadly Straussian persuasion) have argued that although Aristotle says this, he does not mean it; by reading between the lines we can decipher a secret argument for the equality of men and women and for the abolition of slavery. See, for example, Harold Levy, "Does Aristotle Exclude Women from Politics?" *Review of Politics* 52 (1990), 397–416. This sort of interpretation does not seem plausible to me. For one thing, various reliable sources (not to mention the maddening compression of the argument) testify that while Aristotle published dialogues for a wide readership, the surviving Aristotelian corpus is "acroamatic," that is, a rough accompaniment of some sort to his oral teaching. It would be odd for this kind of text to be carefully seeded with an esoteric message. For a survey of the arguments against this position, see Mulgan, "Aristotle on the Political Role of Women," 179–202.
36 See *Pol.* III.4 1277b25–29. "Φρόνησις is the only virtue peculiar to the ruler. The other [virtues], it would seem must necessarily be common to both rulers and ruled, but φρόνησις is not the excellence of the subject is not φρόνησις, but true opinion"; and *EN* VI.8, 1141b23–8: "Πολιτική and φρόνησις are the same state, but their being is not the same. Of practical wisdom concerning the city, the ruling part is legislative science, while the part concerned with particulars has the name common to both, i.e., political science. This part deals with action and deliberation, for the decree is to be acted on as the last thing."
37 *Theat.* 148e5–151d7.
38 In still another register, we might add Foucault's famous examples of the productive "pastoral" power exhibited in the confessional booth and the psychoanalyst's couch, where (far from restricting their actions) power leads

subordinates to produce certain kinds of truth about themselves and contributes to the formation of their identities. See especially "Omes et singulatum: Vers un critique de la raison politique," *Le débat* 41 (1986), 5–35, and "The Subject and Power," *Critical Inquiry* 8:4 (1982), 777–95.

39 Fred Miller, *Nature, Justice, and Rights in Aristotle's* Politics (Oxford: Clarendon, 1995), provides an interesting discussion of one supposed objection to this approach, the "theory of spontaneous order," which he associates with Adam Smith.

40 *Pol.* III.16, 1287a18–32; *NE* V.6 1134a35–b2 makes the related claim that political justice is found only among people "whose mutual relations are governed by law."

41 I am grateful to Josiah Ober for helping me to understand the strength of this worry.

42 *Pol.* III.15, 1286a15–20.

43 Ronald Dworkin defends a highly influential twentieth-century version of this sort of view.

44 Examples include *Pol.* III.15, 1286a7–9, *Pol.* IV.4, 1292a32, and *Pol.* IV.5, 1292b6–7.

45 *Pol.* III.15, 1286a3.

46 Dennis Vlahovic, *The Sovereignty of the Lawcode in Aristotle* (PhD. diss., McGill University, 2002).

47 *Pol.* III.14, 1285b22.

48 There is a fascinating parallel case in the discussion of political animals at the beginning of the *HA* (I.12). Aristotle distinguishes between two kinds of political animals: some, like humans and bees, "have a leader" (ὑφ'ἡγεμόνα) while others, like ants, are "anarchic" (ἄναρχα). Thompson's translation, which tells us that the ones "submit to a ruler" while the others "are every one his own master," encourages the idea that Aristotle conceived of groups, worthy of the moniker πολιτίκα, in which every member rules itself and none rule any others. Not only, however, is nonhuman rule different from its animal counterparts because infused with *logos*, but notwithstanding Thomson's translation, this passage does not seem to me to suggest that each "anarchic" animal rules itself—just as likely, Aristotle's point is that those species don't have *fixed* roles, like the queen in a bee colony or a human city.

49 *Pol.* VII. 8, 1328a25–28. John Cooper's work on friendship stresses the importance of valuing friends for their own sake, even in so-called "utility friendship" and "political friendship." See also Curzer, *Aristotle and the Virtues*, 252–53, for an argument that narrowly commercial relationships cannot count as friendships or, therefore, communities.

50 *Pol.* I.7, 1255b16–19.

51 Another version of the same mistake is to treat women as a special kind of *children*. This is the problem with the interpretation of Francis Sparshott ("Aristotle on Women," *Philosophical Inquiry* 7 (1985), 177–200), who argues that Aristotle's claims about women are grounded in a difference in age between husbands and wives.
52 *EN* VIII.10, 1160b25–6.
53 *EN* VIII.10, 1161a4–7.
54 *EN* VIII.10, 1160b32–61a4, trans. Pakaluk.
55 Aristotle is applying an idea of competing conceptions of justice that he develops at *Pol.* III.9, 1280a22–25: Men and women in bad marriages make the same kind of mistake in assigning power as democrats and oligarchs: "The ones, if they are unequal in a certain thing, such as goods, suppose they are unequal generally, while the others suppose that if they are equal in a certain thing, such as freedom, they are equal generally. But of the most authoritative thing [i.e. virtue] they say nothing." For more about heiresses, see Lockwood, "Justice in Aristotle's Household and City," 12–13.
56 *Pol.* IV.15, 1300b10–12. τῶν προσόδων καὶ τὴν κυρίαν τῆς φυλακῆς.
57 *Pol.* IV. 15.
58 *Pol.* III.1, 1275a27–33. See also *Laws* VI, 767a.
59 Riesbeck's argument that rule is a matter of degree is therefore almost but not quite correct. It is certainly true that Aristotle imagines a wide range of greater and lesser contributions to shared action, higher and lower positions on a hierarchy of ends, and greater and lesser ability to control the ruler of one's community. But he overlooks the qualitative, binary difference between the being at the top of the hierarchy and being anywhere else. For my discussion of indefinite office, I am indebted to an unpublished paper by Marie-Noëlle Ribas.
60 *Pol.* IV.15, 1299a25–28.
61 It is standard at this point to suggest that Aristotle may have shared widespread views about the duties of women, as preserved in sources like Xenophon's *Oeconomicus*. An overview of the sources suggests that preservation of the *oikos*, the woman's task on Aristotle's account, was a crucial duty for fourth-century Athenians. Not only did the household provide the material conditions necessary for free man's activities, but it also was also a gift from the past generations to be preserved and passed on, on pain of severe dishonor. Women had major responsibilities in the estate's day-to-day operation. And they played an equally important role in providing legitimate sons who would provide for the *kurios* in his old age and carry the *oikos* into the future. Thus a husband had to trust his wife with significant responsibilities. The literature on these topics is vast.

For one useful and infrequently cited discussion, see Wolfgang Detel, "The Assymetrical Relationship," in *Foucault and Classical Antiquity*, trans. David Wigg-Wolf (Cambridge: Cambridge University Press, 2005).

62 I draw the contrast between trusting people and merely relying on them from Annette Baier's "Trust and Antitrust" (*Ethics* 96 [1986], 231–60), although I don't use it quite the way she does.

63 Deslauriers' *Aristotle on Sexual Difference* contains extensive discussion. Deslauriers has over the course of her career defended several versions of the social rather than biological interpretation of the "unauthoritative" claim. For a recent version of the biological interpretation, grounded in a rich account of Aristotle's natural philosophy, see Leunissen, *From Natural Character to Moral Virtue in Aristotle*. For a nuanced recent discussion that overlaps in some ways with mine, see Karbowski, "Aristotle on the Deliberative Abilities of Women," 435–60.

64 *Pol.* I.12, 1259b5–9.

65 *Ibid.*

66 For an example of a scholar who finds a contradiction between the passages, see Mulgan, "Aristotle on the Political Role of Women," 188.

67 *EN* VIII.10, 1160b4.

68 The kings he describes in the *EN* are evidently highly idealized—real-world kings must always delegate tasks to a wide range of subordinates, and in some cases, like Sparta, they seem to have very little power at all. For an excellent account of the shifting roles of idealized discussions of kingship, see Atack, *The Discourse of Kingship in Classical Greece*.

69 *EN* II.4, 1105a20–30. For the classic discussion of learners' virtue, see Myles Burnyeat, "Aristotle on Learning to be Good," in *Essays on Aristotle's Ethics*, ed. Amélie Rorty (Berkeley and Los Angeles: University of California Press, 1980), 69–92.

70 Heath, "Natural Slaves." See the subsection 'Being Ruled' in Chapter 2.

71 *EN* VIII.11, 1161a25–7.

72 See Riesbeck's excellent discussion of the phrase κατὰ μέρος in *Aristotle on Political Community*, 248–53. Aristotle's use of the term (and Greek usage more generally) rules out the possibility of translating it as "sharing in rule." In Adriel Trott's discussion of ruling and being ruled by turn (in *Aristotle on the Nature of Political Community*, 143–52), she argues that where ἀρχή refers to political office, ruling and being ruled are zero sum—either you are in office or you are not. By contrast, she suggests that the activity of ruling, which she understands in terms of deliberating together about the common good, involves the shared,

mutual activity of all concerned. For reasons we saw in the section on aristocratic rule earlier, she is right to reject the idea that where one person rules, the other must submit passively and can contribute nothing. But I do not think the alternative Aristotle has in mind is as symmetrical and undifferentiated as she suggests. For more on the distinction between "rule" and "office," see the section "Ruling, Holding Office, and Controlling the City" in Chapter 5.

73 For more on the difference in virtue between rulers and subjects, see Dorothea Frede, "Citizenship in Aristotle's Politics," in *Aristotle's Politics: Critical Essays*, ed. Richard Kraut and Steven Skultety (Lanham: Rowman and Littlefield, 2005), 176–84, a revised version of "Staatsverfassung und Staatsbürger," in *Aristoteles' Politik*, ed. O. Höffe (Berlin: Akademie Verlag, 2001), 75–92.

74 *EN* VIII.10, 1161a8.

Chapter 4

1 *Pol.* III.4, 1277a14–15. For the connection between φρόνησις and πολιτική, see especially *EN* VI.8, which opens with the claim that φρόνησις and πολιτική "are the same state though their being is different." (I take it that this means at least that ruling presupposes φρόνησις and perhaps also that ruling over a city is among the highest ways of exercising rule.)

2 *Pol.* III.4, 1277a31–33. My trans. For the ideal of learning to rule by being ruled, see, for example, Xenophon's *Constitution of the Spartans* II–IV. Such texts are an important influence on *Politics* VII and VIII.

3 *Pol.* III.4, 1277a35. For contempt for banausic arts, see *Pol.* I.11, 1258b37, and VIII.2, 1337b8–11, as well as Xenophon, *Oec.* IV.2, and *Mem.* II.1.6 and Plato *Rep.* VI, 495d–e. For an interesting argument that contempt for banausic work was not as widespread as these philosophers imply, see Maurice Balme, "Attitudes to Work and Leisure in Ancient Greece," *Greece & Rome*, Second Series 31:2 (1984), 140–52.

4 *Pol.* III.4, 1277b7.

5 *Pol.* VII.3, 1325a24–29.

6 He doesn't expand on this point either, although he does gesture back to an earlier discussion of it elsewhere, which is presumably the discussion of natural slavery in Book I.

7 There is an enormous literature on this question. Distinguished entries include Richard Kraut's *Aristotle on the Human Good* (Princeton: Princeton University Press, 1991) and Broadie, *Ethics with Aristotle*.

8. For this possibility, see Ober, *Political Dissent in Democratic Athens*.
9. *EN* X.9.
10. See also Richard Mulgan, "Aristotle on the Value of Political Participation," *Political Theory* 18:2 (1990), 195–215.
11. The quietist tradition was presumably at home in the Academy; see *Rep.* IX, 591e1–5, where Socrates says that true philosophers will decline to practice politics anywhere but in Kallipolis. This passage is discussed by Stephen Menn, "On Plato's Πολιτεία," *Proceedings of the Boston Area Colloquium in Ancient Philosophy* 21 (2005), 1–55. The opportunistic camp is of course associated with the sophists.
12. See Chapter 1. There is at least one place—in his initial attempt to classify the constitutions—where Aristotle does seem to identify correct rule with πολιτική and deviant rule with δεσποτική: "It is evident, then, that those constitutions that look to the common benefit turn out, according to what is unqualifiedly just, to be correct, whereas those which look only to the benefit of the rulers are mistaken and are deviations from the correct constitutions. For they are like δεσποτεία, whereas a *polis* is a community of free people" (*Pol.* III.6, 1279a16–21).
13. *Pol.* III.4, 1277a36–b3: "Now we speak of several forms of slave; for the sorts of work are several. One sort is that done by menials [οἱ χερνῆτες]: as the term itself indicates, these are people who live by their hands; the manufacturing artisan [βάναυσος] belongs among them. Hence among some peoples the craftsmen did not partake in offices in former times, prior to the emergence of rule of the people in its extreme form."
14. All human beings are political animals: see for example, *EN* I.7, 1097b11, *Pol.* I.2, 1253a2–3; all communities are for the sake of the political community: *Pol.* I.1, 1252a5–7.
15. For a helpful sketch of some of the difficulties of articulating ancient political thought with later ways of thinking about the concept of "politics," see Paul Cartledge, *Ancient Greek Political Thought in Practice* (Cambridge: Cambridge University Press, 2009), 11–13.
16. *Pol.* VI.1, 1317a5–7.
17. In this chapter, I will use "neighbors" as a quasi-technical term, to refer to fellow members of a given community. I have in mind, for example, the "others" Aristotle refers to when he says that justice is virtue πρὸς τοὺς ἄλλους.
18. *Pol.* I.7, 1255b19–20.
19. Aristotle doesn't say explicitly how freedom should be defined, but he does single out what he considers the most common mistaken definitions. The reason

extreme democracies are unstable, he says, is that they define freedom badly, as doing whatever one wants. *Pol.* V.9, 1310a28–35. Similarly, at *Pol.* VI.2, 1317b1–15, he says that this false conception of freedom leads people to wrongly resist submitting to the rule of others. For more on the general Greek definition of freedom, see Hansen, "Democratic Freedom," 1–27.

20 Although note that Aristotle also describes marriage as a qualified kind of political rule. See Chapter 3.

21 This is not, I want to stress, the question of *Ethics* V about what it means to *treat people equally* (though we will get to that soon enough), but rather a question about the meaning of equality as a *property* that people may have as a group or in relation to each other.

22 *Pol.* III.9, 1280a10–24. For similar uses of "ἴσος," see, for example, *EN* V. 3, 1131a22 and *Pol.* II.7, 1267a1–2.

23 See Kraut, *Aristotle: Political Philosophy*, for an argument that the standard is contribution-to-the-common-good.

24 We may note in passing that this picture corresponds to a conception of politics in liberal political philosophy. Equality, or a right to equal consideration, is on this picture the fundamental pre-political fact and the central consideration necessary to give an account of political justice. A just political regime, on this picture, would preserve and recognize that pre-political equality, building it into the basic structure of society. As we will see, that is not what Aristotle is saying. I return to the question of Aristotle and liberal political philosophy in the Conclusion.

25 *EN* V.6, 1134a27.

26 *Pol.* II.2, 1261a30–34. In the passage from the *Ethics*, Aristotle says that reciprocity plays an important role in the city, but he doesn't refer by name to something called "reciprocal *equality.*"

27 *EN* V.2, 1130b35.

28 *EN* V.3, 1131a24–30.

29 *EN* V.3, 1131a20–b15. Trans. Rowe, modified.

30 *EN* V.3, 1131a11. Commentaries that explain the mathematical bent of *EN* V in terms of Aristotle's interest in the mean include Michael Pakaluk, *Aristotle: Nicomachean Ethics VIII and IX*, Clarendon Aristotle Series (Oxford: Oxford University Press, 1998) and Kraut, *Aristotle: Political Philosophy*.

31 Stephen Menn has pointed out to me that this statement involves Aristotle in a controversy in the philosophy of mathematics of the time. Euclid avoids speaking of ratios as equal, presumably because they aren't magnitudes.

32 Neither the puzzle nor the solution here is original to Aristotle. The second *endoxon*, that justice is equality, is obviously a democratic claim and a trace of

a real rhetorical victory by the champions of democracy. But as F.D. Harvey shows in a classic discussion, the association of democracy with equality was by Thucydides' time coming to be seen as a problem for democrats. Thus Pericles' funeral oration is remarkably defensive about equality: he worries about critics who think that "democracy is not intelligent or ἴσον," and he insists that "while the law secures equality to all alike in their private disputes, the claim of excellence is also recognized; and when a citizen is in any way distinguished, he is generally preferred to the public service, not in rotation, but for merit." Harvey shows that the distinction between arithmetic and geometric proportion comes from Pythagorian musical theory. In a fragment by Archytas, we learn that the series 6, 4, 2 instantiates arithmetic proportion, since 6 exceeds 4 *by the same amount* as 4 exceeds 2. By contrast, the series 8, 4, 2 exemplifies geometrical proportion: 8 "stands in the same relation" to 4 that 4 does to 2. The difference between these sorts of proportion is relevant to politics because geometric proportion *acknowledges the value* of the numbers involved, just as distributors should acknowledge the value of the people to whom they distribute (Harvey, "Two Kinds of Equality," 101–146). Plato winks at this view at *Gorg.* 337–8.

33 *Pol.* V.1, 1301b30–33.
34 *EN* V.4, 1132a2–10.
35 *EN* V.4, 1132b19–21.
36 *Pol.* II.2, 1261a30. On the exchange of honor for benefits, see Marguerite Deslauriers, "Political Unity and Inequality," in *The Cambridge Companion to Aristotle's Politics*, ed. Deslauriers and Pierre Destrée (Cambridge: Cambridge University Press, 2013, 117–43).
37 *EN* V.2, 1131a3–4. This reading goes back at least to Aquinas. For comparatively recent interpretations along these lines, see, for example, Finley's "Aristotle on Economic Analysis," 3–25 and Gabriel Danzig, "The Political Character of Aristotelian Reciprocity," *Classical Philology* 95:4 (2000), 399–424.
38 *EN* V.5, 1132b25–6. Proponents of this interpretation include Gauthier and Jolif, *Aristote: L'Éthique à Nicomaque* (Louvain : Nauwerlaerts, 1959).
39 *EN* V.5, 1332b35–9.
40 *EN* V.5, 1133a17–25, trans. Irwin. My italics, of course.
41 Moses Finley approvingly quotes Joachim as describing the core doctrine as "unintelligible" ("Aristotle on Economic Analysis," 9). He gives a useful survey of earlier attempts to interpret the passage up to 1970. For a helpful recent discussion, including a good bibliography, see Danzig, "The Political Character of Aristotelian Reciprocity," 399–424.
42 *EN* VIII.7, 1158b24–29.

43 *EN* VIII.8, 1159b2–3.
44 In the same way, women are parties to distributive justice within the household. Maybe nonhuman animals are too.
45 This quote is from *Ancient Greek Political Thought in Practice*; his full version of the argument is in *The Greeks: A Portrait of Self and Others* (Oxford: Oxford University Press, 1993).

Chapter 5

1 For example, *EN* VIII.10, 1160a35; *Pol.* III.13, 1284b25–34; *Pol.* IV.2, 1289a40.
2 *Pol.* III.4, 1277a1.
3 For a useful discussion of the inferiority of the βάναυσοι, see Julia Annas, "Aristotle's *Politics:* A Symposium: Aristotle on Human Nature and Political Virtue," *Review of Metaphysics* 49:4 (1996), 731–53. See also Ober, *Political Dissent in Democratic Athens*, 307–10.
4 *Pol.* VII.9, 1329a2–b17.
5 *EN* V.4, 1131b34–32a7.
6 Pol. II.2, 1261a39–b6, trans. Lord : ἐν οἷς δὲ μὴ δυνατὸν διὰ τὸ τὴν φύσιν ἴσους εἶναι πάντας, ἅμα δὲ καὶ δίκαιον, εἴτ' ἀγαθὸν εἴτε φαῦλον τὸ ἄρχειν. πάντας αὐτοῦ μετέχειν, τοῦτό γε μιμεῖται τὸ ἐν μέρει τοὺς ἴσους εἴκειν τό ἀνομοίους εἶναι ἔξω ἀρχῆς· οἱ μὲν γὰρ ἄρχουσιν οἱ δ' ἄρχονται κατὰ μέρος ὥσπερ ἂν ἄλλοι γενόμενοι. There are many textual problems with this passage, and there is no possible solution that doesn't require editorial intervention.

For our purposes, the problems begin with "there is at least an imitation of this." For the relevant sentence, Ross's Oxford edition has πάντας αὐτοῦ μετέχειν, τοῦτό γε μιμεῖται τὸ ἐν μέρει τοὺς τὸ ἐν μέρει τοὺς ἴσους εἴκειν τό θ' ὁμοίους εἶναι ἔξω ἀρχῆς. Ross (like the most modern editors, including Aubonnet and Newman) mostly follows the first of the two families of manuscripts of Aristotle's *Politics*. The main problem with the second family is that it uses the infinitive μιμεῖσθαι in the place of μιμεῖται. If we adopted this infinitive verb, we would have to read Aristotle as saying that where people are natural equals, it's *better* for imitation to take place, though this may or may not happen. But in context, this reading doesn't make sense. The following sentence (οἱ μὲν γὰρ ἄρχουσιν οἱ δ' ἄρχονται κατὰ μέρος . . .) makes it clear that Aristotle is describing what *does* happen under these conditions, not what should happen. So we turn to the first family, which has the indicative μιμεῖται. If μιμεῖται is the verb, then it's apparently in the middle voice, and we should take τοῦτο as its object and the phrase "τὸ ἐν μέρει τοὺς ἴσους εἴκειν" as its subject. As I argue in the main text, Aristotle's broader argument makes it clear that the referent for the pronoun must be the inequality of rulers and ruled.

The phrase that follows in the manuscripts is more controversial (though less important to the present argument). Here, the manuscripts suggest all sorts of possibilities: τὸ δ' ὡς ὁμοίους εἶναι ἐξ ἀρχῆς, τό θ'ὡς ὁμοίους ἔξω ἀρχῆς, and various others. Some editors and translators take the phrase as a gloss (a decision that Lord follows in his translation). Others have added to the confusion with a variety of other suggestions and speculations, such as replacing τὸ δ' ὡς ὁμοίους with ἀνομοίους. This suggestion, due to Susemihl, is adopted by Ross' Oxford edition; it would allow us to read Aristotle as saying that the members of political communities are similar in some respects but not in others. If we stick to language found in the manuscripts and adopt a variant with ἔξω ἀρχῆς, the idea is that citizens are similar when they aren't in power, or in nonpolitical respects. Newman suggests that if we accept ἐξ ἀρχῆς and ἀνομοίους the idea may be that rule by turns "imitates an original inequality."

Perhaps it will help give a sense of the range of possible interpretations to offer up some of the ways translators have dealt with this passage. Jowett says "an approximation to this is that equals should in turn retire from office and should, apart from official position, be treated alike." Aubonnet's Budé has "on en a une imitation où des homes égaux cèdent à tour le pouvoir, et sont tous considérés comme pareils hors de leur charge." Reeve has "it is at least possible to approximate to this if those who are equal take turns, and are similar when out of office." Saunders writes "the principles (a) that equals should yield place in turn, and (b) that out of office they should be similar, approximate to that practice." For a full discussion of the textual issues, see W.L. Newman, *The Politics of Aristotle*, vol. II (Cambridge: Cambridge University Press, 2010) (reprint of the original 1884 edition), 234–5.

7 As far as I have been able to find, this interpretation is the predominant view among commentators. As Newman (*ibid.*) paraphrases, "since it is better that the same men should always rule . . . and that there should be a permanent difference between rulers and ruled, men seek, where this is out of the question, to get as near to this state of things as possible (μιμεῖται), and by alternation of office to create two different classes, rulers and ruled, thus conjuring up a difference where it can hardly be said to exist." For a similar interpretation, see, Peter Simpson, *A Philosophical Commentary on the Politics of Aristotle* (Chapel Hill: UNC Press, 1998). Compare, however, Riesbeck, *Aristotle on Political Community*, 155n34. He claims that what is imitated is "an arrangement in which everyone shares in rule."

8   For a related point, see Kostas Vlassopoulos, "Free Spaces: Identity, Experience and Democracy in Classical Athens," *Classical Quarterly* 57:1 (2007), 33–52. Vlassopoulos emphasizes the ways that status categories could be obscured and unknowable in public spaces like the marketplace.
9   *Pol.* I.12, 1259b4–9.
10 Herod. 2.172.
11 *Pol.* VII.14, 1332b15–26.
12 *Pol.* III.4, 1277b7. See also *Pol.* VII.8, 1328a35–6.
13 For one example among many, see Miller, "The Rule of Reason," 62, which concludes by saying that in spite of Aristotle's regrettable views about women and slaves, he remains relevant because he recognized "that shared governance when citizens have comparable rational capabilities."
14 *Pol.* III.13, 1284a9–11.
15 *EN* VIII.7, 1158b30–59a4.
16 Some scholars interpret Aristotle's references to the superiority of gods in terms of the claim *Politics* III.11 that if a king's virtue is greater even than the total created by adding together everyone else's virtue, then the many truly have no claim to rule. See Miller, "The Rule of Reason," 38–66.
17 He allows, however, a possible exception in the best constitution. A group of virtuous free men might agree to the justice of assigning different political powers based on age, charging young men with war, mature ones with civic duty, and very old ones with religion.
18 *Pol.* III.9, 1280a15. About five lines later, Aristotle repeats the point: people disagree about the "οἷς" of justice "διότι κρίνουσι τὰ περὶ αὑτοὺς κακῶς." This doctrine is connected to the claim late in the discussion of friendship to the effect that one of the benefits of having virtue friends is that they allow a clear glimpse of one's own virtue, which would otherwise be hard to behold clearly.
19 *Pol.* III.16, 1287a26–b2.
20 Cf. *Pol.* V.10, 1313a3–5, where he writes that kingships no longer come to into existence. ("If monarchies do arise," he says, "they tend to be tyrannies.")
21 Does Aristotle's doctrine of the *phronimos* (an exemplary virtuous person) contradict this position? The idea of a *phronimos* does indeed suggest that we can imagine (and quite possibly identify) people who are more virtuous than we are and who could therefore serve as models for imitation. But the figure of the *phronimos* cannot help with the problems we are considering here. For while judgments about who is and who is not a *phronimos* are not, strictly speaking, judgments about one's own value, they are closely akin to them. For one thing, if I peg some set of people as *phronimoi*, I will likely find them among my friends

and ancestors—that is, they will broadly belong to the class of things that are mine. Moreover, my judgments about who is a *phronimos* will reflect my values. If I am a money-loving oligarch, I may think the Ischomachus of Xenophon's *Oeconomicus* is a *phronimos*, while my political opponents will think otherwise. In short, disagreements about *phronimoi* will closely track disagreements arising from people's poor judgment about their own worth.

22 As tragedy and comedy amply demonstrate (and as we could guess in any case), many women and slaves did not themselves think that their subordination was grounded in unquestionable differences in value. Aristotle does not seem to have thought much about their testimony.

23 *Pol.* VII.14, 1332b37–40.

24 See not only *Pol.* V on how to prevent faction but also such passages as *Pol.* II.5, 1264b8–10: "Also, the way that Socrates selects the rulers is hazardous; for he has the same persons always ruling. This can become a cause of factional conflict."

25 *Pol.* V.1, 1302a16.

26 We are, in this scenario, much like Glaucon and Adeimantus in the *Republic*. See Chapter 1 of G.R.F. Ferrari's *City and Soul in Plato's* Republic (Chicago: University of Chicago Press, 2005).

27 *Pol.* V.1, 1301a39–40.

28 *Pol.* V.4 1304b2–5.

29 *Pol.* I.5, 1254a25.

30 This is an important part of the famous argument for the "wisdom of the multitude" in III.11. On this point, see Kraut, *Aristotle: Political Philosophy*, 408.

31 *Pol.* III.10.

32 *Pol.* V.1, 1302a2–7.

33 *Pol.* IV.9.

34 Melissa Lane, "Popular Sovereignty as Control of Office-Holders: Aristotle on Greek Democracy," in *Popular Sovereignty in Historical Perspective*, ed. Richard Bourke and Quentin Skinner (Cambridge University Press, 2016), 52–72. See also her companion articles on the role of offices in Plato, "How to Turn History into Scenario: Plato's *Republic*," in *How to Do Things with History: New Approaches to Ancient Greece*, by Paul Cartledge (Oxford: Oxford University Press, 2018), 81–108 and in *Plato's Statesman: Proceedings of the Eight Symposium Platonicum Pragense*, ed. Aleš Havlíček, Jakub Jirsa, and Karel Thein (Prague: OIKOYMENH, 2013).

35 Lane writes "In general, as Emily Hulme has suggested to me in a private communication, we should remember that in Greek, verbs of professions, competencies, or capacities, are used more broadly than associated nouns:

'I write, but Hemingway's a writer; Patrick sings, but Sinatra is a singer; and Alcibiades plays the *kithara*, but would surely bristle at the insult of being called a *kitharistes*'" ("How to Turn History into Scenario," 84).
36 Esther Rogan, *La Stásis dans la politique d'Aristote: La cité sous tension* (Paris: Classiques Garnier, 2018).
37 *Pol.* V.3, 1303b12–15.
38 *Pol.* VI.4, 1319b12.
39 *Pol.* VII.13, 1332a10–16. Trans. Reeve, modified.
40 Faint glimpse versus precise knowledge: *PA* 644b32–5a1; "ignoble": *PA* 645a7 and a15; "much repugnance": *PA* 645a29.
41 *GA* II.1, 731b29–35. I'm attached to the basset hound example both because of its remarkable features and because it's a charming creature. But I should acknowledge that the basset hound is a breed, not a species, and that its peculiarities are a result of breeding by humans, a practice inconsistent with Aristotle's biology.
42 The *IA*, *HA*, and *PA* are full of discussions of features like this. See, for example, the discussion of the telescoping undulations of leeches and worms at *IA* 9, 709a25–30.
43 For a general statement of the relationship between the human goods that presuppose evils and the divine ones that don't, see *EN* X.8, 1178b8–22. There are many examples of antecedents. See, for example, the Isles of the Blessed in Hesiod's *Works and Days*, and Calypso's island in Books V and VI of the *Odyssey*.
44 *Met.* V.5, trans. Ross. Cf. the definition of "necessary goods" in the *Republic*, VIII 558e: "Desires that we cannot divert or suppress may be properly called necessary, and likewise those whose satisfaction is beneficial to us, may they not? For our nature compels us to seek their satisfaction." Trans. Shorey.
45 *Pol.* IV.1, 1288b22–26.
46 *Pol.* IV.11, 1295a25–32.
47 *Pol.* IV.11, 1295b25.
48 *Pol.* II.2, 1261a34–b5.
49 *Statesman* 275c.
50 *Laws* VI, 757a–c.
51 *EN* V.10, 1137b11–31.
52 *EN* VIII.7, 1158b29–33. "Equality in friendship, however, does not seem to be like equality in matters of justice. In the sphere of justice, 'equal' means primarily according to desert, whereas equality of number is secondary." Trans. Rackham, modified: ἔστι γὰρ ἐν μὲν τοῖς δικαίοις ἴσον πρώτως τὸ κατ' ἀξίαν, τὸ δὲ κατὰ ποσὸν δευτέρως, ἐν δὲ τῇ φιλίᾳ τὸ μὲν κατὰ ποσὸν πρώτως, τὸ δὲ κατ' ἀξίαν δευτέρως.

53 Kant, *Idea for a Universal History from a Cosmopolitan Point of View*, 6th thesis. Trans. Lucas.

Conclusion

1 Diogenes Laertius, *Lives of Eminent Philosophers*, V.20 (μία ψυχὴ δύο σώμασιν ἐνοικοῦσα) and V.31 (ἐρασθήσεσθαι δὲ τὸν σοφὸν καὶ πολιτεύσεσθαι, γαμήσειν τε μὴν καὶ βασιλεῖ συμβιώσεσθαι).
2 Liberalism is notorious for eluding definition. I take it, though, that it's uncontroversial to assume that it would mark an affinity with liberalism to believe (i) that rational beings are entitled a fundamental equality of status and a concomitant set of equal rights; (ii) that just social arrangements prevent (or minimize) hierarchies in which one person imposes his or her will on another without consent; or (iii) that one of the main goals of politics—and perhaps the only one—is to acknowledge and protect the freedom and equality of human beings, taken as autonomous individuals. These are the claims that I think are often attributed to Aristotle and that I have been claiming he doesn't hold.
3 On some of the problems with communitarian readings of Aristotle's politics, see Yack, *The Problems of a Political Animal*.
4 Will Kymlicka, *Contemporary Political Theory: An Introduction*, 2nd ed. (Oxford: Clarendon Press, 2002), 3 (1990 is the date of the first edition). Kymlicka builds mainly on arguments by Ronald Dworkin in *Taking Rights Seriously* (London: Duckworth, 1977). I take it that the status quo represented by Kymlicka is tattered but still in place.
5 Indeed, the very words "democracy" and "oligarchy" entered vernacular language as specifically Aristotelian jargon: they first appeared alongside hundreds of other Greek-isms, in Nicole Oresme's French translation and commentary of the *Politics*. See Albert Douglas Menut, ed., "Le Livre de Politiques d'Aristote, Published from the Text of the Avranches Manuscript 233," *Transactions of the American Philosophical Society*, New Series 60:6 (1970), 1–392.
6 *Two Treatises of Government*, 2.2
7 J.S. Maloy, "The Aristotelianism of Locke's Politics," *Journal of the History of Ideas* 70:2 (2009), 235–57. Maloy argues that in doing this, Locke allied himself with a broader radical seventeenth-century tradition of using the Aristotelian distinction between political rule and despotism to criticize monarchy.
8 For the period immediately following Aristotle, see D.E. Hahm, "Kings and Constitutions: Hellenistic Theories," in *The Cambridge History of Greek and*

Roman Political Thought, ed. Malcolm Schofield and Christopher Rowe (Cambridge: Cambridge University Press, 2000), 457–76. For the renaissance, see Quentin Skinner, *The Foundations of Modern Thought* (Cambridge: Cambridge University Press, 1978).

9. See Dominic O'Meara, *Platonopolis: Platonic Political Philosophy in Late Antiquity* (Oxford: Clarendon Press, 2005).

10. For a helpful survey of early Christian discussions of obedience and docility, I'm indebted to Amy Barnes' McGill doctoral thesis, *Authenticity and the Ascetic Self*. Barnes connects Augustine to a tradition including figures like Athanasius and John Cassian, concerned with the virtue of obedience and the value of docility. In this tradition, she argues, hierarchical relationships don't simply involve removing the agency of the person ruled and replacing it with the will of the authority figure: "great strength is shown by these men when they overcome pride and attain docility or a true capacity to be shaped by authoritative instruction and to imitate the examples of those they understand to be good."

11. Richard Whately (ed.), *Bacon's Essays* (London: John W. Parker and Son, 1856), 87. I don't know of much work by philosophers that focuses on themes of service or obedience, but I understand that it has lately become a central concern among scholars of early modern English literature. See especially David Schalkwyk's *Shakespeare on Love and Service* (Cambridge: Cambridge University Press, 2008), which surveys the ways the question "how should one serve" runs through Shakespeare's plays and sonnets. Some characters, like Kate, progress from unhappy service-as-bondage to loving service-as-freedom; others, like Cordelia, show that the truest, deepest service involves disobeying or challenging a master; others, like Iago, exploit the access and trust granted to servants.

Bibliography

Annas, Julia. "Plato's *Republic* and Feminism." *Philosophy* 51:197 (1976), 307–21.
Annas, Julia. "Aristotle's *Politics*: A Symposium: Aristotle on Human Nature and Political Virtue." *The Review of Metaphysics* 49:4 (1996), 731–53.
Annas, Julia and Robin Waterfield (eds.). *Plato: Statesman*. Cambridge: Cambridge University Press, 1995.
Arendt, Hannah. *The Human Condition*. Chicago: Chicago University Press, 1998.
Atack, Carol. *The Discourse of Kingship in Classical Greece*. New York: Routledge, 2020.
Baier, Annette. "Trust and Antitrust." *Ethics* 96 (1986), 231–60.
Balme, Maurice. "Attitudes to Work and Leisure in Ancient Greece." *Greece & Rome*, Second Series, 31:2 (1984), 140–52.
Baragwanath, Emily. "The Wonder of Freedom: Xenophon on Slavery." In *Xenophon: Ethical Principles and Historical Enquiry*, edited by Fiona Hobden and Christopher Tuplin. Leiden: Brill, 2012, 631–3.
Belfiore, Elizabeth. "Family Friendship in Aristotle's Ethics." *Ancient Philosophy* 21:1 (2001), 113–32.
Blythe, James. "The Mixed Constitution and the Distinction between Regal and Political Power in the Work of Thomas Aquinas." *Journal of the History of Ideas* 47:4 (1986), 547–65.
Bobonich, Christopher. "Persuasion, Compulsion, and Freedom in Plato's *Laws*." *Classical Quarterly*, New Series 41:2 (1991), 365–88.
Bodéüs, Richard. *Le philosophe et la cité*. Paris: Belles Letters, 1982.
Bodéüs, Richard. "De l'âme servile affranchi de lois." In *Le veritable politique et ses vertues selon Aristote*. Louvain-la-Neuve, Dudley, MA : Peeters, 2004, 79–106.
Bordes, Jacqueline. *Politeia dans la pensée grecque jusqu'à Aristote*. Paris: Belles Lettres, 1982.
Broadie, Sarah. *Ethics with Aristotle*. New York: Oxford University Press, 1991.
Broadie, Sarah. "What Should We Mean by 'the Highest Good'?" In *Aristotle and Beyond: Essays in Metaphysics and Ethics*. Cambridge: Cambridge University Press, 2007, 153–65.
Brunschwig, Jacques. "Rhétorique et dialectique, *Rhétorique* et *Topiques*." In *Aristotle's Rhetoric: Philosophical Essays*, edited by David Furley and Alexander Nehamas. Princeton: Princeton University Press, 1994, 57–96.

Burnyeat, Myles. "Aristotle on Learning to Be Good." In *Essays on Aristotle's Ethics*, edited by Amélie Rorty. Berkeley and Los Angeles: University of California Press, 1980, 69–92.

Burnyeat, Myles. "Enthymeme: Aristotle on the Logic of Persuasion." In *Aristotle's Rhetoric: Philosophical Essays*, edited by David Furley and Alexander Nehamas. Princeton: Princeton University Press, 1994, 3–56.

Buxton, R.G.A. *Persuasion in Greek Tragedy: A Study of Peitho*. Cambridge: Cambridge University Press, 1982.

Callard, Agnes. "Aristotle on Deliberation." *The Routledge Handbook of Practical Reason*, edited by Ruth Chang and Kurt Sylvan. Forthcoming.

Calogero, Guido. "Gorgias and the Socratic Principle *Nemo Sua Sponte Peccat*." *Journal of Hellenistic Studies* 77:1 (1957), 12–17.

Cambiano, Giuseppe. "Aristotle and the Anonymous Opponents of Slavery." *Slavery and Abolition Studies* 8:1 (1987), 22–41.

Cartledge, Paul. *The Greeks: A Portrait of Self and Others*. Oxford: Oxford University Press, 1993.

Cartledge, Paul. *Ancient Greek Political Thought in Practice*. Cambridge: Cambridge University Press, 2009.

Case, Kim and Jonathan Iuzini (eds.) "Special Issue: Systems of Privilege: Intersections, Awareness, and Applications." *Journal of Social Issues* 68:1 (2012).

Chroust, Anton-Hermann. "Aristotle's Flight from Athens in the Year 323 BC." *Historia: Zeitschrift für Alte Geschichte* 15:2 (1966), 185–92.

Connell, Sophia M. *Aristotle on Female Animals*. Cambridge: Cambridge University Press, 2016.

Cooper, John M. "Aristotle on the Forms of Friendship." *Review of Metaphysics* 30:4 (1977), 619–48.

Cooper, John M. "Some Remarks on Aristotle's Moral Psychology." *The Southern Journal of Philosophy* 27 (1988): 25–42.

Cooper, John M. "Ethical-Political Theory in Aristotle's *Rhetoric*." In *Aristotle's Rhetoric: Philosophical Essays*, edited by David Furley and Alexander Nehamas. Princeton: Princeton University Press, 1994, 193–210.

Cooper, John M. (ed.). *Plato: Complete Works*. Associate editor, D.S. Hutchinson. Indianapolis/Cambridge: Hackett, 1997.

Curzer, Howard. *Aristotle and the Virtues*. Oxford: Oxford University Press, 2012.

Danzig, Gabriel. "The Political Character of Aristotelian Reciprocity." *Classical Philology* 95:4 (2000), 399–424.

Deslauriers, Marguerite. "Aristotle on the Virtues of Slaves and Women." *Oxford Studies in Ancient Philosophy* 25 (2003), 213–31.

Deslauriers, Marguerite. "The Argument of Aristotle's *Politics* I." *Phoenix* 60 (2006), 48–69.

Deslauriers, Marguerite. "Political Unity and Inequality." In *The Cambridge Companion to Aristotle's* Politics, edited by Marguerite Deslauriers and Pierre Destrée. Cambridge: Cambridge University Press, 2013, 117–43.

Deslauriers, Marguerite. *Aristotle on Sexual Difference*. Oxford: Oxford University Press, forthcoming.

Deslauriers, Marguerite and Zoli Filotas. "Aristotle's Human Beings." In *Human*. Oxford Philosophical Concepts. Oxford: Oxford University Press, forthcoming.

Detel, Wolfgang. "The Assymetrical Relationship." in *Foucault and Classical Antiquity*, translated by David Wigg-Wolf. Cambridge: Cambridge University Press, 2005.

Devere, Heather. "Reviving Greco-Roman Friendship: A Bibliographical Review." *Critical Review of International Social and Political Philosophy* 2:4 (1999), 149–87.

Dorion, Louis-André. "Socrate et la basiklikê tekhnê: Essai d'exegèse comparative." In *Socrates: 2400 Years Since His Death (399 BC - 2001 AD)*. Athens: European Cultural Centre of Delphi, 2004.

Dorion, Louis-André. "Socrate οἰκονομικός." In *Xénophon et Socrate: Actes du colloque d'Aix-en-Provence*, edited by Michel Narcy and Alonzo Tordesillas. Paris : Vrin, 2008, 253–82.

Dorion, Louis-André. *L'autre Socrate: Études sur les écrits socratiques de Xénophon*. Paris: Belles Letters, 2013.

Dover, Kenneth. *Greek Popular Morality in the Time of Plato and Aristotle*. Oxford: Basil Blackwell, 1974.

Dow, Jamie. *Passions & Persuasion in Aristotle's Rhetoric*. Oxford: Oxford University Press, 2015.

Dworkin, Ronald. *Taking Rights Seriously*. London: Duckworth, 1977.

Ferrari, G.R.F. *City and Soul in Plato's Republic*. Chicago: University of Chicago Press, 2005.

Filotas, Zoli. "Review of *From Natural Character to Moral Virtue in Aristotle*, by Mariska Leunissen." *The Philosophical Review* 128:2 (2019), 224–8.

Filotas, Zoli. "Social Science and Universalism in Xenophon's *Oeconomicus* IV." In *Foreign Influences. The Circulation of Knowledge in Antiquity*, edited by B. Castelnérac, L. Gili and L. Monteils-Laeng. Turnhout: Brepols, forthcoming.

Finley, Moses. *Ancient Slavery and Modern Ideology*. Expanded edition, edited by Brent Shaw. Princeton: Markus Wiener, 1998.

Finley, Moses. "Aristotle on Economic Analysis." *Past and Present* 47:1 (1970), 3–25.

Foreman, P. Gabrielle et al. "Writing About/Teaching About Slavery: This Might Help" (Community sourced document, June 17, 2020, 12:37 PM https://naacpculpeper.org/resources/writing-about-slavery-this-might-help/).

Forsdyke, Sara. "Athenian Democratic Ideology and Herodotus' Histories." *American Journal of Philology* 122:3 (2001), 329–58.

Fortenbaugh, William. "Aristotle on Slaves and Women." In *Articles on Aristotle 2*, edited by Jonathan Barnes, Malcolm Schofield, and Richard Sorabji. London: Duckworth, 1975.

Foucault, Michel. "Nietzsche, la généalogie, l'histoire." In *Hommage à Jean Hyppolite*, edited by Suzanne Bachelard. Paris: P.U.F., 1971.

Foucault, Michel. "The Subject and Power." *Critical Inquiry* 8:4 (1982), 777–95.

Foucault, Michel. "Omes et singulatum: Vers un critique de la raison politique." *Le débat* 41 (1986), 5–35.

Frede, Dorothea. "Citizenship in Aristotle's *Politics*." In *Aristotle's* Politics: *Critical Essays*, edited by Richard Kraut and Steven Skultety. Lanham: Rowman and Littlefield, 2005, 176–84. (Revised version of "Staatsverfassung und Staatsbürger." in *Aristoteles' Politik*, edited by O. Höffe [Berlin: Akademie Verlag, 2001], 75–92.)

Frede, Dorothea. "On the So-Called Common Books of the *Eudemian* and the *Nicomachean Ethics*." *Phronesis* 64:1 (2018), 84–116.

Frede, Dorothea. "The Social Aspects of Aristotle's Theory of Action." *Philosophical Topics* 44:1 (2016), 39–57.

Gagarin, Michael. "The Torture of Slaves in Athenian Law." *Classical Philology* 91:1 (1996), 1–18.

Garnsey, Peter. *Ideas of Slavery from Aristotle to Augustine*. Cambridge: Cambridge University Press, 1996.

Garsten, Bryan. "Deliberating and Acting Together." In *The Cambridge Companion to Aristotle's* Politics, edited by Marguerite Deslauriers and Pierre Destrée. Cambridge: Cambridge University Press, 2013.

Gauthier, René Antoine and Jean Yves Jolif (translation and commentary). *Aristote: L'Éthique à Nicomaque*, 2 vols. Louvain : Nauwerlaerts, 1959 (2002).

Goldschmidt, Victor. "La théorie Aristotélicienne de l'esclavage et sa methode." In *Zetesis: Album amicorum*. Antwerp: De Nederlandsche Boekhandel, 1973, 153–58.

Graham, Daniel W. *The Texts of Early Greek Philosophy*, vol. II. Cambridge: Cambridge University Press, 2010.

Gray, Vivienne. *Xenophon's Mirror of Princes: Reading the Reflections*. Oxford: Oxford University Press. 2011.

Hahm, D.E. "Kings and Constitutions: Hellenistic Theories." In *The Cambridge History of Greek and Roman Political Thought*, edited by Malcolm Schofield and Christopher Rowe. Cambridge: Cambridge University Press, 2000, 457–76.

Hanink, Johanna. *The Classical Debt: Greek Antiquity in an Era of Austerity*. Cambridge: Harvard University Press, 2017.

Hansen, Mogens. "Seven Hundred *Archai* in Classical Athens." *Greek, Roman and Byzantine Studies* 21 (1980), 151–73.

Hansen, Mogens. "Democratic Freedom and the Concept of Freedom in Plato and Aristotle." *Greek, Roman and Byzantine Studies* 50 (2010), 1–27.

Harvey, F.D. "Two Kinds of Equality." *Classica et Medievalia* 26 (1965), 101–46.

Heath, Malcolm. "Aristotle on Natural Slavery." *Phronesis* 53 (2008), 243–70.

Held, Virginia. "Non-Contractual Society." In *Science, Morality & Feminist Theory*, edited by Marcha Hanen and Kai Nielsen. *Canadian Journal of Philosophy*, Supplementary Volume XIII (1987).

Hunt, Peter. "Chapter 2: Slaves in Greek Literary Culture." In *The Cambridge World History of Slavery*. Vol. 1, edited by Keith Bradley and Paul Cartledge. Cambridge: Cambridge University Press, 2011, 22–47.

Johnstone, Steven. "Virtuous Toil, Vicious Work: Xenophon on Aristocratic Style." *Classical Philology* 89 (1994), 219–40.

Kamtekar, Rachana. "The Profession of Friendship." *Ancient Philosophy* 25:2 (2005), 319–39.

Karbowski, Joseph. "Slaves, Women, and Aristotle's Natural Teleology." *Ancient Philosophy* 32 (2012), 323–50.

Karbowski, Joseph. "Aristotle on the Deliberative Abilities of Women." *Apeiron* 47:4 (2014), 435–60.

Kelsen, Hans. "The Philosophy of Aristotle and the Hellenic-Macedonian Policy." *International Journal of Ethics* 48:1 (1937), 1–64.

Kennedy, Rebecca Futo. "We Condone It by Our Silence: Confronting Classics' Complicity in White Supremacy." *Eidolon*. Last modified May 11, 2017. https://eidolon.pub/we-condone-it-by-our-silence-bea76fb59b21.

Kennedy, Rebecca Futo. "On the History of Western Civilization, Part 1." *Medium*. Last modified Apr 2, 2019. https://medium.com/@rfutokennedy/on-the-history-of-western-civilization-part-1-3c7d6f3ebb10.

Kirby, John. "The 'Great Triangle' in Early Greek Rhetoric and Poetics." *Rhetorica: A Journal of the History of Rhetoric* 8:3 (1990), 213–28.

Kirwan, Christopher. *Aristotle: Metaphysics Books Γ, Δ, and E*. 2nd ed. Clarendon Aristotle Series. Oxford: Clarendon, 1993.

Kosman, Aryeh. "Being Properly Affected: Virtues and Feelings in Aristotle's Ethics." In *Essays on Aristotle's Ethics*, edited by Amélie Rorty. Berkeley: University of California Press, 1980, 103–16.

Kraut, Richard. *Aristotle on the Human Good*. Princeton: Princeton University Press, 1991.

Kraut, Richard. *Aristotle: Political Philosophy*. Oxford: Oxford University Press, 2002.

Kymlicka Will. *Contemporary Political Theory: An Introduction*. 2nd ed. Oxford: Clarendon Press, 2002.

Laerke, Mogens, Justin E. H. Smith, and Eric Schliesser (eds.). *Philosophy and Its History*. Oxford and New York: Oxford University Press, 2013.

Lane, Melissa. "Political Expertise and Political Office in Plato's *Statesman*." In Plato's *Statesman. Proceedings of the Eighth Symposium Platonicum Pragense*, edited by Aleš Havlíček, Jakub Jirsa, and Karel Thein. Prague: OIOYMENH. 2013, 51–79.

Lane, Melissa. "Popular Sovereignty as Control of Office-holders: Aristotle on Greek Democracy." In *Popular Sovereignty in Historical Perspective*, edited by Richard Bourke and Quentin Skinner. Cambridge: Cambridge University Press, 2016.

Lane, Melissa. "How to Turn History into Scenario: Plato's *Republic*." In *How to Do Things with History: New Approaches to Ancient Greece*, by Paul Cartledge. Oxford: Oxford University Press, 2018, 81–108.

Leunissen, Mariska. *From Natural Character to Moral Virtue in Aristotle*. Oxford: Oxford University Press, 2017.

Levy, Harold. "Does Aristotle Exclude Women from Politics?" *Review of Politics* 52 (1990), 397–416.

Lockwood, Thornton. "A Topical Bibliography of Scholarship on Aristotle's *Nicomachean Ethics*: 1880 to 2004." *Journal of Philosophical Research* 30 (2005), 78–85.

Lockwood, Thornton. "Justice in Aristotle's Household and City." *Polis* 20:1/2 (2003), 1–21.

Lord, Carnes (ed. and trans.). *Aristotle's* Politics, 2nd ed. Chicago and London: Chicago University Press, 2013.

Lorenz, Hendrik. *The Brute Within*. Oxford: Oxford University Press, 2006.

MacDowell, D.M. (ed. and trans.) *Gorgias: Encomium of Helen*. Bristol: Bristol Classical Press, 1982

Maloy, J.S. "The Aristotelianism of Locke's Politics." *Journal of the History of Ideas* 70:2 (2009), 235–57.

Mayhew, Robert. "Rulers and Ruled." In *A Companion to Aristotle*, edited by G. Anagnostopoulos. Oxford: Blackwell, 2009.

McCoskey, Denise. *Race: Antiquity and Its Legacy*. Oxford: Oxford University Press, 2012.

McDowell, John. "Some Issues in Aristotle's Moral Psychology." In *Mind, Value and Reality*. Cambridge: Cambridge University Press, 1998, 23–40.

McIntosh, Peggy. "White Privilege and Male Privilege: A Personal Account of Coming to See Correspondences Through Work in Women's Studies." Wellesley Centers for Women, Working Paper 189: 1989.

Menn, Stephen. "Collecting the Letters." *Phronesis* 43:4 (1998), 291–305.

Menn, Stephen. "On Plato's Πολιτεία." *Proceedings of the Boston Area Colloquium in Ancient Philosophy* 21 (2005), 1–55.

Menn, Stephen. "Aristotle." in *Encyclopedia of Philosophy*, edited by Donald Borchert, 2nd ed., Detroit: Macmillian, 2006, I: 263–82.

Menut, Albert Douglas, ed. "Le Livre de Politiques d'Aristote, Published from the Text of the Avranches Manuscript 233." *Transactions of the American Philosophical Society*, New Series 60:6 (1970), 1–392.

Miller, Fred D. Jr. *Nature, Justice, and Rights in Aristotle's Politics*. Oxford: Clarendon Press, 1995.

Miller, Fred D. "The Rule of Reason." In *The Cambridge Companion to Aristotle's Politics*, edited by Marguerite Deslauriers and Pierre Destrée. Cambridge: Cambridge University Press, 2013, 38–66.

Moraux, Paul. *À la recherche de l'Aristote perdu: Le dialogue "Sur la justice."* Louvain: Publications Universitaires de Louvain, 1957.

Morrisson, Donald. "Tyrannie et royauté selon le Socrate de Xénophon." *Les études philosophiques* 69: 2 (2004), 177–92.

Morrison, Donald. "The Common Good." In *The Cambridge Companion to Aristotle's Politics*, edited by Marguerite Deslauriers and Pierre Destrée. Cambridge: Cambridge University Press, 2013, 38–66.

Morrow, Glenn. "Plato and Greek Slavery." *Mind*, New Series 48:190 (1939), 186–201.

Morrow, Glenn. *Plato's Law of Slavery in Its Relation to Greek Law*. New York: Arno Press, 1976.

Morrow, Glenn. "Tyrannie et royauté chez le Socrate de Xenophon." *Les Etudes philosophiques* 69 (2004/2), 177–92.

Moss, Jessica. *Aristotle on the Apparent Good: Perception, Phantasia, Thought, and Desire*. Oxford: Oxford University Press, 2012.

Motte, André et al. (eds.). *Philosophie de la forme: Eidos, Idea, Morphe dans la philosophie Grecque des origines à Aristote*. Liège: Peeters, 2003.

Mulgan, Richard. "Aristotle on the Value of Political Participation." *Political Theory* 18:2 (1990), 195–215.

Mulgan, Richard. "Aristotle on the Political Role of Women." *History of Political Thought* 15:2 (1994), 179–202.

Nelis, Jan. "Constructing Fascist Identity: Benito Mussolini and the Myth of the 'Romanità.'" *The Classical World* 100:4 (2007), 391–415.

Nelsestuen, Grant. "*Oikonomia* as a Theory of Empire in the Political Thought of Xenophon and Aristotle." *Greek, Roman, and Byzantine Studies* 57 (2017), 74–104.

Newman, W.L. *The Politics of Aristotle*. 4 vols. Cambridge: Cambridge University Press, 2010 (reprint of 1884 edition).

Nussbaum, Martha. "Aristotle on Human Nature and the Foundations of Ethics." In *World, Mind, and Ethics: Essays on the Philosophy of Bernard Williams*, edited by J. E. J. Altham and Ross Harrisson. Cambridge: Cambridge University Press, 1995, 86–131.

Nussbaum, Martha. *The Therapy of Desire*. Princeton: Princeton University Press, 1994.

Ober, Josiah. *Political Dissent in Democratic Athens*. Princeton: Princeton University Press, 1996.

Ober, Josiah. "The Original Meaning of Democracy: Capacity to Do Things, Not Majority Rule." *Constellations* 15 (2008), 3–9.

O'Meara, Dominic. *Platonopolis: Platonic Political Philosophy in Late Antiquity*. Oxford: Clarendon Press, 2005.

Pakaluk, Michael. *Aristotle: Nicomachean Ethics VIII and IX*. Clarendon Aristotle Series. Oxford: Oxford University Press, 1998.

Pellegrin, Pierre. "Natural Slavery." Translated by Zoli Filotas. In *The Cambridge Companion to Aristotle's Politics*, edited by Marguerite Deslauriers and Pierre Destrée. Cambridge: Cambridge University Press, 2013.

Pomeroy, Sarah. "Slavery in the Greek Domestic Economy in Light of Xenophon's *Oeconomicus*." *Index* 17 (1989), 11–88, reprinted in *Oxford Readings in Classical Studies: Xenophon*, ed. Vivienne Gray. Oxford: Oxford University Press, 2010, 31–40.

Pomeroy, Sarah. *Xenophon Oeconomicus: A Social and Historical Commentary*. Oxford: Clarendon Press, 1994.

Price, A.W. *Love and Friendship in Plato and Aristotle*. Oxford: Oxford University Press, 1990.

Raaflaub, Kurt. "Democracy, Oligarchy, and the Concept of the 'Free Citizen' in Late Fifth Century Athens." *Political Theory* 11:4 (1983), 517–44.

Reeve, C.D.C. "Platonic Politics and the Good." *Political Theory* 23:3 (1995), 411–24.

Rhill, T.E. "Classical Athens." In *The Cambridge World History of Slavery*. Vol. 1, edited by Keith Bradley and Paul Cartledge. Cambridge: Cambridge University Press, 2011. 48–73.

Riesbeck, David. *Aristotle on Political Community*. Cambridge: Cambridge University Press,

Rosler, Andrés. *Political Authority and Obligation in Aristotle*. Oxford Aristotle Studies. Oxford: Clarendon Press, 2005.

Ross, David (trans.) *Aristotle: The Nicomachean Ethics*. Oxford: Oxford University Press, 1954.

Saunders, Trevor. (trans. with commentary) *Aristotle: Politics I*. Clarendon Aristotle Series. Oxford: Oxford University Press, 1996.

Schalkwyk, David. *Shakespeare on Love and Service*. Cambridge: Cambridge University Press, 2008

Schlaifer, Robert. "Greek Theories of Slavery from Homer to Aristotle." *Harvard Studies in Classical Philology* 47 (1936), 165–204.

Schofield, Malcolm. *Saving the City: Philosopher Kings and Other Paradigms*. New York: Routledge, 1999.

Schofield, Malcolm. "Aristotle's Political Ethics." In *The Blackwell Guide to Aristotle's Nicomachean Ethics*, edited by Richard Kraut. Oxford: Blackwell, 2006, 305–22, 305.

Schollmeier, Paul. *Other Selves: Aristotle on Personal and Political Friendship*. New York: State University of New York Press, 1994.

Segal, Charles. "Gorgias and the Psychology of Logos." *Harvard Studies in Classical Philology* 66 (1962), 99–155.

Sihova, Julia. "Aristotle on Sex and Love." In *The Sleep of Reason*, edited by Martha Nussbaum and Juha Sihova. Chicago: Chicago University Press 2002, 200–221.

Simpson, Peter. *A Philosophical Commentary on the Politics of Aristotle*. Chapel Hill: UNC Press, 1998.

Skinner, Quentin. "Meaning and Understanding in the History of Ideas." *History and Theory* 8:1 (1969), 3–53.

Skinner, Quentin. *The Foundations of Modern Thought*. Cambridge: Cambridge University Press, 1978.

Smith, Nicholas D. "Aristotle's Theory of Natural Slavery." *Phoenix* 37:2 (1983), 109–22.

Sparshott, Francis. "Aristotle on Women." *Philosophical Inquiry* 7 (1985), 177–200.

Stern-Gillet, Susan. *Aristotle's Philosophy of Friendship*. New York: SUNY Press. 1995.

Striker, "Emotions in Context: Aristotle's Treatment of the Passions in the Rhetoric and His Moral Psychology." In *Essays on Aristotle's Rhetoric*, edited by Amélie Rorty. Berkeley: University of California Press, 1980, 286–302.

Tamiolaki, Melina. "Virtue and Leadership in Xenophon: Ideal Leaders or Ideal Losers?" In *Xenophon: Ethical Principles and Historical Enquiry*, edited by Fiona Hobden and Christopher Tuplin. Leiden: Brill, 2012, 563–89.

Taylor, Alfred Edward. "The Words Εἶδος, Ἰδέα in Pre-Socratic Literature." In *Varia Socratica*. Oxford: James Baker, 1911.

Taylor, C.C.W. (trans. with commentary). *Aristotle: Nicomachean Ethics II-IV*. Clarendon Aristotle Series. Oxford: Oxford University Press, 2006.

Trott, Adriel M. *Aristotle on the Nature of Political Community*. Cambridge: Cambridge University Press, 2014.

Veloso, Claudio William. "La relation entre les liens familiaux et les constitutions politiques." in *Politique D'Aristote: Famille, régimes, education*, edited by Emmanuel Bermon, Valéry Laurand, and Jean Terrel. Bordeaux: Presses Universitaires de Bordeaux, 2011, 23–40.

Vlahovic, Dennis. *The Sovereignty of the Lawcode in Aristotle*. PhD diss., McGill University, 2002.

Vlassopoulos, Kostas. "Free Spaces: Identity, Experience and Democracy in Classical Athens." *Classical Quarterly* 57:1 (2007), 33–52.

Vlastos, Gregory. "Slavery in Plato's Thought." In *Platonic Studies*. Princeton: Princeton University Press, 1973.

Ward, Julie. "*Ethnos* in the *Politics*: Aristotle on Race." In *Philosophers on Race*, edited by Julie Ward and Tommy Lott. Oxford: Blackwell, 2002, 14–37.

Whitely, Richard (ed.). *Bacon's Essays*. London: John W. Parker and Son, 1856.

Williams, Bernard. *Shame and Necessity*. Berkeley: University of California Press, 1993.

Williams, Bernard. "The Actus Reus of Dr. Caligari." *University of Pennsylvania Law Review* 142:5 (1994): 1661–73.

Yack, Bernard. *The Problems of a Political Animal: Community, Justice, and Conflict in Aristotelian Political Thought*. Berkeley and Los Angeles: University of California Press, 1993.

General Index

academy 147 n. 8
Aeschines 22, 152 n. 4
agency 60, 69–70, 76, 186 n. 10
Amasis 120
Annas, Julia 50
Archê. *See also* rule
   architectonic craft as 62–4, 165 n. 33
   as political office 11, 81, 88–9, 129–31, 175 n. 72
   as rule 6, 62, 104, 126
aretê. *See* virtue
aristocracy 11–12, 48, 87–92, 94, 150 n. 31
Aristophanes 32
Athens
   attitude to freedom 28, 30
   constitution of 28, 30–1
   democracy in 31, 79, 142
   isonomia in 115
   political offices in 13, 89, 93–4, 129–30
   slavery in 26–7, 41–2, 48, 159 n. 73
Augustine 144, 186 n. 10

Bacon, Francis 144
Barbarians. *See* foreigners
best 117, 134, 137, 177 n. 12, 182 n. 16.
   See also aristocracy; democracy; monarchy; oligarchy
   and friendship 72–6, 78–81, 169 n. 14, 171 n. 30
   and household 72–5, 81, 86–8, 150 n. 31, 168 n. 3, 168 n. 5
   and political faction 79, 125, 127
   as power structure 80–1, 88
   types of 7, 10–11, 72, 78, 129, 171 n. 25
Broadie, Sarah 59
brotherhood 72–4, 87, 91, 93, 103

Cartledge, Paul 115
children
   care of 47

deliberative capacity of 24, 61, 65, 92
friendship with 74, 169 n. 8
as parts of their parents 169 n. 13
rule over 1–2, 5, 80, 85–6, 91–3, 104, 124, 171 n. 30
city (*polis*)
   and education 38
   and household 74, 103, 169 n. 9
   and justice 132
   prior to its parts 76
   ruled by law 83 (*see also archê*, as political office; conflict)
community (*koinônia*)
   always involves rule 6–8, 82–3
   and cooperation 76–7
   of equals 8, 13, 14, 65, 83, 100, 104–7, 111–14, 119–20, 123, 135
   of exchange 113
   and friendship 77–9, 81, 169 n. 14
   and justice 77, 128, 169 n. 14
   kinds of 75–6, 78–9
   political 7–8, 13, 64, 93–4, 103, 112–14, 117–18, 121–3, 126, 135
   of self-rulers 84–5
conflict 14, 124–8, 130
constitution (*politeia*)
Cooper, John 71, 171 n. 27, 173 n. 49
craft (*technê*)
   as *archê* 62–4, 165 n. 33
   hierarchy of 9–10, 63–4
   of ruling 3–4, 39, 44–5, 152 n. 9
Cronos 135
Curzer, Howard 171 n. 30

Dahl, Robert 145
decision (*proairesis*)
   and deliberation 62–3, 90
   made by ruler 10–11, 53, 62–3, 92–3, 149 n. 21
   psychology of 65–8

subordinate's role in   60, 63, 66–8, 90, 100–1, 162 n. 3
and virtue   63, 65, 82
deliberation. *See also under* decision
   and agency   60–1
   and *phronêsis*   64–5
democracy. *See also under* Athens
   and equality   107–8, 112, 116, 178 n. 32
   and freedom   27–8, 30, 32, 105–6, 177 n. 19
   and rule of law   31, 131
Democritus   35, 157 n. 52
Demosthenes   28
Deslauriers, Marguerite   61, 147 n. 13, 175 n. 63
despotism. *See* rule, despotic
difference
   artificial   114, 120–1, 181 n. 7
   and conflict   130–1
   and equality   115
   natural   11, 42, 85–6
   sexual   17, 47, 173 n. 51
Dow, Jamie   163 n. 7

Empedocles   35
equality
   arithmetic   111–12, 127–8, 135–6
   and freedom   104, 116
      and friendship   78, 87, 123
   geometrical   127–8, 135–6
   and justice   105–6, 108–13, 178 n. 32
   and mathematics   105, 108–11, 178 n. 31, 178 n. 32
   proportional   107–11, 127–8
   reciprocal   112–14, 119
   (*see also isonomia*)
Eudaimonia. *See* happiness

faction (*stasis*). *See* conflict
family. *See* household
Finley, Moses   179 n. 41
foreigners   4, 27–8, 41, 43, 68, 78
Fortenbaugh, William   25, 29, 48, 153 n. 18
Foucault, Michel   145, 173 n. 38
friendship (*philia*). *See also under* equality
   as community   76–8, 169 n. 14
   and constitutions   75–9
   and happiness   7, 45–6, 75
   within household   73–5, 86–7, 103, 169 n. 8
   and justice   77–8, 170 n. 22, 182 n. 18
   of master and slave   80, 171 n. 28
   and rule   7–8, 45, 72–3, 81–5
   types of   75, 80–1
   as virtue   75–7

Gauthier, René   72, 149 n. 28
god   14, 23, 121–4, 132–3, 135–6, 144
Gorgias   32–6, 69, 156 n. 47, 157 n. 52, 157 n. 56, 158 n. 62, 159 n. 77

happiness (*eudaimonia*). *See also under* friendship
   and persuasion   45, 47
   and rule   14, 101, 126, 129
   of subordinates   46, 50
Harvey, F.D.   178 n. 32
Helen of Troy   32–3
Herodotus   28, 120, 171 n. 25
Hobbes, Thomas   142–3
household
   and city   23, 74, 81–2, 103, 169 n. 9
   and constitution   74–5, 87, 168 n. 3
household. *See also* friendship, within household; rule, within household; women, role in

imagination   67
Isocrates   119, 144
isonomia (equality before the law)   114–16

Jolif, J.Y.   72, 149 n. 28
justice. *See also under* city; community; equality; friendship
   corrective   118, 120, 132, 136
   distributive   108–10, 118, 128, 180 n. 44
   and *isonomia*   114–15
   and law   30, 173 n. 40
   and slavery   41, 48–9

kalon (noble)   48, 64, 99, 132
Kant, Immanuel   69–70, 137, 142
Karbowski, Joseph   152 n. 15
Kirwan, Christopher   62

Lane, Melissa   129–30, 183 n. 35
language. *See* speech

leisure 106, 126, 133–4
liberalism 25, 48, 140–4, 153 n. 18,
    162 n. 3, 178 n. 24, 185 n. 2
Locke, John 142–3, 185 n. 7

Machiavelli, Niccolò 144
Maloy, J.S. 143, 185 n. 7
marriage 7, 13, 87–8, 91, 174 n. 55,
    178 n. 20. *See also* women, role
    in household
Menn, Stephen 178 n. 31
Miller, Fred D. Jr. 149 n. 20, 173 n.
    39, 182 n. 13
monarchy 22–3, 44–6, 72–3, 79–80, 87,
    92–3, 104, 117, 122–4, 136, 144
Moraux, Paul 147 n. 12, 152 n. 7

Newman, W.L. 148 n. 18, 180 n.
    6, 181 n. 7

Ober, Josiah 150 n. 34
oligarchy 28, 87–8, 103, 105–7, 127,
    130

Pakaluk, Michael 169 n. 14
Panthea 48
Pericles 23, 178 n. 32
persuasion. *See also under* rule
    causes of 56
    through character 55–7, 63,
        163 n. 7, 164 n. 16
    through emotion 54–5
    and freedom 31–2, 35, 38
    and *logos* 32, 158 n. 62
    means of 54–7
    psychology of 33–5, 58–61, 67–8
    and slavery 25, 36
    and violence 28, 30, 32–5, 38–42,
        47, 156 n. 46
Phantasia. *See* imagination
Philip of Macedon 28
philosophy
    natural 17, 77, 132–3, 175 n. 63
    practical 17, 150 n. 31
phronêsis (practical wisdom) 2, 56, 60–1,
    65–6, 82, 98, 125–9
Plato
    on education 24–5, 38
    on imagination 67
    on law 38–41, 152 n. 11, 158 n. 70

and paternalism 38–9, 41,
    142, 158 n. 64
on persuasion 36–7, 40–1,
    157 n. 59, 158 n. 62
on rule 1–2, 22–3, 135–6, 144,
    164 n. 20, 171 n. 25
on slavery 18, 24, 26, 41–2, 158 n. 66,
    159 nn. 72, 73, 74
on women 50
pleonexia (greed) 128
polis. *See* city
Pomeroy, Sarah 48
Popper, Karl 40

Ribas, Marie-Noëlle 174 n. 59
Riesbeck, David 148 n. 18, 162 n. 3, 169 n.
    9, 174 n. 59, 175 n. 72, 181 n. 7
rule
    alternating 8, 14, 91, 93–4, 119–20,
        134, 181 n. 7
    benevolent 11, 12, 79–80, 85, 87,
        101–2, 104
    best kind of 12–14, 134
    craft of 44–5
    and decision 62–3, 66
    democratic 92–4
    despotic 98–100
    among equals 8, 13–14, 119
    exploitative 80, 101
    within household 82, 85, 87–93,
        150 n. 31, 172 n. 35
    kinds of 10–12, 85–7
    kingly 12, 92–3
    of law 30–1, 83–4, 131, 149 n. 21
    permanent 85–6, 93, 101, 119–20,
        135, 137
    and persuasion 9, 28, 31, 42, 47,
        69, 157 n. 59
    political 12–13, 98–104, 125–9,
        134–6 (*see also archê*; women,
        rule over)

Salamis 22
Saunders, Trevor 148 n. 17, 180 n. 6
Schofield, Malcolm 16, 17, 147 n. 13
Scylax 121, 124
Skinner, Quentin 151 n. 38
slavery. *See also under* Athens; justice;
    persuasion; Plato; Xenophon
    and admonishment 24–26, 29, 50

natural 29, 39, 42, 47–9, 68, 92–3, 115, 124
and violence 26–9, 36, 40–2, 47–9
Socrates 1–3, 22, 25, 36–8, 40, 43–9, 82, 144
Solon 28
soul. *See also* decision, psychology of; persuasion, psychology of
parts of 37, 58–61, 67, 90, 131
Sparshott, Francis 174 n. 51
speech 32–8, 42, 47, 54, 57–61, 68–9
sunesis (comprehension) 60

Themistocles 22
Thrasymachus 22, 157 n. 57
Thucydides 32, 178 n. 32
Trott, Adriel M. 149 n. 20, 153 n. 17, 175 n. 72

virtue 45–6, 55, 60–1, 65–6, 98, 106, 135–6. *See also* decision, and virtue; friendship, as a virtue; justice; *sunesis*
Vlastos, Gregory 39

Weber, Max 145
Wiedemann, Thomas 28
Williams, Bernard 26, 69–70
women
and deliberation 61, 65, 90
and female animals 17, 90
role in household 11, 47, 87–92, 174 n. 61, 180 n. 44 (*see also under* rule)
and slaves 50, 61, 90

Xenophon
on psychology 46
on the royal science 44–5
on self-control 43–5, 49, 161 n. 105
on slavery 48–50

Index Locorum

Aeschylus
Persians
241–242   154 n.25

Antiphon
I Tetral
2.7   153 n. 20

Aristotle
De Anima
III.3, 429a4-8   67
III.7, 431a7-10   67
III.10, 433a10-16   67

Constitution of Athens
I.2   28
I.5   28

Eudemian Ethics
II.10, 1226b9-10   166 n. 49
II.10, 1227a7-8   166 n. 49
III.5 1230a27-29   63
VII.9, 1241b12-17   78
VII.10, 1242b1-2   168 n. 3

Generation of Animals
II.10, 731b29-35   133

De Incessu Animalium
9, 709a25-30   184 n. 42

Metaphysics
V.1, 1013a10-11   62

De Motu Animalium
8, 702a15-17   67

Nicomachean Ethics
I.1, 1094a11-13   10
I.7, 1097b11   103
I.13, 1102a27-33   168 n. 7
I.13, 1102b26-33   167 n. 64
I.13, 1102b28   167 n. 64
I.13, 1102b33-1103a3   59
II.4, 1102a20-30   92

II.4, 1105a24   165 n. 40
II.5, 1105b26   55
III.1, 1110b30-1111a4   167 n. 69
III.2, 1112a16-18   63
III.2, 1111b5   63
III.3, 1112b11-16   65
III.3, 1112b33-34   166 n. 49
III.3, 1112b24   62
III.3, 1112b27   60
III.3, 1112b28   60
III.3, 1112b30-1   60
III.3, 1113a8-9   60
V.2, 1130b35   108
V.2, 1131a3-4   112
V.3, 1131a11   110
V.3, 1131a18-24   77
V.3, 1131a20-b15   108
V.3, 1131a22   178 n. 22
V.3, 1131a24-30   108
V.3, 1131a29   109
V.4, 1131b34-32a7   118
V.4, 1132a2-10   111
V.4, 1132b19-21   112
V.5, 1132b25-6   113
V.5, 1132b35-9   113
V.5, 1133a17-25   113
V.6, 1134a27   106
V.6, 1134a35-b2   83
V.10, 1137b11-31   136
VI.1, 1139a22   63
VI.2, 1139a23   62
VI.3, 1139a31-34   66
VI.5, 1140a25-8   64
VI.5, 1140a26   65
VI.5, 1140b10   65
VI.8, 1141b23-8   82
VI.10, 1143a7   61
VI.10, 1143a14-16   61
VIII.1, 1155a4   75
VIII.1, 1155a29   170 n. 22
VIII.1, 1155a34-b9   77
VIII.1, 1155b5-14   68

VIII.1, 1155b9-10	75	I.8, 1256b26	153 n. 16
VIII.1, 1155b23-31	171 n. 27	I.11, 1258b37	176 n. 3
VIII.5, 1157b7	76	I.12, 1259b4-9	120
VIII.7, 1158b12-19	74	I.12, 1259b5-9	91
VIII.7, 1158b24-29	114	I.13, 1259b37	53
VIII.7, 1158b29-33	136	I.13, 1260a7-14	61, 65
VIII.7, 1158b30-59a4	123	I.13, 1260a12	68
VIII.8, 1159b20-24	77	I.13, 1260a31-3	61
VIII.8, 1159b2-b3	114	I.13, 1260b5-8	24
VIII.9, 1159b25-28	77	II.2, 1261a25-35	61
VIII.9, 1160a27-30	78	II.2, 1261a30	112, 119
VIII.10, 1160a35	117	II.2, 1261a30-4	107
VIII.10, 1160b4	92	II.2, 1261a34-b5	134
VIII.10, 1160b9	12	II.2, 1261a39-b6	119, 180 n. 6
VIII.10, 1160b23-24	168 n. 3	II.5, 1264b8-10	183 n. 24
VIII.10, 1160b25-26	87	II.7, 1267a1-2	178 n. 22
VIII.10, 1160b32-61a4	87	III.1, 1275a27-33	89
VIII.10, 1161a4-7	87	III.1, 1275a32	11
VIII.10, 1161a8	94	III.1, 1275b19	61
VIII.11, 1161a25-7	93	III.4, 1277a1	117
VIII.11, 1161a30-34	80	III.4, 1277a14-15	98
X.8, 1178b8-22	184 n. 43	III.4, 1277a15	61
X.8, 1178b15	132	III.4, 1277a15-20	65
X.9, 1179b25	50	III.4, 1277a31-33	98
		III.4, 1277a35	98
Parts of Animals		III.4, 1277a36-b3	102
I.5, 644b32-5a1	133	III.4, 1277b7	98, 122
I.5, 645a7	133	III.4, 1277b25-9	61, 82
I.5, 645a29	133	III.4, 1277b25-30	61
		III.4, 1277b28-9	64
Politics		III.6, 1278b9-10	80
I.1, 1252a5-7	103	III.6, 1278b15	81
I.1, 1252a7-9	22	III.6, 1278b31-32	168 n. 7
I.1, 1252a8-16	4	III.6, 1278b32	171 n. 25
I.1, 1252a20-26	4	III.6, 1279a16-21	177 n. 12
I.2, 1252a25-31	76	III.9, 1280a10-24	105
I.2, 1252b5-9	68	III.9, 1280a15	124
I.2, 1253a2-3	103	III.9, 1280a22-25	174 n. 55
I.2, 1253a7-15	167 n. 64	III.13, 1284a9-11	123
I.2, 1253a9-18	58	III.13, 1284b25-34	117
I.3, 1253b18-20	22	III.14, 1285a19-21	68
I.3, 1253b20-23	29	III.14, 1285b22	84
I.5, 1254a19-21	6	III.15, 1286a3	84
I.5, 1254a25	126	III.15, 1286a7-9	84
I.5, 1254a26-33	5	III.15, 1286a15-20	83
I.6, 1255b11-14	171 n. 28	III.16, 1287a18-32	83
I.7, 1255b16-19	4, 85	III.16, 1287a26-b6	124
I.7, 1255b19-20	104	IV.1, 1288b22-6	134
I.7, 1255b19-36	64	IV.2, 1289a40	117
I.7, 1255b20	22	IV.4, 1291a21-24	6

IV.4, 1292a32	84		*Against Androtion*	
IV.5, 1292b6-7	84		22.3	153 n. 20
IV.11, 1295a25-32	134			
IV.11, 1295b25	134		Democritus	
IV.15, 1299a25-8	89		DK B31	35
IV.15, 1300b10-12	88			
V.1, 1301a39-40	125		Diogenes Laertius	
V.1, 1301b30-3	111		*Vitae*	
V.1, 1302a2-7	127		V.20	139
V.1, 1302a16	125		V.31	139
V.3, 1303b12-15	131			
V.4, 1304b2-5	126		Empedocles	
V.9, 1310a28-35	177 n. 19		DK B112	35
V.10, 1313a3-5	182 n. 20		DK B114	35
VI.1, 1317a5-7	103			
VI.2, 1317b1-15	177 n. 19		Gorgias	
VI.4, 1319b12	131		*Helen*	
VII.2, 1324a39-40	160 n. 79		8-14	32
VII.2, 1324b30-32	167 n. 70		9	34
VII.2, 1324b32-35	22		11	33
VII.3, 1325a24-29	99		12	33
VII.8, 1328a25-28	84			
VII.8, 1328a35-6	122		*Palamedes*	
VII.9, 1329a2-b17	118		33-34	156 n. 47
VII.13, 1332a10-16	132			
VII.14, 1332b15-26	121		Herodotus	
VII.14, 1332b37-40	124		*Histories*	
VIII.2, 1337b8-11	176 n. 3		II.172	120
			VII.135.3	154 n. 25
Rhetoric			VII.104.4	155 n. 37
I.2, 1356a1-12	54			
I.2, 1356a7	57		Isocrates	
I.2, 1356a13-14	55		*Against Lochites*	
I.3, 1358a37-8	57		20.10	155 n. 35
I.9, 1366b20	65			
I.13, 1373b5-20	154 n. 33		*Busiris*	
I.15, 1376b31	153 n. 20		11.8	119
II.1, 1378a8	57			
II.1, 1378a9-10	56		Lysias	
II.4, 1380b35-81a2	78, 171 n. 27		*Funeral Oration*	
			4.10-17	153 n. 20
Aristides			18-19	29
In Defense of the Four				
348	22		Parmenides	
			KRS 291.3-4	41
Demosthenes				
Philippic 3			Plato	
9.36	28		*Apology*	
Philippic 4			26a	25
10.4	155 n. 35			

Gorgias
452d   35

Meno
72c   53
77b2-78c   160 n. 84
80a2-b3   36

Phaedrus
261a7-b2   157 n. 59
268d1   157 n. 57
271c10   157 n. 59

Philebus
16b5-18d2   149 n. 25
39a-b   67
58a-b   156 n. 48

Republic
I, 327c-28a   157 n. 59
IV, 431c2   39
VI, 493a-d   157 n. 59
VI, 493c-d   37
VI, 495d-e   176 n. 3
VII, 519e3   38
IX, 590c-d   164 n. 20
IX, 590d3-5   40
IX, 591e1-5   177 n. 11

Sophist
229e5-230a2   25
235b7   36
253c   39

Statesman
259c1-5   23
274e1-4   23
275c   135

Symposium
218a   157 n. 58

Theaetetus
158e5-151d7   82

Timaeus
51e   158 n. 62

Laws
III, 697c-d   154 n. 25
IV, 712e9-10   147 n. 10

IV, 722b5-c4   39
IV, 723a7   40
VI, 757a-c   136
VI, 767a   174 n. 58
VI, 777a   42
VI, 777e   24
VIII, 838d-e   42
IX, 879a   159 n. 73

Lysis
207d-10b   1
209a4   2
210b1-c3   2
210a1-7   2

Xenophon
Constitution of the Spartans
II-IV   176 n. 1

Cyropaedia
VIII.8.5   160 n. 87

Memorabilia
II.1.6   176 n. 3
II.2.10   47
II.1.8   43
II.1.11   43
II.1.13   43
II.1.16-17   49
III.2.4   46
III.3.7   47
III.3.8   46, 47
III.3.11   47
III.4.6   44
III.4, 6-11   22
IV.2.11   160 n. 86
XII.19   49

Oeconomicus
I   45
I.17   162 n. 105
III.12-13   48
IV.2   49, 176 n. 3
VII.26   47
IX.11   46
X.10   162 n. 105
XIII.5   152 n. 5
XIII.6-9   46
XXI.5-6   46

www.ingramcontent.com/pod-product-compliance
Lightning Source LLC
Chambersburg PA
CBHW061827300426
44115CB00013B/2272